CHEESESPOTTING

'You have to be a romantic to invest yourself, your money, and your time in cheese'

Anthony Bourdain, 'Medium Raw', 2010

'Britain makes without a doubt the best cheeses in the world'

Steve Parker, 2023

Following a long corporate career working for an international brewer and wine distributor, Steve Parker opened an award-winning cheese shop, delicatessen and wine bar in South West London.

He judges in international food and drink competitions, including the British, International and World Cheese Awards and has featured in industry publications including *Speciality Food Magazine, Decanter, Off Licence News and Wine Merchant*.

He now organises food and drink tasting events and is a writer and speaker on his favourite subjects of cheese and wine, with a particular interest and focus on the cheeses and wines of Britain.

His first book *'British Cheese on Toast'* was published in 2020 by Headline Home (Hachette) and is available from good bookshops or from Amazon.

CHEESESPOTTING

An enthusiast's guide
to British Cheeses

www.steveparkercheeseandwine.com

steve@steveparkercheeseandwine.com

Twitter : @stevecheesewine

Instagram : stevecheesewine

TO MY MOTHER, OLIVE

CONTENTS

Baron Bigod & Tunworth

Cornish Kern

Weywood

Teesdale Cheesemakers

Caws Penhelyg Abaty

Winterdale Shaw

Honour Natural Foods

Thornby Moor Dairy

Daylesford Organics

Beenleigh Blue

Colston Bassett

Wiltshire Loaf

Appleby's Cheshire

Golden Cross

Sinodun Hill

Rollright

West County Cheeses

AN INTRODUCTION TO CHEESESPOTTING

Serious Cheesespotting
2023 International Cheese and Dairy Awards

Since the dawn of time, humankind has collected things. Sometimes we collect physical objects such as stamps or coins but more often than not, we collect our own sightings, observations or experiences using lists. In 1948 Charles Warrell published the first four volumes in what was to become a series of small books called I-SPY. 'At the Circus', 'Secret Codes', 'In the Country' and 'Dogs' were the first four books which soon grew to cover over more than 100 different topics appealing to children of all ages ever since. Also in the 1940s, Ian Allen published the first book listing locomotives of the Southern Railway and such was its demand that further volumes were published covering all of the railway companies and even their carriages and wagons. Bus spotting, plane spotting, lorry spotting soon followed as hobbies for people of all ages. At the same time there was an increasing interest in collecting sightings of birds, butterflies and other wildlife and it wasn't long before books of lists of them appeared and were snapped up by an eager spotting public.

By the start of the 21st century, such was the interest in food and drink that our collecting and spotting habits had extended to beers, wines, whiskies and various foods. One of the most popular foods in the world is without a doubt cheese. It is actually is the most widely stolen food in the world, such is its popularity. It is therefore time that Cheesespotting is brought to the world.

Without a doubt, Britain has the widest range and most diverse choice of cheese styles anywhere in the world. For several years now, I have travelled the length and breadth of Britain visiting dairies, cheesemakers and cheesemongers, sometimes working alongside them to make their wonderful cheeses, tasting, sampling and writing about them.

Cheesespotting is a fairly comprehensive listing of every cheese made in Britain at the time of writing. It includes traditionally made artisan farmhouse cheeses, larger volume dairy cheeses and industrial scale commercially made cheeses. They are all in this book, with variants of each cheese shown where relevant.

With room to write your own tasting notes and tick when you have spotted or tasted each cheese, there are many hours, days and weeks of seeking out and sampling ahead.

HAPPY CHEESESPOTTING

NOTES ABOUT THE CHEESES

In this main part of this book, dairies and cheesemakers are listed in alphabetical order with the cheeses they make listed, also alphabetically, under the dairy information. In some cases the selling dairy will have some or all of their own name cheeses made by another cheesemaker. In these examples, the relevant cheese will be listed under the seller with a note of who actually made the cheese. If you are looking for a specific cheese but don't know who makes it, there is an alphabetical index of cheeses at the back of the book along with an index of cheesemakers and dairies and a listing of recommended cheese shops where you can go to buy your favourite cheeses.

There is a built in challenge with compiling a book of this nature and that is the ever changing nature of the British cheese scene. Almost daily, a new cheese is launched or a new variation of an existing cheese is created. Sadly the occasional cheesemaker ceases production, either closing the business altogether or selling to another dairy. The result of these changes is that as soon as the book is fully up to date, another day passes and it needs amending. So please forgive me if there's a cheese that is missing or one that is no longer made, I am only human. One cheesemaker did ask not to be included and I have respected their wishes and have albeit reluctantly left out their diary and their cheeses. Do please drop me a line notifying me of any changes, errors or omissions that you are aware of and I will make sure they are corrected for the next edition.

One further complication is the definition of British and the definition of cheese. On the surface these would seem to be simple, but alas it is not so. For the purposes of this book, I have included cheeses that either actually made or finished in either England, Northern Ireland, Scotland or Wales even if the style is generally accepted as originating in other countries. There are many great examples of classic cheeses such as Halloumi, Ricotta, Feta or Brie that are made in Britain and these have been included. I have not included cream cheese, mascarpone, cottage cheese or any non-dairy plant based products. As excellent as some of these products are, I have not included them for the purposes of this book.

A number of British cheeses have been granted *protected geographical status* in order to ensure that the reputation of regional products and traditional agricultural practices are safeguarded and imitation products are prevented from entering the market. There are three classifications in use and any cheeses that have been granted a status are identified by the three letters shown in the relevant section of the book and are also listed below.

Protected Designation of Origin (PDO) : Products that are produced, processed **and** prepared in a specific area, using a particular, usually traditional, method.

Protected Geographical Indication (PGI) : Products that are produced, processed **or** prepared in a specific area, using a particular, usually traditional, method.

Traditional Speciality Guaranteed (TSG) : Products with *traditional character* or *customary names* distinguishing them from similar products. Unlike PDO and PGI they do not need to be linked to a particular area but they must be able to show that the materials and methods used have been consistent for at least 30 years. At the time of writing, only 7 British products in total have been granted TSG status, with no cheeses amongst them.

Protected Designation of Origin (PDO	Protected Geographical Indication (PGI
Beacon Fell	Dorset Blue
Bonchester	Exmoor Jersey Blue
Buxton Blue	Orkney Scottish Island Cheddar
Dovedale	Teviotdale
Single Gloucester	Yorkshire Wensleydale
Staffordshire	Traditional Ayrshire Dunlop
Stilton (Blue & White)	Traditional Welsh Caerphilly
Swaledale	
West Country Farmhouse Cheddar	

Each dairy and cheese entry has key information included and the layout is shown below with a key to abbreviations.

NAME OF DAIRY OR CHEESE COMPANY
County
Name of Cheesemaker or Owner
Notes about the dairy

Name of Cheese	STYLE	MILK	TRT	REN	ORG	RIND	SHAPE
Notes about the cheese							
Variants :							
Notes :							

KEY & GUIDE TO ABBREVIATIONS

COUNTY
Throughout the four countries of England, Northern Ireland, Scotland and Wales, the use of the word county is far more complicated than I had ever believed possible. Historical counties, ceremonial counties, administrative counties all lead to potential confusion. Some people prefer to use older traditional county names, including where I live which many people still refer to as Middlesex, despite the name having ceased to exist officially several decades ago. Other people use the modern county names that were introduced in the 1970s but have since faded into official history. Faced with the dilemma of which system to use, which varies in each of the four countries, I decided to use the county name referred to by the dairy, cheesemaker or cheesemonger. This has led to rather a hybrid solution but one that keeps the true heroes of this book happiest.

STYLE
There are numerous ways of categorising cheeses around the world but there is no standardised system, so for the purposes of this book, I am using my own system. The categories I have used are as follow.

Fresh : Young soft newly made cheeses that haven't had time to develop any rind and are intended to be eaten almost immediately.

Soft : Cheeses that have had only a few weeks maturing so that the centre is chalky turning to yielding and a soft rind or no rind at all with a tendency to become runny.

Semisoft : Rinds can be soft or starting to become firmer with a texture that is still yielding, but will not become fully runny

Crumbly : Larger cheeses with a fully set texture but as the curd doesn't hold together the cheese often crumbles when it is cut.

Firm : Generally larger cheeses, often cooked or pressed, which have lost more moisture and have a creamy solid texture which holds together when cut and a range of complex flavours.

Hard : Aged cheeses which have lost moisture and dried to a brittle texture, cracking when cut and a full and complex range of flavours.

Blue : Cheeses that have been injected with a blue mould that develops as the cheese matures, forming a sticky or a crusty rind and flavours ranging from mildly tangy to very salty.

MILK

Although cheese can be made from the milk of most mammals, in Britain we nearly always use four animals as follows :   **C** = Cow   **G** = Goat   **S** = Sheep   **B** = Buffalo
In a few cases a blend of milks is used and two letters are used to indicate the blend.

TREATMENT (TRT)

P = Pasteurised milk goes through a process of heating to kill all the naturally occurring bacteria and enzymes. Designed to kill off any detrimental bacteria but in doing so it kills everything. Usually undertaken when milk from more than one source is used, as any traceability is impossible in the event of a problem. Some cheeses have regulations that prohibit the use of unpasteurised milk, e.g. Stilton. To distinguish it from other processes, pasteurisation involves heating the milk to 72°C for 15 seconds or heating it to 63°C for 30 minutes.

T = Thermised milk has been heated to between 57°C and 68°C for at least 15 seconds. This process kills some, but not all, of the natural bacteria and enzymes in the milk, thereby retaining more of the natural flavours. Thermised milk is technically unpasteurised.

U = Unpasteurised milk refers to all milk that is not, by definition, pasteurised.

U/P = Available as either unpasteurised or pasteurised.

RENNET (REN)

Rennet is an essential part of the cheesemaking process as it is used to coagulate the milk and set the curd into a solid form. It was probably discovered by accident when the only method of transporting or storing liquids was an animal's stomach.

A = Animal rennet, sometimes referred to as traditional rennet, is an enzyme obtained from the stomach lining of an unweaned veal calf, kid or lamb.

V = Vegetarian rennet can be made either by using moulds that produce enzymes that are similar to rennet, or by genetically modifying moulds to produce the rennet enzyme called *Chymosin.*

L = In the case of some cheeses, no rennet is used and instead the curds are set by the action of lactic acid, which is converted from naturally occurring lactose in the milk.

A/V = Available as either animal or vegetarian rennet.

ORGANIC (ORG)

Where indicated with an 'O', the milk has been produced using organic farming methods. (O) indicates that the cheese is made as an organic version and a non-organic version.

RIND

As cheeses mature they usually develop a rind which is in effect dried cheese. These rinds vary massively depending on the type of cheese, ranging from very thin rinds to soft white bloomy rinds to harder crusty rinds. In some cases, the cheese is enclosed using a number of different artificial materials.

XR = No Rind : Usually applying to very young cheeses where no rind develops at all due to its freshness or the cheese has been shrink-wrapped during maturation to prevent a rind forming, usually prior to the cheese being portioned for retail packs.

NR= Natural Rind : The rind formed by a cheese drying on the outside with the nature and thickness dependent on the style and age of the cheese, with some forming a hard crust that is inedible.

BR = Bloomy Rind : The white soft velvety rind formed on the outside of many soft creamy cheeses, by the action of *Penicillium candidum* and/or *Penicillium Geotrichum* which grow in the presence of oxygen on the outside of the cheese.

WR = Washed Rind : Cheeses are washed in brine or alcohol (beer, cider, wine, brandy, etc) to form a soft, sticky thin rind, usually pink or orange colour and developing a fruity, pungent aroma due to the action of *Brevibacterium linens*.

FR = Flavoured Rind : Cheeses where an additional flavour has been used to rub into or coat the outside the cheese enhancing it with a wide variety of tastes including nettles, wild garlic, hops, black pepper, herbs, dried grapes and many more.

PC = Plastic Coating : A synthetic coating which is painted on to the cheese and acts as a breathable protective barrier, allowing the cheese to mature with a natural ripening process in controlled conditions.

WC = Wax Coated : An impermeable barrier is formed by coating the cheese in wax, usually black or brightly coloured which allows the cheese to mature whilst retaining all the moisture, a process most commonly used on Cheddar style cheeses.

SHAPE

Cheeses are made in a variety of different shapes and sizes, some more common than others. There is no official definition of shapes, so this book uses its own descriptions. Most of them are self-explanatory, but some require a few words to clarify what is meant.

Disc : small flat round weighing less than 1kg

Wheel : large flat round weighing more then 1kg

Drum : tall round with the diameter greater than the height

Half Drum : half of a disc or drum

Rounded Drum : drum but with rounded sides

Cylinder : tall round with the height greater than the diameter

Log : long horizontal cylinder

Barrel : shorter squat version of a log

Ball : sphere or globe

Block : large rectangular shape, usually used for large volume commercial cheesemaking

Brick : small rectangular shape

Square : flat square

Cube : equal square sided

Rounded Square : square with curved sides

Heart : heart shaped

Ammonite : similar to a flat spiral

Flying Saucer : round with pointed rim around centre

Pyramid : four-sided pyramid

Flat Pyramid : truncated pyramid with flat top and no point

Triangle : flat with three points

Cone : conical with round flat base

Flat Cone : truncated cone with flat top and no point

Bell : shaped like a bell

Millstone : disc with a hole in the centre

Button : small round disc

Ingot : small flat brick

Lozenge : similar to an ingot with rounded ends

Bomb : similar to a ball with a 'fuse'

Rock : unsymmetrical lump

Star : generally a five pointed star

Hourglass : a ball tied in the middle to resemble a number 8

Slices : thin pieces cut from a log

Stick : small snacking size brick

Basket : holed basket used to hold ricotta

Pot : small tub used to hold soft fresh cheeses

Bag : small bag used to hold small pieces of cheese (eg curds)

Rope : long strands of cheese rolled up into a ball shape

THE CHEESES

ABBEY FARM COTTAGE
North Yorkshire
Cheesemaker : Suzanne & Jonty Birrell-Gray

Small farm in the North York Moors making a range of dairy products and running a holiday business.

Bell End Blue Blue G U V BR Disc

Made as a 150g - 200g cheese with a Camembert style appearance and texture with minimal blue veining.

Variants :

Notes :

Rosedale Soft G U V BR Disc, Button

Made as a Camembert style cheese in various sizes between 250g and and a 100g Crottin style.

Variants :

Notes :

ABBEY HOME FARM
Gloucestershire
Cheesemaker : Sarah Dibben

Farmed by descendants of the first 16th century owners, now organic with their own Dairy Shorthorn cows.

Abbey Home Farm Halloumi Style Semisoft C P V O XR Block

Made as a 200g block suitable for slicing and grilling.

Variants :

Notes :

Abbey Home Farm Soft Cheese Soft C P V O FR Cylinder

Made as a soft cheese during the summer months and coated in herbs.

Variants :

Notes :

Patience Firm C P V O XR Drum

Made as a mild cheese and matured for 3 -5 weeks.

Variants :

Notes :

Wiggold Cheddar Firm C P V O NR Drum

Made as a traditional Cheddar and matured as a mature and vintage version.

Variants :

Notes :

ABERDYFI CHEESE COMPANY
Gwynedd

Cheesemaker : Hamish Dunkinson, Roman Hackelsberger

Own flock of Lacaune sheep grazing on the slopes above the sea at the mouth of the River Dyfi.

Caws Dyfi   Hard   S   P   A   NR   Drum

Based on a Pecorino style cheese and matured for at least 6 months.

Variants :

Notes :

Caws y Bugail   Hard   S   P   A   NR   Drum

Based on a Manchego style cheese and matured for at least 6 months.

Variants :

Notes :

===

ABERGAVENNY FINE FOOD CO
Monmouthshire

Commercial Cheesemaker

Started as a hill farm near Abergavenny, growing to become a large company based in Blaenavon.

Pant ys Gawn   Soft   G   P   V   XR   Log

Named after the founders' farm, it is made as a 125g cheese.

Variants : Original, Garlic & Herb, Honey & Ginger

Notes :

===

ALEX JAMES CHEESES
Oxfordshire

Cheesemakers : Ford Farm, Shepherds Purse, Caws Cenarth, Rosary, Nettlebed, High Weald

Alex James, bass guitarist with Blur has collaborated with several cheesemakers to create a range of cheeses.

No. 1 Cheddar   Firm   C   P   V   NR   Block

Made by Ford Farm Cheesemakers in Dorset and matured for 15 months.

Variants :

Notes :

No. 2 Blue Monday   Blue   C   P   V   NR   Drum

Made by Shepherds Purse in North Yorkshire as a 1.4kg cheese.

Variants :

Notes :

No. 3 Valley Brie   Soft   C   P   V   BR   Drum

Made by Caws Cenarth in Carmarthenshire as a 200g individual cheese.

Variants :

Notes :

No. 4 Goat's   Soft   G   P   V   NR   Drum

Made by Rosary Goat's Cheese in Wiltshire as a 100g single cheese.

Variants :

Notes :

No. 5 Grunge   Semisoft   C   P   A   O   WR   Triangle

Made by Nettlebed Creamery in Oxfordshire as a 150g pungent cheese.

Variants :

Notes :

No. 6 Sheep's   Semisoft   S   P   V   O   XR   Drum

Made by High Weald Dairy in West Sussex as a 100g single cheese blended with garlic and herbs.

Variants :

Notes :

====================

ALSOP & WALKER

East Sussex

Cheesemaker : Arthur Alsop

Started in 2008 when the son of a beef farmer and apprentice chef bought an existing business from a friend.

Ewe Eat Me   Hard   S   P   V   NR   Drum

Made as a 3kg cheese with a pink rind and matured for 4 months.

Variants :

Notes :

Idle Hour   Firm   C   P   V   NR   Drum

Made as a 2.5kg cheese and matured for 16 - 20 weeks.

Variants :

Notes :

Lord London   Semisoft   C   P   V   BR   Bell

Originally made to celebrate the 2012 London Olympics, made as a 500g cheese and matured for 6 weeks.

Variants : Original, Smoked

Notes :

| **Mayfield** | Firm | C | P | V | | WC | Drum |

Made as a large 18kg cheese and matured for 6 months.
Variants : Original, Smoked
Notes :

| **Sussex Blue** | Blue | C | P | V | | NR | Drum |

Made as a 2.5kg cheese and matured for 4 months.
Variants :
Notes :

| **Sussex Brie** | Soft | C | P | V | | BR | Disc |

Made as a 1.2kg cheese and matured for 6 weeks.
Variants : Original, Truffle
Notes :

| **Sussex Camembert** | Soft | C | P | V | | BR | Disc |

Made as a 1kg cheese and matured for 6 weeks.
Variants :
Notes :

| **Sussex Farmhouse** | Firm | C | P | V | | WR | Drum |

Made as a 15kg cheese and matured for 6 months.
Variants :
Notes :

| **Woodside Red** | Firm | C | P | V | | NR | Drum |

Made as a 2.5kg cheese and matured for 4 months.
Variants :
Notes :

APPLEBY CREAMERY
Cumbria

Cheesemaker : Maurice Walton

Made in the Eden valley using milk from a herd of Ayrshire cows across the border in Scotland.

| **Black Dub Blue** | Blue | C | P | V | | NR | Drum |

Made as a 2.5kg cheese.
Variants :
Notes :

Blencathra   Crumbly   C   P   V   XR   Half Drum
Made as a 1.5kg cheese based on a Caerphilly style.
Variants :

Notes :

Border Reiver   Firm   C   P   V   WC   Disc
Made as a 200g cheese based on a Cheddar style.
Variants :

Notes :

Eden Chieftain   Firm   C   P   V   XR   Half Drum
Made as a 1.5kg Cheddar style cheese.
Variants : *Original, Smoked*

Notes :

Eden Ivory   Hard   S   P   V   XR   Half Drum
Made as a 1.5kg cheese.
Variants :

Notes :

Eden Pearl   Soft   S   P   V   BR   Disc
Made as a 125g individual cheese.
Variants :

Notes :

Eden Smokie   Soft   C   P   V   XR   Disc
Made as a 230g version of Eden Valley Brie which has been smoked over apple and oak wood.
Variants :

Notes :

Eden Sunset   Firm   C   P   V   XR   Half Drum
Made as a 1.5kg cheese based on Double Gloucester and coloured orange with annatto.
Variants :

Notes :

Eden Valley Brie   Soft   C   P   V   BR   Disc
Made as a 1kg & 230g Brie style cheese.
Variants :

Notes :

| **Flakebridge** | Firm | C | P | V | XR | Half Drum |
| | | | | | | |

Made as a 1.5kg cheese based on Red Leicester and coloured orange with annatto.

Variants :

Notes :

| **Hootenanny** | Firm | G | P | V | XR | Half Drum |
| | | | | | | |

Made as a 1.5kg cheese.

Variants : Original, Smoked

Notes :

| **Nanny McBrie** | Soft | G | P | V | BR | Disc |
| | | | | | | |

Made as a 125g individual cheese.

Variants :

Notes :

| **Old Applebian** | Crumbly | C | P | V | XR | Half Drum |
| | | | | | | |

Made as a 1.5kg cheese based on a traditional Westmoreland recipe with a creamy lemony flavour.

Variants :

Notes :

APPLEBY'S

Shropshire

Cheesemaker : Paul Appleby

Third generation cheesemaker using the same techniques started by his grandmother over 70 years ago.

| **Appleby's Cheshire** | Crumbly | C | U | A | NR | Cylinder |
| | | | | | | |

Made as a 8kg cheese, clothbound and matured for 3 months.

Variants : Coloured, White

Notes :

| **Appleby's Double Gloucester** | Firm | C | U | A | NR | Cylinder |
| | | | | | | |

Made as a 8kg cheese, clothbound and matured for 4 months.

Variants :

Notes :

ARGYLL AND BUTE CHEESES
Argyll & Bute
Cheesemaker : Ian Rutledge

Previously based on Arran but now moved to a new dairy in Argyll but is using milk from Arran.

Largie Crumbly C P V NR Drum

Based on Caerphilly and matured for 3 months.

Variants :

Notes :

===

ARTISAN FARM
Lancashire
Commercial Cheesemaker

Created by actor Sean Wilson and now made in the true home of Lancashire cheese, the Trough of Bowland.

How's Yer Father Firm C P V WC Drum

Made as a creamy Lancashire, matured for 6 - 8 weeks and coated in green wax.

Variants :

Notes :

Mouth Almighty Firm C P V WC Drum

Made as a tasty Lancashire, matured for 3 - 12 months and coated in yellow wax.

Variants :

Notes :

Muldoon's Picnic Crumbly C P V WC Drum

Made as a modern style crumbly Lancashire and coated in red wax.

Variants :

Notes :

Smelly Ha'peth Blue C P V XR Drum

Made as a soft creamy Gorgonzola style blue cheese.

Variants :

Notes :

===

BALCOMBE DAIRY
West Sussex
Cheesemaker : Chris Heyes

Made in 'cheese pods' (shipping containers) the other side of the wall from Lodgelands Farm milking parlour

Balcombe Breeze	Firm	C	P	V	NR	Drum

Made as a 3.5kg Tomme style cheese matured for 12 - 16 weeks.

Variants :

Notes :

Blue Clouds	Blue	C	P	V	NR	Drum

Named in honour of Chris's mentor's Kenyan farm, it is made as a 3.5kg cheese and matured for 8 weeks.

Variants :

Notes :

BALLOCHMYLE FINE CHEESE
Ayrshire
Cheesemaker : Robert Shaw

Family dairy farmers for over 100 years with their own herd of Ayrshires.

Ayrshire Farmhouse Brie	Soft	C	P	V	BR	Disc

Traditionally made as an individual small cheese or a larger cutting version.

Variants :

Notes :

BALLYLISK OF ARMAGH
Armagh
Cheesemaker : Dean Wright

Fifth generation farmers who started making cheese in 2015 using milk from their own closed pedigree herd.

The Single Rose	Soft	C	P	V	BR	Disc

Made as a 200g & 110g cheese single cream Brie style cheese.

Variants :

Notes :

Triple Rose	Soft	C	P	V	BR	Disc

Made as a 230g & 130g triple-cream cheese by adding double cream to the curds.

Variants : Original, Smoked

Notes :

BARBER'S FARMHOUSE CHEESE
Somerset
Commercial Cheesemaker
The oldest surviving Cheddar makers in the world, and guardians of last remaining traditional starter cultures.

Barber's 1833 Vintage Reserve Cheddar Firm   C   P   V   XR   Block
Made as a large block cheese before maturing for 24 months and cutting into 1.2kg bricks and 190g wedges.
Variants :
Notes :

Barber's Farmhouse Cheddar   Firm   C   P   V   XR   Block
Made as a 20kg cheese before maturing and cutting into smaller blocks.
Variants : Mellow (4 months), Mature (12 months), Vintage (18 months)
Notes :

Barber's Mature Cheddar Truckle   Firm   C   P   V   WC   Drum
Made as a 900g, 400g & 200g cheese, matured for 12 months then coated in black wax.
Variants :
Notes :

Barber's Haystack Tasty   Firm   C   P   V   XR   Block
Made as a 20kg cheese before maturing and cutting into small blocks for retail.
Variants :
Notes :

Barber's Red Leicester   Firm   C   P   V   XR   Block
Made as a 5kg block coloured orange with annatto and matured for 4 months before cutting into blocks.
Variants :
Notes :

===

BATCH FARM CHEESEMAKERS
Somerset
Cheesemakers : Jean Turner, Malcolm & Stephen Dyer
Family cheesemakers for over 50 years with milk from the family farm overlooked by Glastonbury Tor.

Batch Farm Cheese Curds   Fresh   C   U   V   XR   Bag
Made as fresh curd for use in traditional Canadian poutine.
Variants : Somerset Red, Classic, Cider, Chilli, Garlic & Herb, Chilli & Chive, Garlic & Herb
Notes :

Batch Farm Clothbound Cheddar   Firm   C   U   V   NR   Cylinder

Made as a 1kg & 600g cheese, clothbound and aged for 2 years.

Variants :

Notes :

Batch Farm Goat's Cheese   Firm   G   U   V   WC   Disc

Made for Batch Farm who flavour and wax coat the 180g cheeses.

Variants : Traditional, Oak Smoked, Cranberry, Spring Onion, Tomato & Basil

Notes :

Batch Farm Waxed Cheddar   Firm   C   U   V   WC   Cylinder

Made as a 2kg cheese, wax coated and matured for 12 months, often smoked or blended with flavourings.

Variants : Original, Mild, Vintage, Extra Tasty, Garlic & Herb, Hot Chilli & Chive, Fiery Fred

Notes :

Batch Farm Farmhouse Cheddar   Firm   C   P   A   NR   Cylinder

Made as a 2kg & 1kg cheese, clothbound and matured for 9 - 12 months.

Variants :

Notes :

Batch Farm Mild Cheddar   Firm   C   P   V   XR   Cylinder

Made as a 2kg cheese, clothbound and matured for 3 - 6 months.

Variants :

Notes :

Batch Farm Somerset Red Cheddar   Firm   C   P   V   XR   Cylinder

Made as a traditional Cheddar but coloured orange with annatto.

Variants : Original, Oak Smoked

Notes :

BATH SOFT CHEESE COMPANY
Somerset

Cheesemakers : Graham & Hugh Padfield

Third and fourth generation farmers and cheesemakers at Park Farm, certified organic in 2000.

Bath Blue   Blue   C   P   A   O   NR   Cylinder

Supreme Champion in the World Cheese Awards 2014, made as an 8kg cheese and aged for 8 - 10 weeks.

Variants :

Notes :

Bath Soft Soft C P A O BR Square
Allegedly the cheese sent by his father to Admiral Nelson, it is a 250g cheese matured for 6 weeks.
Variants :
Notes :

Kelston Park Semisoft C P V O BR Disc
Named after the cows' grazing pastures and made as a 500g cheese as a vegetarian alternative to Bath Soft.
Variants :
Notes :

Merry Wife Firm C P V O WR Drum
Made as a 3kg & 400g cheese, washed in cider made by Graham on the farm and matured for 4 weeks.
Variants :
Notes :

Wyfe of Bath Firm C P V O NR Ammonite
Named after the character in Chaucer's Canterbury Tales, made as a 3kg cheese and matured for 6 months.
Variants : Original, Extra Mature
Notes :

===

BELLEVUE CREAMERY
Ayrshire
Cheesemaker : Calum Chaplin
Owned by Arran Cheese Shop, a former milking shed on the west coast of Arran converted to a creamery.

Arran Blue Blue C P V NR Drum
Made as a 1.5kg cheese and twice winning the Best Scottish Cheese award.
Variants :
Notes :

Arran Camembert Soft C P V BR Disc
Made as a 180g cheese based on Camembert and matured for 3 weeks.
Variants :
Notes :

Arran Mist Soft C P V BR Disc
Made as a 180g triple-cream cheese based on Brie.
Variants :
Notes :

===

BELTON FARM
Shropshire
Commercial Cheesemaker

Owned by the Beckett family for over 100 years, using milk from local farms and their own starter cultures.

Belton Farm Caerphilly Crumbly C P V XR Block, Wheel
Made to a traditional bespoke recipe to produce a crumbly, moist cheese.
Variants :
Notes :

Belton Farm Cheddar Firm C P V XR Block
A sweet, nutty Cheddar made in a range of different maturities, with the flavour intensifying as it ages.
Variants : Mild, Mature, Vintage, Organic Mild, Organic Mature
Notes :

Belton Farm Cheshire Crumbly C P V XR Cylinder, Block
Made as a 20kg block, 12kg & 6kg traditional cylinder & 4kg wheel and as a white or coloured Cheshire.
Variants : White, Coloured
Notes :

Belton Farm Double Gloucester Firm C P V XR Cylinder, Block
Made as a 20kg block, 12kg & 6kg traditional cylinder & 4kg wheel coloured orange with annatto.
Variants : Original, Chives
Notes :

Belton Farm Lancashire Crumbly C P V XR Wheel, Block
Made as a 20kg block & 4kg wheel with a crumbly texture and refreshing zesty flavour.
Variants :
Notes :

Belton Farm Port Wine Derby Firm C P V XR Wheel
Made as an 8kg creamy Derby cheese with Port added during the making to give rich red marbling.
Variants :
Notes :

Belton Farm Red Leicester Firm C P V XR Wheel, Block
Made as a 20kg block & 4kg wheel with a savoury nutty caramel flavour and coloured orange with annatto.
Variants : Original, Cracked Black Pepper
Notes :

Belton Farm Sage Derby　　　　Firm　　　C　P　V　　　　XR　Drum

Made as a 4kg creamy Derby cheese with a sage infusion added during the making to give green marbling.

Variants :

Notes :

Belton Farm Wensleydale　　　Crumbly　　C　P　V　　　　XR　Block, Drum

Made as a 20kg block & 4kg wheel with a crumbly delicate texture and a mild acidic and wild honey flavour.

Variants :

Notes :

Red Fox　　　　　　　　　　　Firm　　　C　P　V　　　　XR　Drum, Block

Aged Red Leicester matured as a 20kg block for 16 months and 12kg vintage drum aged for 18 months.

Variants : Original, Vintage, Smoked

Notes :

White Fox　　　　　　　　　　Firm　　　C　P　V　　　　XR　Block

Uncoloured Leicester matured as a 20kg block for 16 months and 12kg vintage drum aged for 18 months.

Variants : Original, Vintage

Notes :

BERKSWELL CHEESE
West Midlands

Cheesemakers : Stephen Fletcher, Julie Hay

Second generation sheep farmer/cheesemaker, later discovering a history of cheesemaking at Ram Hall Farm.

Berkswell　　　　　　　　　　Hard　　　S　U　A　　　　NR　Flying Saucer

Made as a 3kg Manchego based cheese but unpressed and drained in colanders and matured for 4 months.

Variants :

Notes :

BEVISTAN DAIRY
Bedfordshire

Cheesemaker : Beverley Beales

Family farm with herd of cows and a flock of milking sheep producing milk, yogurt and cheese.

Bevistan Blue　　　　　　　　Blue　　　S　U　V　　　　NR　Drum

Made by Gary Bradshaw at Hamm Tun Fine Foods using Bevistan milk and matured for 6 weeks.

Variants :

Notes :

Bevistan Smoked Semisoft S P V XR Disc
Made as a 120g - 150g cheese and smoked over applewood.
Variants :

Notes :

Bevistan Tomme Firm S P V NR Wheel
Made as a 3kg Alpine style cheese and matured for 3 months.
Variants :

Notes :

Carlton Semisoft S P V XR Disc
Made as a 120g - 150g cheese with a fondant texture and a fresh citrus flavour.
Variants :

Notes :

BLACK COW
Dorset
Cheesemaker : Jason Barber
Own herd of cows milk is used to make cheese from the curds and vodka from the whey.

Black Cow Cheddar Firm C P V WC Drum, Disc
Made by Somerset cousins' Barber's Cheesemakers as a 900g & 200g cheese and matured for 12 months.
Variants :

Notes :

BLACKWOODS CHEESE COMPANY
Kent
Cheesemaker : David Holton
Australian cheesemaker then affineur at Neal's Yard Dairy, now cheesemaker at Commonwork Organic Farm.

Edmund Tew Soft C U A O WR Drum
Made as a 150g cheese based on Langres., annatto washed and matured for 3 weeks.
Variants :

Notes :

Graceburn Fresh C U A O XR Cubes
Based on Persian Fetta and made in small cubes in a 250g jar .
Variants :

Notes :

BLAENAFON CHEDDAR COMPANY
Monmouthshire
Cheesemakers : Susan & Gerry Woodhouse & Charlotte Hill
Family run business who buy large blocks from a Welsh dairy co-operative for blending and waxing.

Bara Brith Firm C P V WC Drum
Made as a 200g Cheddar flavoured with raisins and mixed fruit infused with 'Black Mountain' liqueur.
Variants :
Notes :

Blaenafon Firm C P V WC Drum
Made as a 200g Cheddar flavoured with ginger and Celtic Spirit Company's Danzy Jones Welsh whisky.
Variants :
Notes :

Blaenafon Caerphilly Crumbly C P V WC Block
Made as a 200g young crumbly wax coated Caerphilly.
Variants :
Notes :

Blaenafon Oak Smoked Mature Firm C P V XR Drum
Made as a 200g Cheddar smoked over oak chippings for 36 hours in Crickhowell.
Variants :
Notes :

Capel Newydd Firm C P V WC Drum
Made as a 200g Cheddar flavoured with Sugarloaf Vineyard wine, garlic, elderflower and thyme.
Variants :
Notes :

Cymru Crunch Firm C P V WC Drum
Made as a 200g Cheddar flavoured with pickled onions, chives and Watkins Cwru Braf beer.
Variants :
Notes :

Dragon's Breath Firm C P V WC Drum
Made as a 200g Cheddar flavoured with chilli mustard, chilli jelly and Brains SA beer.
Variants :
Notes :

Lion Hotel 1868 Cheddar   Firm   C   P   V   WC   Drum

Matured in the cellar of The Lion Hotel in Blaenafon, famed for the 1868 political riots in the town.

Variants :

Notes :

Pwll Ddu   Firm   C   P   V   WC   Drum

Made as a 200g Cheddar flavoured with wholegrain mustard, leek and Reverend James Welsh Ale.

Variants :

Notes :

Taffy Apple   Firm   C   P   V   WC   Drum

Made as a 200g mature Cheddar flavoured with onion marmalade and Taffy Apple Cider from Swansea.

Variants :

Notes :

BLUE SKY CHEESE
Lincolnshire

Cheesemakers : Jeremy & Becky Cooper

The milk from their from flock of Zwartbles sheep is high in butterfat and produced rich creamy cheese.

Hal-Ewe-Mee   Semisoft   S   U   V   XR   Block

Based on Halloumi and sold as a 180g block.

Variants :

Notes :

BOOK & BUCKET CHEESE COMPANY
Dorset

Cheesemakers : Peter & Mandy Morgan

Started in 2019 by making bespoke cheeses and expanded into a wide range mainly named after writers.

Austen   Semisoft   S   P   V   XR   Block

Made as a 1kg cheese based on Feta and matured for 5 weeks.

Variants :

Notes :

Blyton   Semisoft   C   P   V   BR   Drum

Made as a 1kg cheese based on Brie and matured for 2 weeks.

Variants : Original, Smoked

Notes :

Burns   Semisoft   S   P   V   XR   Block

Made as a 2.5kg cheese based on Halloumi and matured for 5 weeks.

Variants : Original, Smoked

Notes :

Cranborne Blue   Blue   C   P   V   NR   Drum

Made as a 3kg cheese.

Variants :

Notes :

Golding   Hard   S   P   V   NR   Drum

Based on Ricotta Salata and made exclusively for The Pig Hotel.

Variants : Original, Truffle

Notes :

Hardy's   Hard   S   P   V   NR   Drum

The first cheese they made is a 3kg cheese inspired by Manchego and matured for 9 months.

Variants :

Notes :

Huxley   Semisoft   C   P   V   XR   Block

Made as a 2kg cheese as a cow's milk version of Halloumi and matured for 4 weeks.

Variants : Original, Smoked, Fire (Naga Chilli)

Notes :

Orwell   Semisoft   S   P   V   XR   Disc

Made as a 150g cheese and matured for 10 days.

Variants : Original, Pink Peppercorns, Edible Flowers

Notes :

Potter   Fresh   C   P   V   XR   Pot

Made as a 1kg & 200g cheese as a cross between a soft cheese and a curd cheese.

Variants : Original, Truffle

Notes :

Shakespeare   Soft   S   P   V   BR   Disc

Made as a 1kg & 200g sheep's milk version of Brie and matured for 4 weeks.

Variants :

Notes :

Wilde   Fresh   C   P   V   XR   Pot

Made as a 1kg & 200g cheese flavoured with locally foraged wild garlic.

Variants :

Notes : ☐

Wordsworth   Firm   C   P   V   NR   Drum

Made as a 3kg cheese based on Gouda.

Variants : Original, Smoked, Truffle

Notes : ☐

BOOKHAM HARRISON FARMS
West Sussex
Cheesemaker : Rob Booker

Made by Lye Cross Farm using milk from Harrison Farms in West Sussex.

Sussex Charmer   Firm   C   P   V   XR   Brick, Cube

Made as a 1kg & 200g cheese for Bookham Harrison by Lye Cross Farm and matured for 14 months.

Variants :

Notes : ☐

BOTTON CREAMERY
North Yorkshire
Cheesemaker : Ruth Wells

Part of a working community for adults with learning difficulties using milk from their cows to make cheese.

Botton Gouda   Firm   C   U   V   O   NR   Rounded Drum

Made as a 4 - 6 kg cheese and matured for 6 weeks.

Variants : Original, Cumin, Chilli

Notes : ☐

Dale End Cheddar   Firm   C   U   V   O   NR   Cylinder

Made as an 8kg cheese and matured for 18 months.

Variants :

Notes : ☐

Moorland Tomme   Firm   C   U   V   O   NR   Rounded Drum

Based on a traditional French style Tomme and matured for 12 months.

Variants :

Notes : ☐

Summerfield Alpine Firm C U V O NR Drum
Alpine style cheese only made in summer when cows are eating fresh grass and matured for 3 months.
Variants :

Notes :

BRADBURY'S CHEESE
Derbyshire
Commercial Cheesemaker
Founded in 1884 and now owned by the Paul family, specialising in blending, cutting and waxing cheeses.

Bradbury's Waxed Truckles Firm C P V WC Disc
A range of popular cheeses blended with various flavours, shaped and wax coated as 200g cheeses.
Variants : Mature Cheddar, Smokey, Red Hot Dutch, Caramelised Onion, Gin & Lemon, Gingerbread, Chipotle & Ale, Double Gloucester Chive & Onion, Wensleydale & Cranberry, White Stilton & Apricot, White Stilton Mango & Ginger

Notes :

Saxon Cross Firm C P V XR Block
Made as a Cheddar by J J Sandham for Bradbury's, matured for 13 months and smoked over oak chippings.
Variants :

Notes :

BRADFIELDS FARM DAIRY
Essex
Cheesemaker : Clare Lambert
Third generation family farm with own herd, Essex's only cheesemaker as well as a range of dairy products.

Blackwater Firm C P V WC Drum
Made as a 3kg & 800g Gouda style cheese matured for 3 months.
Variants :

Notes :

Bures Essex Fresh C P V XR Disc
Made as a 150g - 180g lactic-set cheese matured for 5 days, designed to be eaten young and fresh.
Variants : Original, Baby Bures (70 - 100g)

Notes :

Cam   Fresh   C   P   V   BR   Disc

Made as a 150g cheese similar to Bures Essex but with a bloomy geotrichum rind and matured for 2 weeks.

Variants :

Notes :

Chalvedon   Hard   C   P   V   NR   Cylinder

Made as a 3kg & 800g cheese based on a Manchego recipe and matured for 6 months.

Variants :

Notes :

Essex Soft   Fresh   C   P   V   XR   Disc

Made as a 150g lactic-set cheese drained in muslin instead of moulds to give a very delicate cheese.

Variants : Original, Basil, Mint, Chilli, Chive

Notes :

Roding Red   Firm   C   P   V   WC   Drum

Made as a 3kg cheese using a Cheddar recipe and coloured orange with annatto.

Variants :

Notes :

BRIDDLESFORD FARM DAIRY
Isle of Wight

Cheesemakers : Griffin Family

Third generation farmers producing dairy products for 100 years and now using rich Guernsey milk.

Briddlesford Cheddar   Firm   C   P   V   PC   Drum

Made as a 4.5kg cheese and matured for at least 3 months.

Variants :

Notes :

Briddlesford Fetter   Semisoft C   P   V   XR   Disc

Made as a 200g cheese based on Feta and sold in brine.

Variants :

Notes :

Briddlesford Gouda   Firm   C   P   V   XR   Drum

Made as a 4.5kg cheese and matured for at least 2 months.

Variants :

Notes :

| Briddlesford Halloumi | Semisoft | C | P | V | | XR | Block |

Made as a 1kg cheese coated in salt and mint.

Variants :

Notes :

| Briddlesford Red | Firm | C | P | V | | XR | Drum |

Made as a 4.5kg cheese and matured for at least 3 months.

Variants :

Notes :

===

BRIDGE FARM
Borsetshire
Cheesemaker : Helen Archer

Started cheesemaking on family farm in 2001 using milk from their own herd of Montbeliardes.

| Borsetshire Blue | Blue | C | U | V | O | NR | Drum |

Made using old recipes discovered by Helen's aunt, Jennifer Aldridge and matured for 10 weeks.

Variants :

Notes :

| Sterling Gold | Firm | C | U | V | | NR | Drum |

Named after Oliver Sterling, originally made with Jersey milk at Grange Fam, but now made at Bridge Farm.

Variants :

Notes :

===

BRINKWORTH DAIRY
Wiltshire
Cheesemaker : Ceri Collingborn

Family farm for over 120 years with fifth generation cheesemaker using milk from own herd of Friesian cows.

| Avebury | Soft | C | P | V | | BR | Disc |

Made as a 200g individual cheese.

Variants :

Notes :

| Brinkworth Blue | Blue | C | P | V | | NR | Drum |

Made as a 4kg cheese and matured for 2 months as a harder blue.

Variants :

Notes :

Gallipot Eyes Firm C P V NR Drum

Made as a 3kg Gouda style cheese and matured for 6 - 12 months.

Variants :

Notes :

Ramps Hill Firm C P V NR Drum

Made as a 3kg Alpine style cheese named after the local version of an alpine peak.

Variants :

Notes :

Royal Bassett Blue Blue C P V NR Drum

Made as a 200g individual soft creamy blue cheese.

Variants :

Notes :

The Cheese with no Name Semisoft C P V WR Drum

Made as a 2kg cheese to a St Paulin recipe with a sticky orangey pink rind and an oozing centre.

Variants :

Notes :

Wiltshire Blue Blue C P V NR Drum

Made as a 3kg cheese.

Variants :

Notes :

Wiltshire Loaf Firm C P V NR Wheel

Made as a 3kg cheese to the same recipe as Ceri's great grandfather and mentioned in Jane Austen novels.

Variants :

Notes :

BROOKE'S WYE VALLEY DAIRY
Monmouthshire

Cheesemakers : Robert & Irene Brooke

Family farm producing fresh milk, double cream, ice cream and cheese using milk from their Jersey herd.

Angiddy Soft C P V BR Disc

Made as a 900g & 200g cheese and named after the river flowing through the farm.

Variants :

Notes :

| **Blue Wenalt** | Blue | C | P | V | NR | Disc |

Made as a 250g cheese using Jersey milk to give a rich, creamy, buttery blue cheese.

Variants :

Notes :

| **Fedw** | Semisoft | C | P | V | XR | Brick |

Named after local woods and made as a 200g cheese similar to a creamy cross between Feta and Caerphilly.

Variants :

Notes :

BRUE VALLEY
Somerset
Cheesemaker : Simon Clapp

Close by Glastonbury Tor, the Clapp family have farmed here since 1538 making a range of dairy products.

| **Fior di Latte Mozzarella** | Fresh | C | P | V | XR | Ball |

Made as a 265g cheese.

Variants :

Notes :

BUCKSHAW MILK SHEEP
Dorset
Cheesemaker : Rachel Dustan

Family farm where sheep are milked by hand and used to hand make a range of cheeses.

| **Buckshaw Blewe** | Blue | S | U | V | NR | Drum |

Made as a 550g cheese.

Variants :

Notes :

| **Buckshaw Crumbly** | Crumbly | S | U | V | NR | Drum |

Made as a 550g cheese with a mild flavour.

Variants :

Notes :

| **Buckshaw Fela** | Semisoft | S | U | V | XR | Block |

Based on Feta.

Variants :

Notes :

Buckshaw Hallewemi   Semisoft   S   U   V   XR   Block
Based on Halloumi.
Variants :
Notes :

Buckshaw White   Semisoft   S   U   V   NR   Drum
Made as an unpressed 2.3kg cheese with a strong mature flavour.
Variants :
Notes :

====

THE BUFFALO DAIRY
Cornwall
Cheesemakers : Duncan & Julie Aitkenhead
Family farm started adding Italian Water Buffaloes in 2001 and now has herd of 70 animals.

Mount's Bay Mozzarella   Fresh   B   P   V   XR   Ball
Using expertise from Trento, Italy to develop an authentic recipe for this traditional style of cheese.
Variants :
Notes :

====

THE BUFFALO FARM
Fife
Cheesemakers : Steve Mitchell, Jim Ritchie, Juan Vicente Reggeti
Scotland's only buffalo mozzarella maker also makes a full range of products from the milk of 500 buffalo.

Scottish Buffalo Mozzarella   Fresh   B   P   V   XR   Ball
Inspired to make mozzarella after a TV visit by chef Gordon Ramsey, it is made as a traditional 125g ball.
Variants :
Notes :

====

BURNSIDE CHEESE
Orkney
Cheesemaker : Barry Graham
Orkney's newest cheesemaker started in 2021 and now has four variants of their cheese.

Burnside   Semisoft   C   P   V   XR   Drum
Made as a 320g cheese with a smooth texture suitable for eating fresh or for cooking similar to Halloumi.
Variants : Original, Smoked, Chilli Flakes, Pepper & Chive
Notes :

====

BURT'S CHEESE
Cheshire
Cheesemakers : Claire Burt, Tom Partridge

Won a gold medal for her home-made cheese in 2010 so set up a dairy and now uses milk from Bidlea Farm.

Burt's Blue   Blue   C   P   V   NR   Ammonite, Disc

Made as a 1.1kg and 180g cheese.

Variants :

Notes :

DiVine   Soft   C   P   V   WR   Disc

Made as a 1.2kg and 180g cheese, washed in Gwatkins Cider and wrapped in vine leaves.

Variants :

Notes :

Drunken Burt   Blue   C   P   V   WR   Disc

Made as a 1.2kg and 180g cheese based on Burt's Blue, but unpierced and washed in Gwatkins Cider.

Variants :

Notes :

Little Burtles   Firm   C   P   V   NR   Ball

Made as a 80g cheese flavoured with garlic and rolled in black pepper to give an intense flavour.

Variants :

Notes :

BUTLERS FARMHOUSE CHEESES
Lancashire
Cheesemakers : Matthew & Daniel Hall

Fourth generation family cheesemakers using milk from surrounding farms often run by extended family.

Beacon Blue   Blue   G   P   V   XR   Drum

One of the few blue goat's cheeses in Britain, made as a 2.5kg cheese.

Variants :

Notes :

Blacksticks Blue   Blue   C   P   V   NR   Drum

Made as a 2.5kg cheese, coloured with annatto and matured for 3 months.

Variants :

Notes :

Burland Bloom   Soft   C   P   V   BR   Disc

Described as a British Brie and made as a 150g cheese.

Variants :

Notes :

Button Mill   Soft   C   P   V   BR   Disc

Made as a 150g cheese based on Camembert and Brie and matured for 2 weeks.

Variants :

Notes :

Goosnargh Gold   Firm   C   P   V   NR   Drum

Based on Double Gloucester and matured for 5 months.

Variants :

Notes :

Kidderton Ash   Soft   G   P   V   BR   Log

Based on a French style Chèvre as a 150g cheese and rolled in ash.

Variants :

Notes :

Mrs Butlers   Firm   C   P   V   XR   Cylinder

Farmhouse creamy Lancashire, clothbound and matured for 3 - 5 months.

Variants :

Notes :

Parlick Brie   Soft   S   P   V   BR   Disc

Named after nearby Parlick Fell and made as a 1kg cheese.

Variants :

Notes :

Parlick Original   Firm   S   P   V   XR   Block

Named after nearby Parlick Fell and made using local sheep's milk.

Variants : Original, Olive

Notes :

Ravens Oak   Soft   G   P   V   BR   Disc

Handmade as a 150g cheese and matured for 3 weeks.

Variants :

Notes :

Rothbury Red   Firm   C   P   V   XR   Drum

Based on Red Leicester coloured orange with annatto and matured for 7 months.

Variants : Original, Smouldering Ember (Smoked)

Notes :

Smouldering Ember   Firm   C   P   V   XR   Block

Red Leicester smoked and matured for 7 months.

Variants :

Notes :

Stratford Blue   Blue   C   P   V   NR   Drum

Made as a 2.5kg cheese.

Variants :

Notes :

Sunday Best   Crumbly   C   P   V   XR   Cylinder

Made a a traditional Lancashire using a 50 year old family recipe and matured for 18 months.

Variants :

Notes :

This Is Proper Double Gloucester   Firm   C   P   V   XR   Block

Made as a large block, matured and portioned into 250g blocks, coloured orange with annatto.

Variants :

Notes :

This Is Proper Goat's Cheese   Firm   G   P   V   XR   Block

Made using milk from goats on family farms as a large block, matured and portioned into 250g blocks.

Variants :

Notes :

This Is Proper Lancashire   Crumbly   C   P   V   XR   Block

Made as a large block, matured and portioned into 250g blocks, in three different styles.

Variants : Creamy, Tasty, Crumbly

Notes :

This Is Proper Red Leicester   Firm   C   P   V   XR   Block

Made as a large block, matured and portioned into 250g blocks, coloured orange with annatto.

Variants :

Notes :

Trotter Hill   Firm   C   P   V   NR   Cylinder

Made a a traditional Lancashire, clothbound and matured for 12 months.

Variants :

Notes :

CAERFAI FARM
Pembrokeshire

Cheesemakers : Wyn & Christine Evans

Organic, sustainable third generation family farm located on the coast in Pembrokeshire Coast National Park.

Caerfai Caerffili   Crumbly   C   U   V   O   NR   Drum

Made as a 3.4kg cheese, clothbound and matured for 6 months.

Variants : Original, Leek & Garlic

Notes :

Caerfai Cheddar   Firm   C   U   V   O   NR   Drum

Made as a 5kg cheese, clothbound and matured for 9 months.

Variants :

Notes :

CAERPHILLY CHEESE COMPANY (CWMNI CAWS CAERFFILI)
Caerphilly

Cheesemakers : Huw Rowlands, Deian Thomas

New cheesemaker planning to start making Caerphilly again after 30 years in the town of the same name.

Caerphilly Caerphilly   Crumbly   C   NR   Drum

The cheese has not been named yet and other details are awaiting its release.

Variants :

Notes :

CALEDONIAN CREAMERY (LACTALIS)
Dumfries & Galloway

Commercial Cheesemaker

Opened in 1899 as the Galloway Cheese Co. and is now owned by the world's largest dairy, Lactalis.

Galloway Cheddar   Firm   C   P   V   XR   Block

Launched by McLelland in 1959 and made as a coloured Cheddar using annatto to create the orange colour.

Variants : Medium, Mature

Notes :

Seriously Cheddar Firm C P V XR Block

Made as a large block and matured for 18 - 24 months before being portioned into smaller blocks.

Variants : Mature, Red Mature, Extra Mature, Red Extra Mature, Strong Vintage

Notes :

CALON WEN
Carmarthenshire
Commercial Cheesemaker

Welsh for 'white heart', this co-operative of 25 organic farms has their cheese made for them at Belton Farm.

Calon Wen Cheddar Firm C P V O XR Block

Made as a 20kg Cheddar with organic milk from the cooperative, matured then cut into 200g blocks.

Variants : Mellow Creamy, Extra Mature

Notes :

Rossett Red Firm C P V O XR Block

Made as a 20kg Red Leicester with organic milk from the cooperative, matured then cut into 200g blocks.

Variants :

Notes :

CAMBRIDGE CHEESE COMPANY
Cambridgeshire
Cheesemongers : Jacky & Paul Sutton-Adam

Cheesemonger in Cambridge city centre since 1994 who has a range of cheeses exclusively made for them.

Cambridge Bleat Soft G P A BR Cylinder

Made by Neal's Yard Creamery as a 180g cheese, ash coated and matured for 4 - 5 weeks.

Variants :

Notes :

Cambridge Blue Blue C U A NR Drum

Made exclusively for and matured for 6 - 24 months by Cambridge Cheese Company.

Variants :

Notes :

Lord Nelson Soft G U A BR Flat Pyramid

Made by Neal's Yard Creamery as a 180g cheese and matured for 4 - 7 weeks.

Variants :

Notes :

CAMBUS O'MAY CHEESE CO
Aberdeenshire
Cheesemaker : Alex Reid

Situated in Royal Deeside with cheesemaker Alex basing his cheeses on those made by his mother years ago.

Ardmore   Firm   C   U   A   NR   Drum

Handmade as a 12kg cheese, infused with Ardmore Single Malt Whisky and matured for 6 weeks.

Variants :

Notes :

Auld Reekie   Firm   C   U   A   NR   Drum

Handmade as a 1.5kg cheese, matured for 8 months and smoked over whisky barrel shavings.

Variants :

Notes :

Cambus O'May   Firm   C   U   A   NR   Drum

Handmade as a 12kg cheese, hand-pressed, cloth wrapped and matured for 6 weeks.

Variants :

Notes :

Lairig Ghru   Crumbly   C   U   A   NR   Drum

Named after a Grampian mountain pass, handmade as a 12kg cheese and matured for 2 months.

Variants :

Notes :

Lochnagar   Hard   C   U   A   NR   Drum

Handmade as a 12kg cheese and matured for 3 months.

Variants : Original (3 months), Auld Lochnagar (12 months)

Notes :

CARRON LODGE
Lancashire
Cheesemaker : Adrian Rhodes

Second generation farmers who diversified into cheesemaking using 100 year old local recipes.

Carron Lodge Double Gloucester   Firm   C   P   V   XR   Block, Drum

Handmade as a 20kg rindless or traditional 13kg clothbound drum and matured for 3 months.

Variants : Rindless, Clothbound

Notes :

Carron Lodge Goat Cheddar   Firm   G   P   V   XR   Half Drum

Made using locally sourced milk as a Cheddar style 900g cheese and smoked in own smokehouse.

Variants :

Notes :

Carron Lodge Lancashire   Crumbly   C   P   V   XR   Block, Drum

Made as a tangy, moist crumbly 20kg block and 4 kg drum and matured with no rind.

Variants :

Notes :

Carron Lodge Red Leicester   Firm   C   P   V   XR   Block, Drum

Made as a 20kg rindless or 4kg clothbound drum, coloured with annatto and matured for 3 months.

Variants :

Notes :

Charcoal Briquette   Firm   C   P   V   WC   Lozenge, Log

Made as a 1kg & 200g cheese blended with charcoal and wax coated.

Variants :

Notes :

Dambuster   Firm   C   P   V   WC   Drum

Made as a 1.5kg & 200g mature Cheddar.

Variants :

Notes :

Farmhouse Caerphilly   Crumbly   C   P   V   XR   Block, Drum

Handmade as a 20kg block and 4kg drum.

Variants :

Notes :

Inglewhite Buffalo   Firm   B   P   V   NR   Drum

Made as a 2kg Cheddar style cheese using milk from own herd of water buffalo and clothbound.

Variants :

Notes :

Lincoln Blue   Blue   C   P   V   WC   Drum

Made as an 800g creamy mature blue cheese.

Variants :

Notes :

Lincoln Imp Firm C P V WC Drum
Made as a 500g & 200g extra mature Cheddar and wax coated.
Variants :

Notes :

Shipston Blue Blue B P V NR Disc
Made as a 850g cheese which is very creamy due the high fat content of buffalo milk.
Variants :

Notes :

===

CAWS CENARTH
Carmarthenshire
Cheesemaker : Carwyn Adams
Organic family farm and cheesemakers drawing on traditions from great, great grandparents.

Becca Firm S P V NR Drum
Made as a limited edition cheese.
Variants :

Notes :

Black Sheep Firm S P V WC Drum
Made as a 150g individual cheese.
Variants :

Notes :

Caws Cenarth Cheddar Firm C P V O WC Disc
Made as a 200g individual cheese.
Variants : Original, Leek, Balsamic & Onion, Crystallised Ginger, Chilli & Tomato, Brandy & Apricot

Notes :

Cenarth Brie Soft C P V O BR Disc
Made as a 1kg & 180g Brie style cheese.
Variants :

Notes :

Cryf Firm C P V WC Drum, Heart
Made as a 400g & 200g extra mature Cheddar.
Variants :

Notes :

Name	Type						Shape
Dol Las	Blue	S	P	V		NR	Drum

Made as a 1kg creamy textured cheese.
Variants :
Notes :

Dol Wen	Soft	S	P	V		BR	Drum

Made as a 1kg cheese.
Variants :
Notes :

Ffili	Crumbly	C	P	V	O	WC	Drum

Made as a 200g Caerffili and wax coated.
Variants : Original, Smoked
Notes :

Golden Cenarth	Soft	C	P	V	O	WR	Disc

Made as a 200g cheese.
Variants :
Notes :

Llain	Hard	C	P	V	O	NR	Drum

Made as an Alpine style cheese matured for 10 months.
Variants :
Notes :

Perl Las	Blue	C	P	V	O	NR	Drum

Made as a 2.5kg cheese and matured for 3 months.
Variants :
Notes :

Perl Wen	Soft	C	P	V	O	BR	Disc

Made as a 1.2kg cheese and matured for 7 weeks.
Variants :
Notes :

St Ludoc	Semisoft	C	P	V	O	WR	Wheel

Made as a 1.9kg cheese washed in organic cider.
Variants :
Notes :

Thelma's Traditional Caerffili PGI   Crumbly   C   P   V   O   NR   Drum

Made as a 3kg cheese and matured for 6 weeks.

Variants :

Notes :

CAWS PENHELYG
Ceredigion

Cheesemaker : Roger Yorke

Single herd local organic milk is used to make cheese in small batches in a micro dairy on the family farm.

Abaty   Soft   C   U   V   O   BR   Disc

One of very few single herd raw milk Brie style cheeses made in Britain, made as a 1.6kg & 230g cheese.

Variants :

Notes :

Abaty Glas   Blue   C   U   V   O   NR   Drum

Made as a 2.3kg cheese, creamy and buttery in style.

Variants :

Notes :

CAWS RHYD Y DELYN
Anglesey

Cheesemakers : Menai & Maldwyn Jones

Family farm on Anglesey using milk from their own Holstein Friesian herd and using local Halen Môn sea salt.

Gouda Mon   Firm   C   P   V   NR   Rounded Drum

Made as a 1.5k & 2.5kg cheese based on Gouda.

Variants :

Notes :

Mon Las   Blue   C   P   V   NR   Drum

Made as a 2.5kg cheese based on Gorgonzola.

Variants :

Notes :

CAWS TEIFI
Ceredigion
Cheesemakers : Tim Mitchell

Founded in 1981 by Dutch cheesemakers John & Patrice who realised their vision of organic farming.

Celtic Promise   Crumbly   C   U   A   O   WR   Drum

Based on Teifi Caerphilly. Made as a 475g cheese and matured for 8 weeks.

Variants :

Notes :

Gwyn Bach   Semisoft   C   U   A   O   NR Cylinder

Made as a 150g cheese using Caerphilly curd.

Variants :

Notes :

Saval   Crumbly   C   U   A   O   WR   Drum

Made as a 1.8kg cheese at Caws Teifi before being brine washed.

Variants :

Notes :

Teifi   Firm   C   U   A   O   PC   Rounded Drum

Made as a 3.8kg Gouda.

Variants : Mature, Heritage, Seaweed, Cumin, Nettle, Onion & Garlic, Smoked, Chilli

Notes :

Teifi Caerphilly PGI   Crumbly   C   U   A   O   NR   Drum

Made as a 3.8kg cheese.

Variants : Original, Mature, Oak Smoked

Notes :

Teifi Halloumi   Semisoft   C   U   V   O   XR   Block

Made as a 1kg and 200g block.

Variants :

Notes :

CERNEY CHEESE
Gloucestershire
Cheesemaker : Avril Pratt

Founded by Lady Isabel Angus to make the goat's cheeses that she developed a passion for while in France.

Cerney Mini Ash   Fresh   G   U   V   XR   Drum
Made as a 140g cheese, coated in ash and matured for 4 weeks.
Variants : Original, Pepper, Vine

Notes :

Cerney Pyramid   Fresh   G   U   V   XR   Flat Pyramid
Based on Valencay and made as a 250g cheese, coated in ash and matured for 4 weeks.
Variants : Original, Pepper, Vine

Notes :

===

CHAPEL CROSS TEA ROOM
Somerset
Cheesemaker : Rosie Adams

Family home for over 50 years with cheese being made from her own small herd of Golden Guernsey goats.

Big Nick   Semisoft   G   U   V   WR   Disc
Brine washed cheese which won best new cheese in the 2022 British Cheese Awards.
Variants :

Notes :

Little Benet   Soft   G   U   V   BR   Drum
Made as a 140g lactic cheese coated in ash before the soft white rind develops.
Variants :

Notes :

Mini Mogul   Soft   G   U   V   PC   Rounded Drum
New cheese created in 2023, made as a 250g cheese and matured for 5 weeks.
Variants :

Notes :

Young Louis   Fresh   G   U   V   BR   Drum
Made as a 140g cheese and ready to eat after just a few days but can mature to yield more intense flavours.
Variants :

Notes :

===

CHARLES MARTELL & SON
Gloucestershire
Cheesemaker : Charles Martell

The farm has been home to the Martells for over 50 years when Charles started breeding Gloucester cows.

Double Berkeley   Firm   C   P   A   NR   Drum

Made as a 2.2kg cheese. First mentioned in literature in 1792 but died out until revived by Martell in 1984.

Variants :

Notes :

Hereford Hop   Firm   C   P   A   FR   Drum

Created by Martell in 1987, it is made as a 3kg cheese and coated in dried hops from nearby Herefordshire.

Variants :

Notes :

Martell Double Gloucester   Firm   C   U/P   V   NR   Drum

Had died out in 1950s but revived by Martell in 1973. Made as a 3kg cheese and matured for 3 months.

Variants :

Notes :

Martell Single Gloucester PDO   Firm   C   U/P   V   NR   Drum

Only made on Gloucestershire farms with Gloucester cows, it is a 2.6kg cheese matured for 2 months.

Variants :

Notes :

May Hill Green   Semisoft   C   P   V   FR   Disc

Made as a 1.8kg & a 500g cheese, it is coated with chopped nettles giving a dramatic appearance.

Variants :

Notes :

Slack Ma Girdle   Semisoft   C   P   V   BR   Disc

Developed in 2016 as a non smelly version of Stinking Bishop, it is made as a 700g cheese but not washed.

Variants :

Notes :

Stinking Bishop   Semisoft   C   P   V   WR   Disc

Made as a 1.8kg & 500g cheese, wrapped in a cedar band, washed in perry and matured for 8 weeks.

Variants :

Notes :

CHEDDAR GORGE CHEESE COMPANY (CARRON LODGE)
Somerset
Cheesemakers : Cheddar Gorge Cheese Team

Founded in 2003, the only Cheddar actually made in Cheddar Gorge and matured in the gorge's caves.

Cheddar Gorge Flavoured Cheddar   Firm   C   U   V   NR   Drum
Made as a 25kg cheese, clothbound and matured for at least 12 months.
Variants : Cider Garlic & Chive, Herbs & Wild Garlic, Red Onion & Tomato, Slosh of Port
Notes :

Cheddar Gorge Traditional Cheddar   Firm   C   U   V   NR   Cylinder
Made as a 25kg cheese, clothbound and matured for at least 12 months.
Variants : Mellow, Mature (12m), Extra Mature (15m), Vintage (20m), Smoked
Notes :

Cheddar Gorge Waxed Cheddar   Firm   C   U   V   WC   Disc
Made as a 200g individual cheese and wax coated.
Variants : Especially Strong (24 months), Chilli, Love It or Hate It (Yeast Extract)
Notes :

CHEESE CELLAR DAIRY (H&B)
Worcestershire
Cheesemaker : George Bramham

Goat's dairy owned by cheese wholesaler Harvey & Brockless making Loire valley influenced goat's cheeses

---

Ashlynn   Soft   G   P   V   BR   Cylinder
Made as a 200g cheese, ash coated with a line of ash running through the centre and matured for 2 weeks.
Variants :
Notes :

Blanche   Soft   G   P   V   BR   Log
Made as a 200g cheese and matured for 2 weeks to develop a wrinkled rind and delicate creamy centre.
Variants :
Notes :

Clara   Soft   G   P   V   BR   Log
Made as a 200g cheese the same as Blanche, but ash coated and matured for 2 weeks.
Variants :
Notes :

| **Delilah** | Soft | C | P | V | | BR | Flat Pyramid |

Made as a 200g triple-cream cheese with crushed pink peppercorns as decoration.

Variants :

Notes :

| **Greta** | Semisoft | C | P | V | | BR | Pot |

Made as a cows milk curd similar to Feta and the cubes submerged in a pot of garlic and basil oil.

Variants :

Notes :

| **Luna** | Soft | G | P | V | | BR | Log |

Made as a 200g cheese, similar to Blanche and Clare and ash coated, but drier and easier for slicing.

Variants :

Notes :

| **Trufflynn** | Soft | G | P | V | | XR | Drum |

Made the same as Ashlynn, but with a line of truffle in the centre, ash coated and matured for 2 weeks.

Variants :

Notes :

===

CHEESE GEEK
London

Cheesemonger : Edward Hancock

Online cheesemonger who has worked with two dairies to develop four cheeses of their own.

| **Eastwood** | Soft | C | P | V | | XR | Wheel |

Made as a 2kg cheese based on Brie by Bath Soft Cheese Company and matured for 7 - 8 weeks.

Variants :

Notes :

| **Hendrix** | Blue | C | P | V | | BR | Drum |

Made as a 500 - 600g cheese by Caws Cenarth matured for 5 weeks developing a silky smooth texture.

Variants :

Notes :

| **Swift** | Firm | C | P | V | | BR | Rounded Drum |

Made as a 2.5kg cheese by Bath Soft Cheese Company based on Gouda and matured for 9 months.

Variants :

Notes :

Washington   Soft   C   P   V   WR   Disc

Made by Caws Cenarth as a 1kg cheese washed in cider and matured for 8 weeks.

Variants :

Notes :

CHEESE ON THE WEY
Surrey
Cheesemaker : John Brown

The old dairy building on a Jersey dairy farm is used to make cheeses with low environmental impact.

Alfred's Yellow Jersey   Firm   C   T   V   WC   Rounded Drum

Based on a Gouda and made asa 4kg cheese, flavoured with fenugreek seeds then coated in yellow wax.

Variants :

Notes :

Blackfriar   Firm   C   T   V   FR   Drum

Based on a Tomme de Savoie as a 2.2kg cheese and coated in grape skins from nearby Greyfriars Vineyard.

Variants :

Notes :

Blue Millie   Blue   C   T   V   NR   Drum

Made as a 2.5kg cheese and matured for 5 weeks.

Variants :

Notes :

Colwey   Fresh   C   T   V   XR   Drum

Made as a 2.5kg cheese and matured for 2 weeks.

Variants :

Notes :

Millie   Firm   C   T   V   NR   Drum

Made as a 2.5kg cheese similar to a Caerphilly style and matured for 5 weeks.

Variants :

Notes :

Tilston Blue   Blue   C   T   V   NR   Drum

Made as a 5.0kg cheese and matured for 3 months.

Variants :

Notes :

| **Tommie** | Firm | C | T | V | NR | Drum |

Made as a 2.5kg Alpine style cheese and matured for 2 months.

Variants :

Notes :

| **Weywood** | Semisoft | C | T | V | WR | Brick |

Made as a 180g cheese, washed in locally made cider and matured for 3 weeks.

Variants :

Notes :

CHEESEMAKERS OF CANTERBURY
Kent
Cheesemaker : Jane Bowyer.

Made in a former milk dairy starting with recipes from a Wiltshire dairy, now makes a range of cheeses.

| **Ancient Ashmore** | Hard | C | U | V | NR | Drum |

Made as a 4kg vintage Cheddar style cheese and matured for at least 12 months.

Variants :

Notes :

| **Ashmore Farmhouse** | Firm | C | U | V | NR | Drum |

Made as a 4kg Cheddar style cheese and matured for at least 6 months, some of which is flavoured.

Variants : Original, Smoked, Mustard, Chilli

Notes :

| **Bowyer's** | Soft | C | P | V | BR | Disc |

Made as a 2.5kg Brie style cheese and matured for 2 - 6 weeks.

Variants : Original, Smoked

Notes :

| **Canterbury Cobble** | Firm | C | U | V | WR | Flying Saucer |

Brine washed and forming a natural rind that is matured for 3 months.

Variants :

Notes :

| **Chaucers** | Soft | C | P | V | BR | Disc |

Made as a 200g Camembert style cheese and matured for 3 weeks.

Variants :

Notes :

Dargate Dumpy   Soft   S   P   V   BR   Disc

Made as a 150g sheep's milk Camembert style cheese and matured for 2 - 6 weeks.

Variants :

Notes :

Ellie's Goat   Soft   G   P   V   XR   Disc

Made as a 125 - 150g cheese using some goat's milk supplied by the creator of these cheeses, Ellie's Dairy.

Variants : Original, Chilli, Herb

Notes :

Fremlin's Kentish Log   Soft   G   P   V   XR   Log

Made as a traditional 100g goat's log using some milk supplied by the creator of these cheeses, Ellie's Dairy.

Variants :

Notes :

Gruff   Firm   G   U   V   WR   Flying Saucer

Made as a 1kg cheese, brine washed and matured for 2 - 4 months.

Variants :

Notes :

Kelly's Canterbury Goat   Hard   G   U   V   NR   Drum

Made as a 4kg cheese and matured for 3 months.

Variants :

Notes :

Ramsey   Hard   S   U   V   NR   Drum

Made as a sheep's milk Cheddar style cheese and matured for 4 - 6 months.

Variants :

Notes :

Shaggy's Beard   Soft   G   P   V   XR   Log

Made as a goat's milk Camembert using some milk supplied by the creator of these cheeses, Ellie's Dairy.

Variants :

Notes :

Shawn   Firm   S   U   V   NR   Flying Saucer

Made as a Pecorino style cheese with a hard crusty rind.

Variants :

Notes :

CHESHIRE CHEESE COMPANY (JOSEPH HELER)
Cheshire
Commercial Cheesemaker
Farm based in Nantwich using Cheshire milk, one of only two truckle makers who make their own cheese.

Cheshire Cheese Cheddar Firm C P V WC Disc
Made as a 2kg & 200g cheese and wax coated.
Variants : Black Bob, Vintage, Reserva, Old Hag, Charcoal, Jerk, El Gringo, Masala, Shamrock, Hunter
Notes :

Cheshire Cheese Cheshire Crumbly C P V WC Disc
Made as a 200g cheese and wax coated.
Variants : Traditional Creamy, Gincello
Notes :

Cheshire Cheese Royal Blue Blue C P V NR Disc
Traditionally made as a 200g individual cheese in a presentation box.
Variants :
Notes :

Cheshire Cheese Smokewood Firm C P V WC Disc
Made as a 200g Red Leicester, matured and smoked before being coated in red wax.
Variants :
Notes :

===

THE CHUCKLING CHEESE COMPANY
Lincolnshire
Cheesemongers : Stuart & Emma Colclough
Cheesemongers with several shops sourcing waxed cheeses and selling under their own names.

Chuckling Cheese Cheddar Truckles Firm C P V WC Drum
Made as 200g cheese and wax coated.
Variants : Extra Mature, Black Pepper, Caramelised Red Onion, Cream Tea, Mexican Sweet Chilli, Ale &
Mustard, Margarita, Black as Charcoal, Gin & Tonic, Rum & Pineapple, Garlic & Chive, Sunday Roast
Notes :

Chuckling Cheese Large Truckles Firm C P V WC Drum
Made as 2kg Cheddar and wax coated.
Variants : Extra Mature, Vintage, Smoked
Notes :

===

COACHYARD CREAMERY
Durham
Cheesemaker : Mark Samuelson

Small scale cheesemaker using Holstein-Friesian milk from the neighbouring farm.

Edgedale   Firm   S   U   V   NR   Cylinder

New experimental sheep's milk cheese made as a 850g truckle & 100g crottin and matured for 4 months.
Variants : Original, Truffle

Notes :

Volesdale   Firm   C   U   V   NR   Cylinder

Made as a 2.2kg & 850g Cheddar style truckle matured for 4 - 12 months.
Variants :

Notes :

===

COLSTON BASSETT DAIRY
Nottinghamshire
Cheesemaker : Billy Kevan

Owned by and made using milk from a co-operative of 3 farms within 1.5 miles since 1913.

Colston Bassett Shropshire Blue   Blue   C   P   A/V   NR   Cylinder

Made as a 8kg cheese milder and sweeter than Stilton, coloured with annatto and matured for 3 months.
Variants :

Notes :

Colston Bassett Stilton PDO   Blue   C   P   A/V   NR   Cylinder

Made as a 8kg cheese, hand ladled, hand rubbed and matured for 3 months.
Variants :

Notes :

===

CONNAGE HIGHLAND DAIRY
Highland
Cheesemakers : Jill & Callum Clark

Second generation family owned organic farm with own herd grazing on the shores of Moray Firth.

Connage Cheddar   Firm   C   P   V   O   NR   Drum

Made as a 25kg cheese, clothbound and matured for 12 months.
Variants :

Notes :

Connage Clava Brie   Soft   C   P   V   O   BR   Disc, Heart

Made as a 1.5kg, 250g & 120g cheese and matured for 3 weeks.

Variants : Original, Smoked

Notes :

Connage Cromal   Crumbly   C   P   V   O   NR   Drum

Named after a local hill and made as a 14kg Caerphilly style cheese.

Variants :

Notes :

Connage Crowdie   Fresh   C   P   V   O   XR   Pot

Traditional curd cheese made by hanging curds overnight in muslin bags before going into 160g pots.

Variants :

Notes :

Connage Dunlop   Firm   C   P   V   O   NR   Cylinder

Made as a 25kg cheese, clothbound and matured for 5 - 7 months.

Variants : Original, Smoked

Notes :

Connage Gouda   Firm   C   P   V   O   WC   Rounded Drum

Made as a 12kg cheese and matured for 6 months.

Variants : Original, Cumin, Garlic & Nettle

Notes :

CORNISH CHEESE COMPANY
Cornwall
Cheesemaker : Phil Stansfield

Family farm on the edge of Bodmin Moor who started making cheese in 2001 due to falling milk prices.

Cornish Blue   Blue   C   P   V   NR   Cylinder

Winning World Champion cheese in 2010, it is made as a 5kg cheese and matured for 3 months.

Variants :

Notes :

Cornish Brie   Soft   C   P   V   BR   Disc, Heart

Launched in 2021 after building new dairy separate from the blue, it is made as a 1kg, 600g & 200g cheese.

Variants :

Notes :

Cornish Camembert Soft C P V BR Disc
Introduced in 2023 to complement the Cornish Brie and made as a 1kg & 200g cheese.
Variants :

Notes :

Cornish Cheddar Soft C P V WC Drum
Made for the Cornish Cheese Company as a 200g cheese by Davidstow Creamery.
Variants :

Notes :

Cornish Nanny Blue G P V NR Cylinder
Goat's milk version of Cornish Blue, it is made in various sizes up to 2kg between Easter and Christmas.
Variants :

Notes :

CORNISH GOUDA COMPANY
Cornwall
Cheesemaker : Giel Sprierings
Made using milk from own herd of Holstein-Friesian cows fed using own crops and powered by biomass.

Cornish Gouda Hard C P A WC Curved Drum
Made as a 10kg cheese & 900g truckle and matured for 3 - 36 months with a range of added flavours.
Variants : Mild, Mature, Extra Mature, Vintage, Cumin, Truffle, Fenugreek, Honey Clover, Italian Herb

Notes :

COSYN CYMRU
Gwynedd
Cheesemaker : Carrie Rimes
Started cheesemaking in France and now in the foothills of Snowdonia using milk from local Lleyn sheep.

Brefu Bach Soft S U V BR Drum
Made as a 120g lactic set cheese with very small amount of thistle rennet and matured for 3 - 7 weeks.
Variants :

Notes :

Caws Calan Semisoft S U A NR Drum
Younger 600g truckle version of Caws Chwaral and matured for 2 - 4 months.
Variants :

Notes :

| Caws Chwaral | Firm | S | U | A | | NR | Drum |

Based on a slow aged Caerphilly recipe and made as a 6kg cheese and matured for 2 - 5 months.

Variants :

Notes :

| Olwyn Fawr | Firm | S | U | A | | NR | Drum |

Meaning 'big wheel', made using lamb's rennet as a 6kg cheese, hard pressed and matured for 4 - 9 months.

Variants :

Notes :

COTE HILL FARM

Lincolnshire

Cheesemakers : Mary & Joe Davenport

Mother and son make the cheese on the family farm while father and other son manage the herd.

| Cote Hill Blue | Blue | C | U | V | | NR | Disc |

Made as a 1.2kg cheese and matured for 8 weeks.

Variants :

Notes :

| Cote Hill Lindum | Semisoft | C | U | V | | WR | Square |

Named after the Roman name for Lincoln, made as a 1.5kg cheese washed in FAB Brewery Golden Fleece.

Variants :

Notes :

| Cote Hill Red | Firm | C | U | V | | WR | Drum |

Made as a 4kg Alpine style cheese and matured for 4 months.

Variants :

Notes :

| Cote Hill White | Fresh | C | U | V | | XR | Disc |

Made as a 100g cheese and matured for 3 days to be eaten whilst young and fresh.

Variants :

Notes :

| Cote Hill Yellow | Firm | C | U | V | | WC | Disc |

Made as a 1.42g cheese matured in bright yellow wax as a tribute to the Lincolnshire nickname Yellowbelly.

Variants :

Notes :

Snowdrop   Soft   C   U   V   BR   Disc

Cote Hill White but mould ripened and named after the favourite flower of matriarch, Cynthia Davenport.

Variants :

Notes :

COTHERSTONE DAIRY
Durham

Cheesemakers : Joan & Alwin Cross

Dales style cheese made to a family recipe now made using milk from a local farm.

Cotherstone   Firm   C   P   V   NR   Drum

Made as a 2.3kg firm/crumbly cheese and matured for 2 months, sometimes wax coated.

Variants :

Notes :

THE COTSWOLD CHEESE COMPANY
Gloucestershire

Cheesemakers : Jon & Lisa Goodchild

Cheesemonger who has a house blue cheese made under their name for their three Cotswold shops.

Stow Blue   Blue   C   P   V   NR   Drum

Made by Hartington Creamery as a 2.2kg & 200g cheese with a delicate blue texture and flavour.

Variants :

Notes :

COUNTRY CHEESES
Devon

Cheesemongers : Gary & Elise Jungheim, Rebecca Cleave

Cheesemonger with three cheese shops in Devon who have developed their own range of cheeses.

Bakesy Meadow   Soft   G   P   V   BR   Drum

Made by Sharpham Dairy exclusively for Country Cheeses.

Variants :

Notes :

Bliss   Firm   C   P   V   NR   Drum

Alpine inspired cheese made by Country Cheeses only very rarely and matured in their own cave.

Variants :

Notes :

Blue Bay   Blue   C   P   V   NR   Cylinder

Made by Ticklemore Dairy as a 2kg cheese and matured for 2 - 3 months exclusively for Country Cheeses.

Variants :

Notes :

Celeste   Soft   C   U   V   BR   Disc

Made by Sharpham Dairy exclusively for Country Cheeses using Jersey milk as a Brie style 200g cheese.

Variants :

Notes :

Chemmy   Soft   G   P   V   BR   Log

Made by Sharpham Dairy exclusively for Country Cheeses to their own recipe.

Variants :

Notes :

Devon Sage   Firm   C   P   V   WC   Drum

Made by Curworthy Cheese exclusively for Country Cheeses in the style of a Sage Derby.

Variants :

Notes :

Little Stinky   Semisoft   C   P   V   WR   Disc

Made by Whalesborough Cheese exclusively for Country Cheeses as 200g cheese and washed in cider.

Variants :

Notes :

Shoalgate   Firm   C   U   V   WR   Drum

Appenzeller inspired cheese made by Country Cheeses only very rarely and washed in Buckfast Tonic Wine.

Variants :

Notes :

Sweet Charlotte   Firm   C   P   V   NR   Drum

Alpine inspired cheese made by Country Cheeses only very rarely and matured in their own cave.

Variants :

Notes :

Trehill   Firm   C   P   V   WC   Drum

Made by Curworthy Cheese exclusively for Country Cheeses as a 2.5kg cheese infused with chives and garlic.

Variants :

Notes :

Withybrook   Soft   G   P   V   BR   Flat Pyramid

Made by Sharpham Dairy exclusively for Country Cheeses with a traditional ash coating.

Variants :

Notes :

COW CLOSE FARM
Derbyshire

Cheesemakers : Sophie & James Summerlin

Husband and wife cheesemaking team using milk from a local herd since 2016 in the Peak District.

Stanage Millstone   Soft   C   P   V   BR   Millstone

Handmade as a 725g and 180g cheese with an unusual hole in the centre and matured for 7 weeks.

Variants :

Notes :

CROOME CHEESE
Worcestershire

Cheesemaker : Nick Hodgetts

Family run business using block Cheddar to blend and flavour and shape before cutting or wax coating.

Croome Flavoured Cheddar   Firm   C   P   V   XR   Block

Made as block Cheddar, blended with flavours and cut into 150g wedges.

Variants : Ginger, Prosecco, Stinking Rose, Bramble, Brunswick, Colonel Mustard, Faithful Baron, Jubilee Fig, Lazy Mule, Musketeer, Scrumpy Crunch, Talisman, Whittington Oak, Worcester Gold, Worcester Red

Notes :

Croome Waxed Truckles   Firm   C   P   V   WC   Half Drum, Drum

Made as block Cheddar, blended with flavours and formed into 1kg half drums & 150g wax coated drums.

Variants : Worcester Sauce, Worcesters Gold, Scrumpy & Apple, Honey & Figs, Hot Chilli, Black Truffle, Blackberry & Apple, Onion & Sage, Whittington Oak, Garlic & Parsley, Whittington Red, Honey & Ginger

Notes :

Harlech   Firm   C   P   V   WC   Drum

Made as a Welsh Cheddar blended with horseradish and parsley and formed as a 1.5kg & 150g cheese.

Variants :

Notes :

Tintern Firm C P V WC Drum
Made as a Welsh Cheddar blended with onions, chives and shallots and formed as a 1.5kg & 150g cheese.
Variants :
Notes :

Worcestershire Hop Firm C P V FR Drum
Made as a 4kg & 2kg Welsh Cheddar rolled in roasted hops.
Variants :
Notes :

Y Fenni Firm C P V WC Drum
Made as a Welsh Cheddar blended with wholegrain mustard and ale and formed as a 1.5kg & 150g cheese.
Variants :
Notes :

===

CROPWELL BISHOP CREAMERY
Nottinghamshire
Cheesemaker : Robin Skailes
Cheesemakers since 1847 and now using milk from 9 local farms to make traditional and modern cheeses.

Beauvale Blue C P A NR Cylinder
Made as a 7kg cheese and matured for 3 months.
Variants :
Notes :

Cropwell Bishop Blue Shropshire Blue C P V NR Cylinder
Made as an 8kg cheese, coloured orange with annatto and matured for 3 months.
Variants :
Notes :

Cropwell Bishop Stilton PDO Blue C P A/V NR Cylinder
Made as a 7kg cheese and matured for 3 months.
Variants : Traditional (Animal), Organic (Vegetarian)
Notes :

Cropwell Bishop White Stilton PDO Crumbly C P V XR Cylinder
Made as an 8kg cheese and blended with various fruits.
Variants : Blueberry, Cranberry, Apricot, Mango & Ginger
Notes :

CRYER & STOTT
West Yorkshire
Cheesemongers : Richard & Clare Holmes
Cheesemonger who has range of exclusive Yorkshire themed cheeses made for them by a number of dairies.

Britannia Firm C P V WC Drum
Made as a Cheddar and matured for 16 months.
Variants :
Notes :

Cryer & Stott Coverdale Crumbly C P V NR Drum
Made as an 800g Wensleydale style cheese exclusive to Cryer & Stott, clothbound and matured for 5 weeks.
Variants :
Notes :

Duke of Wellington Blue C P V NR Drum
Created exclusively for British embassies and now made for general use and matured for 15 weeks.
Variants :
Notes :

Endeavour Semisoft C P V WR Drum
Double-cream cheese washed in Mason's Yorkshire Tea Gin.
Variants :
Notes :

Ewe Beauty Firm S U V WR Drum
Made in a Pecorino style and matured for 6 months.
Variants :
Notes :

Flatcapper Brie Soft C P V BR Disc
Made as a 500g Brie style cheese.
Variants :
Notes :

King Charles III Truffle Cheddar Firm C P V NR Drum
Isle of Kintyre Cheddar blended with black truffle then clothbound and buttered to mature.
Variants :
Notes :

Lilibet Blue   Blue   C   P   V   NR   Drum

Created to celebrate Elizabeth II's Platinum Jubilee, matured for at least 70 days and often up to 12 weeks.

Variants :

Notes :

Northern Balls   Firm   C   P   V   WC   Bomb

Mature Cheddar blended with a range of flavours and shaped as a bomb.

Variants : Great Balls of Fire (Jalapeño), Salty Balls (Seaweed), Prickly Balls (Horseradish & Nettle), Old Balls

Notes :

Northern Goats   Firm   G   P   V   XR   Half Drum

Launched in 2022, it is based on a Cheddar style and matured for 3 months.

Variants :

Notes :

Pomfret Monk   Firm   C   P   V   WC   Half Drum

Launched in 2022 as a mature Cheddar blended with powdered liquorice root.

Variants :

Notes :

Rhuby Crumble   Crumbly   C   P   V   WC   Drum

Wensleydale style blended with Yorkshire rhubarb and vanilla pod.

Variants :

Notes :

Sheffield Forge   Firm   C   P   V   WC   Disc

Yorkshire Red cheese blended with Henderson's Relish.

Variants :

Notes :

Stottie   Soft   G   P   V   BR   Drum

Based on Brie and made as an individual cheese.

Variants :

Notes :

Wave   Firm   C   P   V   XR   Half Drum

Mature Cheddar blended with Scarborough seaweed.

Variants :

Notes :

Yorkshire Cask Firm C P V WC Disc

Mature cheddar blended with Kirkstall Virtuous Ale and wholegrain mustard.

Variants :

Notes :

CURDS & CROUST
Cornwall

Cheesemaker : Martin Gaylard

Experienced Cornish cheesemaker now working as an independent in a new purpose built dairy.

Boy Laity Soft C P A BR Disc

Made as a 1kg & 165g cheese based on Camembert.

Variants :

Notes :

Miss Wenna Soft C P V BR Disc

Made as a 165g cheese based on Brie.

Variants :

Notes :

Nanny Florrie Soft G P V BR Disc

Made as a 165g cheese based on Brie.

Variants :

Notes :

Smokey Duke Soft C P V BR Disc

Made as a 150g cheese based on Brie and naturally smoked over oak wood.

Variants :

Notes :

The Truffler Soft C P V BR Disc

Made as a 165g cheese based on Brie and flavoured with truffle.

Variants :

Notes :

CURLEW DAIRY
North Yorkshire
Cheesemakers : Ben & Sam Spence

Started as The Home Farmer before relocating to Wensley Village to make this most traditional of cheeses.

Yoredale Crumbly C U VA NR Cylinder

Made as a 7kg Wensleydale style cheese formerly named Old Roan, clothbound and matured for 3 months.

Variants :

Notes :

CURWORTHY CHEESE
Devon
Cheesemakers : Rachel Stephens, Richard Drake

Started 30 years ago in the shadow of Dartmoor with milk sourced from a single local herd.

Belstone Firm C P V NR Drum

Made as a 2.4kg & 1.2kg cheese based on a 17th century recipe, a vegetarian version of Curworthy.

Variants :

Notes :

Chipple Firm C P V WC Drum

Made as a 2.4kg cheese based on Curworthy with chopped spring onions and coated with green wax.

Variants :

Notes :

Curworthy Firm C P A WC Drum

Based on a traditional 17th century recipe and made as a 2.4kg & 1.2kg cheese coated with black wax.

Variants :

Notes :

Dartmoor Chilli Firm C P A WC Drum

Made as a 2.4kg Curworthy with fresh Dartmoor chillies coated with red wax with a yellow wax top.

Variants :

Notes :

Devon Maid Soft C P V BR Disc

Described as a Brie with Camembert tones, it is made as a 650g & 250g cheese.

Variants :

Notes :

Devon Oke Firm C P A NR Drum

Made as a 4.5kg cheese based on a 17th century recipe, longer matured (5 months) version of Curworthy.

Variants : Original, Smoked (Devon Smoake)

Notes :

Haytor Firm C P V NR Drum

Made as a 3.6kg cheese based on an Alpine style recipe.

Variants :

Notes :

Meldon Firm C P V WC Drum

Made as a 2.4kg & 1.2kg cheese with English mustard and ale, wax coated and matured for 3 months.

Variants :

Notes :

THE DAIRY DOOR

Shropshire

Cheesemaker : Millie Preece

Farming family who set up a cheesemaking business in 2022 using milk from a local Ayrshire herd.

Farley Semisoft C P V XR Square, Heart

Made as a 100 - 120g cheese based on Feta in two shapes and named after a nearby hamlet.

Variants :

Notes :

Harley Semisoft C P V XR Square, Heart

Made as a 100 - 120g cheese based on Halloumi in two shapes and named after a neighbouring village.

Variants :

Notes :

St Barties Soft C P V BR Disc, Heart

Named after a local church and made as a 250g disc and a 150g heart shape based on Brie.

Variants :

Notes :

The Wedge Firm C P V XR Disc

A new cheese named after Wenlock Edge, based on Gouda and matured for 4 months.

Variants :

Notes :

DAIRY PRODUCE PACKERS
Armagh
Commercial Cheesemaker

Part of Kerry Group making a range of cheeses mainly for supermarket customers.

Coleraine Cheddar   Firm   C   P   V   XR   Block
Made as large blocks, matured and cut into smaller blocks for retail.
Variants : Medium, Mature

Notes :

DALTONS DAIRY
Staffordshire
Farmer & Cheesemonger : Dalton Family

Family dairy farm and farm shop supplying milk to local cheesemakers who in turn make cheeses for them.

Daltons Dovedale Blue PDO   Blue   C   P   V   NR   Drum
Made by Staffordshire Cheese Company as a 2.5kg cheese as a continental style blue.
Variants :

Notes :

Daltons Staffordshire PDO   Firm   C   P   V   NR   Cylinder
Made by Staffordshire Cheese Company as an 8.5kg cheese and matured for 3 months.
Variants : Original, Vintage Staffordshire Sage

Notes :

THE DAMN FINE CHEESE COMPANY
Highland
Cheesemonger : Tracey Smedley

Following a career selling speciality foods, set up her own business selling blended wax coated Cheddars.

Damn Fine Waxed Cheddar   Firm   C   P   V   WC   Drum
Mature Cheddar in blocks is blended with various flavours, shaped as a 200g cheese and wax coated.
Variants : Mature, Smoked, Caramelised Red Onion, Black Pepper, Garlic & Chive, Chilli, Cranberry, Whisky & Orange, Wee Yeastie, Black Gold, The Italian Job, Taste of Christmas

Notes :

DART MOUNTAIN CHEESE
Derry

Cheesemaker : Julie & Kevin Hickey

Cheese dairy and food business started in 2009 by two former chef caterers in the Sperrin Mountains.

Banagher Bold   Firm   C   P   V   WR   Drum

Made as a 3.2kg cheese and washed in a locally made pale ale before being matured for at least 3 months.

Variants :

Notes :

Carraig Bán   Fresh   G   P   V   XR   Drum

Made using goat's milk from a neighbouring farm as a 150g - 190g cheese and matured for 5 days.

Variants :

Notes :

Dart Mountain Dusk   Firm   C   P   V   NR   Drum

Made as a 3.2kg cheese, ash coated and matured for at least 3 months.

Variants :

Notes :

Kilcreen   Firm   C   P   V   NR   Drum

Made as an Alpine style 3.2kg cheese and matured for at least 6 months.

Variants :

Notes :

Meeny Hill   Firm   G   P   V   NR   Drum

Made as a 3.2kg cheese and matured for at least 3 months.

Variants :

Notes :

Meeny Hill Blue   Blue   G   P   V   NR   Drum

Made as a 3.2kg cheese and matured for at least 2 months.

Variants :

Notes :

Sperrin Blue   Blue   C   P   V   NR   Drum

Their first cheese, named after the mountains and made as a 3.2kg cheese matured for at least 2 months.

Variants :

Notes :

Tirkeeran   Hard   C   P   A   NR   Drum

Named after an Irish chieftain and made as a 3.2kg cheese matured for 7 months.

Variants :

Notes :

DAVID WILLIAMS CHEESE
Cheshire

Cheesemonger : David Williams

Bowland was originally developed by David's grandfather in 1875 and now made by Belton Farm.

Bowland   Firm   C   P   V   FR   Drum

Made as a 1.5kg Lancashire blended with apple, raisin, cinnamon originally as a Christmas cake alternative.

Variants :

Notes :

DAVIDSTOW CREAMERY (SAPUTO)
Cornwall

Commercial Cheesemaker

Started in 1950 on a former RAF base, the world's largest mature Cheddar plant owned by a Canadian dairy.

Cathedral City Cheddar   Firm   C   P   V   XR   Block

Made as a 20kg cheese and matured for 4 - 24 months depending on the profile before being cut.

Variants : Mild, Mature, Extra Mature, Vintage, Strongest, Black Pepper, Balsamic Onion

Notes :

Davidstow Cheddar   Firm   C   P   V   XR   Block

Made as a 20kg cheese and matured for anything up to 60 months before being cut into portions.

Variants : Classic Mature, Crackler Extra Mature (20 months), Reserve Vintage (36 months), Reserve (40 months), Reserve (60 months)

Notes :

DAYLESFORD ORGANICS
Gloucestershire

Cheesemakers : Peter Kindel, Sasha Serebrinsky

Bamford family owned farm converted to organic in 1994 and built cheese dairy using own milk in 2001.

Adlestrop   Semisoft   C   P   V   O   WR   Drum

Made as a 3.2kg cheese and matured for 10 weeks.

Variants : Original, Waxed 250g

Notes :

Baywell   Soft   C   P   V   O   WR   Heart

Made as a 180g cheese and matured for 5 weeks.

Variants :

Notes :

Bledington Blue   Blue   C   P   V   O   NR   Disc

Made as a 350g cheese and matured for 5 weeks.

Variants :

Notes :

Daylesford Blue   Blue   C   P   V   O   NR   Cylinder

Made as a 1.5kg cheese and matured for 10 weeks.

Variants :

Notes :

Daylesford Cheddar   Firm   C   P   A   O   NR   Cylinder

The first organic British Cheddar, made as a 10kg cheese, clothbound and matured for 9 - 12 months.

Variants : Original, Reserve (18 months), Waxed 250g

Notes :

Daylesford Double Gloucester   Firm   C   P   A   O   NR   Drum

Made as a 3.2kg cheese and matured for 3 months.

Variants : Original, Waxed 250g

Notes :

Daylesford Single Gloucester PDO   Firm   C   P   A   O   NR   Drum

Made as a 3.5kg cheese and matured for 2 months.

Variants :

Notes :

Penyston Brie   Soft   C   P   V   O   BR   Disc

Made as a 250g cheese and matured for 5 weeks.

Variants :

Notes :

DEFAID DOLWERDD
Pembrokeshire
Cheesemakers : Nick & Wendy Holthan
Family sheep farm selling milk until they decided to make their own cheese at Food Centre Wales.

Aur Preseli   Firm   S   P   V   NR   Drum

Made as a 4 to 5kg cheese and rubbed with local golden rape seed oil.

Variants :

Notes :

Frenni   Soft   S   P   V   BR   Disc

Named after the mountain behind the farm and made as a 2 - 2.5kg cheese based on Brie.

Variants :

Notes :

Glas   Blue   S   P   V   NR   Drum

With a name meaning 'blue' in Welsh and made as a 3kg cheese.

Variants :

Notes :

Halwmi   Firm   S   P   V   XR   Block

Made as a block based on Halloumi and cut into 140g smaller blocks for retail.

Variants :

Notes :

Preseli   Semisoft   S   P   V   XR   Disc

Made as a block based on Feta and cut into 140g smaller blocks for retail.

Variants :

Notes :

DELAMERE DAIRY
Cheshire
Commercial Cheesemaker
Started in 1985 making cheese from their own goats but now outsource the making of their dairy range.

Delamere Farmhouse Mild Goat   Firm   G   P   V   XR   Block

Made at Ford Farm for Delamere and matured for 3 months before being cut into 150g blocks.

Variants :

Notes :

Delamere Medium Goat's Cheese   Firm   G   P   V   XR   Block

Made at Ford Farm for Delamere and matured for 4 - 6 months before being cut into 150g blocks.

Variants :

Notes :   ☐

DEWLAY CHEESEMAKERS
Lancashire
Cheesemaker : Nick & Richard Kenyon

Third generation family owned dairy named from the founders Wigan pronunciation of the French 'du lait'.

Beacon Fell Traditional Lancashire PDO Crumbly   C   P   V   XR   Cylinder

Made as a 20kg traditional creamy Lancashire using a two day curd and matured for 8 - 20 weeks.

Variants :

Notes :   ☐

Dewlay Cheddar   Firm   C   P   V   XR   Block

Made as a 20kg block in white and coloured versions at different stages of maturity.

Variants : White, Coloured, Mild, Mature, Extra Mature

Notes :   ☐

Dewlay Cheshire   Crumbly   C   P   V   XR   Block

Made as a 20kg block with a salty tangy citrus flavour.

Variants :

Notes :   ☐

Dewlay Double Gloucester   Firm   C   P   V   XR   Block, Cylinder

Made as a 20kg block and a 10kg drum and matured for 3 - 5 months to give a smooth mature flavour.

Variants :

Notes :   ☐

Dewlay Lancashire Creamy   Firm   C   P   V   XR   Block, Half Drum

Made as a 20kg block using a two day curd and made in a number of flavours as 1.6kg half drums.

Variants : Original, Smoked, Chilli, Garlic

Notes :   ☐

Dewlay Lancashire Crumbly   Crumbly   C   P   V   XR   Block, Cylinder

A younger style, made as a 20kg block or drum and matured quickly to produce a more acidic cheese.

Variants :

Notes :   ☐

| **Dewlay Red Leicester** | Firm | C | P | V | | XR | Block, Cylinder |

Made as a 20kg block and a 10kg drum and coloured with annatto to give a deep orange colour.

Variants :

Notes :

| **Dewlay Wensleydale** | Crumbly | C | P | V | | XR | Block, Cylinder |

Made as a 20kg block with a flaky texture or a smaller drum with cranberries added.

Variants : Original (Block), Cranberry (Drum)

Notes :

| **Garstang Blue** | Blue | C | P | V | | XR | Cylinder |

Made to a Lancashire recipe with the addition of blue mould and matured for up to 12 weeks.

Variants :

Notes :

| **Nicky Nook** | Blue | C | P | V | | XR | Cylinder |

Made as a Lancashire with added blue mould and orange annatto before being matured for up to 14 weeks.

Variants :

Notes :

| **Special Reserve Tasty Lancashire** | Crumbly | C | P | V | | XR | Cylinder |

Made as a 20kg traditional tasty Lancashire using a two day curd and matured for up to 12 months.

Variants :

Notes :

===

DODDINGTON CHEESE
Northumberland

Cheesemaker : Maggie Maxwell

Scottish dairy farmers who moved south and started cheesemaking in 1980s using raw milk from own herd.

| **Admiral Collingwood** | Semisoft | C | U | A | | WR | Square |

Made as a 1.5kg cheese washed in Newcastle Brown Ale and matured for 10 months.

Variants :

Notes :

| **Berwick Edge** | Firm | C | U | A | | WC | Wheel |

Made as an 8kg & 4kg Gouda style cheese, wax coated and matured for 12 - 18 months.

Variants :

Notes :

Capability Brown Crumbly C U A BR Drum

Made as a 2kg cheese and described as being 'like Darling Blue, without the blue', almost Caerphilly like.

Variants :

Notes :

Cuddy's Cave Firm C U A NR Wheel

Made as a 3.5kg Dales style cheese and matured for 3 - 6 months.

Variants : Original, Smoked

Notes :

Darling Blue Blue C P A NR Drum

Made as a 1.8kg - 2.5kg cheese, the only one with pasteurised milk and matured for 2 months.

Variants :

Notes :

Doddington Hard C U A WC Rounded Drum

Made as a 10kg cross Leicester and Cheddar style, wax coated and matured for 18 - 24 months.

Variants :

Notes :

Hotspur Firm C U A FR Brick

Made as a 1kg Dales style cheese, matured for 5 months then coated in olive oil and black pepper.

Variants :

Notes :

DROMONA

Tyrone

Commercial Cheesemaker

Owned by Dale Farm dairy co-operative who make a wide range of dairy products.

Dromona Cheddar Firm C P V XR Block

Made in large blocks before being matured and cut into retail blocks.

Variants : Mild, Medium, Mature, Extra Mature, Cracker

Notes :

DRUMTURK CHEESES
Perthshire
Cheesemaker : Denise Ferguson

Fifth generation family farm with Britain's only herd of pure Toggenburg goats making cheese for 40 years.

Blackthorn Crumble   Crumbly   G   P   V   XR   Drum, Disc
Made as a 3kg & 300g cheese with Blackthorn sea salt, buttered and clothbound before 6 weeks maturing.
Variants :
Notes :

Capercaillie   Semisoft   G   P   V   BR   Disc
Made as a 150g - 200g cheese coated in black pepper then white rind forms during 10 days maturing.
Variants :
Notes :

Drumturk Goat's Curd   Fresh   G   P   V   XR   Pot
Young fresh goat's curd with various flavours added.
Variants : Original, Stem Ginger, Rosemary & Garlic, Turmeric & Cumin, Heart-Beet
Notes :

Granite   Fresh   G   P   V   FR   Disc
Only made rarely as a 75g disc made with with half curd and half double cream and coated in black pepper.
Variants :
Notes :

Megique   Soft   G   P   V   BR   Triangle
Named after one of the goats, made as a square cheese, cut into 125g triangles and matured for 10 days.
Variants :
Notes :

Ptarmigan   Soft   G   P   V   BR   Disc
Made as a 200g cheese, ash coated and matured for 10 days.
Variants :
Notes :

DUNLOP DAIRY
Ayrshire
Cheesemaker : Ann Dorward

Making cheese since the 1980s using milk from their own herd of Ayrshire cows and goats.

Aiket	Soft	C	P	V	BR	Disc

Made as a 1kg & 200g cheese.

Variants :

Notes :

Ailsa Craig	Fresh	G	P	V	BR	Rock

Made as a 180g individual cheese.

Variants :

Notes :

Ayrshire Dunlop PGI	Firm	C	P	V	NR	Cylinder

Made as a 20kg & 3kg cheese and matured for 6 - 12 months.

Variants :

Notes :

Bonnet	Firm	G	P	V	NR	Drum

Made as a 3kg cheese and matured for 8 months.

Variants :

Notes :

Clerkland Crowdie	Fresh	C	P	V	XR	Log

Made as a 100g cheese and matured for 2 weeks.

Variants : Original, Oatmeal & Black Pepper

Notes :

Glazert	Soft	G	P	V	BR	Log

Made as a 250g individual cheese.

Variants :

Notes :

Paddy's Milestone	Fresh	C	P	V	BR	Rock

Made as a 200g individual cheese.

Variants :

Notes :

ELDWICK CREAMERY
West Yorkshire
Cheesemaker : Laura Greenwood

Community focused local business set up in 2022 and located in a converted garage using Aire valley milk.

Airedale   Firm   C   P   V   BR   Drum
Made as a 2.5kg Dales style cheese rubbed in Yorkshire rapeseed oil and matured for 2 months.
Variants :
Notes :

Brie by Gum   Soft   C   P   V   BR   Disc
A triple-cream version of Brie made as a 1.5kg & 230g cheese.
Variants : Original, Italian Truffle
Notes :

Go T' Foot of T' Stairs   Soft   G   P   V   BR   Flat Pyramid
Using local goat's milk to make a 180g Loire valley style individual ash-coated cheese.
Variants :
Notes :

Yorkshire Kay-Soa   Semisoft   C   P   V   FR   Drum
Made as a 1.5kg Mahon style cheese, rubbed with paprika and oil before being matured for 6 months.
Variants :
Notes :

ERRINGTON CHEESE
Lanarkshire
Cheesemaker : Selina Cairns

Second generation family cheesemakers in Upper Clyde Valley with own herd of goats and Lacaune sheep.

Biggar Blue   Blue   G   U   V   NR   Drum
Made as a 3kg cheese and matured for 2-6 months.
Variants :
Notes :

Blackmount   Soft   G   U   A   BR   Flat Pyramid
Made as a 220g cheese with a yeast rind and matured for 2 weeks.
Variants :
Notes :

Bonnington Linn Firm   G   U   A   NR   Drum

Made as an 8kg cheese, clothbound and matured for 6 - 18 months.

Variants :

Notes :

Corra Linn Hard   S   U   A   NR   Drum

Made as a 7.5kg cheese, clothbound and matured for 9 - 24 months.

Variants :

Notes :

Elrick Log Fresh   G   U   V   BR   Log

Made as a 190g cheese with a yeast rind, ash coated and matured for 2 weeks.

Variants :

Notes :

Lanark Blue Blue   S   U   V   NR   Cylinder

Made as a 3.5kg cheese and matured for 2 - 9 months.

Variants :

Notes :

Lanark White Firm   S   U   V   NR   Drum

Made as a 2.5kg cheese and matured for 2-6 months.

Variants :

Notes :

Sir Lancelot Fresh   S   U   A   BR   Disc

Seasonal cheese made infrequently as a 150g cheese with a yeast rind and matured for 2-6 weeks.

Variants :

Notes :

Tinto Firm   G   U   V   NR   Cylinder

Made as a 2kg cheese and matured for 2 months.

Variants :

Notes :

THE ETHICAL DAIRY
Dumfries & Galloway
Cheesemakers : David & Wilma Finlay
Carbon neutral sustainable 'cow with calf' organic dairy at Rainton Farm 40 years after cheesemaking ended.

Barlocco Blue   Blue   C   P   V   O   NR   Drum
Strong blue named after an island off the coast near the farm and matured for 2 - 5 months.
Variants :
Notes :

Bluebell   Blue   C   P   V   O   NR   Drum
Rich, soft creamy blue made as a 240g individual cheese and matured for 6 - 8 weeks.
Variants :
Notes :

Carrick   Firm   C   U   V   O   NR   Drum
Traditional farmhouse cheese matured for 9 - 18 months.
Variants :
Notes :

Ethical Dairy Cheddar   Firm   C   U   V   O   NR   Drum
Traditional farmhouse Cheddar matured for 9 months.
Variants :
Notes :

Fleet Valley Blue   Blue   C   U   V   O   NR   Drum
Firmer blue than most, matured for 2 - 6 months.
Variants :
Notes :

Laganory   Crumbly   C   U   V   O   NR   Drum
Made in a Caerphilly style with a slight crumble and matured for 2 - 6 months.
Variants : Original, Smoked
Notes :

Rainton Tomme   Firm   C   U   V   O   NR   Drum
Named after the family farm, made as an Alpine style cheese and matured for 2 - 6 months.
Variants : Original, Mature (8 months), Smoked
Notes :

| Skinny Cheese | | Firm | C | U | V | O | NR | Drum |

Made at start of year when butterfats are too low for making other cheeses.

Variants : Skinny Gold, Skinny Red (coloured orange with annatto)

Notes :

EWENIQUE DAIRY
Pembrokeshire

Cheesemaker : Bryn Perry, Rebecca Morris

Family pasture-fed sheep farm using the milk to make their own cheese and using the whey to make vodka.

| Ewe Blue | | Blue | S | P | V | | NR | Drum |

Made as a 2.6kg cheese and matured for 4 - 5 weeks.

Variants :

Notes :

FARMVIEW DAIRIES
Antrim

Cheesemaker : Davide Tani

Family owned business since 1988 making a range of dairy products in Belfast.

| Kearney Blue | | Blue | C | P | A | | NR | Drum |

Made as a 500g cheese based on Stilton and matured for 6 weeks.

Variants :

Notes :

FAYREFIELD FOODS
Denbighshire

Commercial Cheesemaker

Colliers was founded by Chris Swire and is now made by Fayrefield alongside their range of bulk cheeses.

| Colliers Mature Celtic Cheddar | | Firm | C | P | V | | XR | Block |

Made as a 20kg cheese using only Welsh milk.

Variants :

Notes :

| Colliers Powerful Cheddar | | Firm | C | P | V | | XR | Block |

Made as a 20kg cheese using only Welsh milk and matured for 20 months.

Variants :

Notes :

FELTHAM'S FARM CHEESES
Somerset

Cheesemakers : Marcus Fergusson, Penelope Nagle

Sustainable organic eco farm using milk from nearby Bruton Organic Dairy to make their range of cheeses.

Gert Lush Soft C P V O BR Disc

Made as a 230g cheese and described as a sophisticated, nuanced take on a Camembert.

Variants :

Notes :

La Fresca Margarita Fresh C P V O XR Pot

Made as a 230g cheese based on typically Latin American Queso Fresco and matured for 1 week.

Variants :

Notes :

Rebel Nun Blue C P V O WR Disc

Milder version of Renegade Monk with more blue flavour made as a 220g cheese and matured for 4 weeks.

Variants :

Notes :

Renegade Monk Blue C P V O WR Disc

Made as a 220g cheese described as 'drunkenly washed in ale with a touch of blue', matured for 4 weeks.

Variants :

Notes :

FEN FARM DAIRY
Suffolk

Cheesemaker : Jonny Crickmore

Third generation family farm who switched to Montbeliarde cows in order to produce their iconic cheese.

Baron Bigod Soft C P A BR Disc

Based on Brie de Meaux. Made as a 3kg, 1kg & 250g cheese and matured for 8 weeks.

Variants : Original, Truffle

Notes :

FERNDALE NORFOLK FARMHOUSE CHEESE
Norfolk

Cheesemaker : Arthur Betts

Family owned mixed use farm producing cheese using milk from a local herd as well as being potato farmers.

Norfolk Dapple   Firm   C   U   V   NR   Cylinder
Made as a 10kg cheese, clothbound and matured for 4 - 6 months developing a distinctive dappled rind.
Variants : Original, Vintage, Smoked, Ruby

Notes :

Norfolk Pinkfoot   Firm   C   U   V   NR   Drum
Made as a 4kg cheese coloured orange with annatto, clothbound and matured for 2 months.
Variants :

Notes :

Norfolk Tawny   Semisoft   C   U   V   WR   Disc
Matured for 6 weeks while being washed in local Norfolk ale.
Variants :

Notes :

==========

FIELDING COTTAGE
Norfolk

Cheesemaker : Sam Steggles

Third generation farmer who started with 9 and now has 800 goats on the farm.

Norfolk Mardler   Firm   G   P   V   WC   Block
Made as a 20kg cheese and matured for 8 weeks prior to cutting and coating in yellow wax.
Variants :

Notes :

Wensum White   Soft   G   P   V   BR   Brick
Made as a 140g Brie style cheese which is matured for 7 days.
Variants :

Notes :

==========

FORD FARM CHEESEMAKERS (BARBER'S)

Dorset

Commercial Cheesemaker

Started 40 years ago as a partnership of two families on the Ashley Park Estate now owned by Barber's.

Billie's Goat Cheese Firm G P V XR Block

Made as a 20kg block based on Cheddar and cut into retail portions.

Variants :

Notes :

Coastal Cheddar Firm C P V XR Block

Made by Barber's as a 20kg cheese and matured for up to 15 months before being cut into smaller blocks.

Variants :

Notes :

Crofter Hard S P V XR Block

Made as a block cheese based on Manchego and matured for up to 6 months.

Variants :

Notes :

Dorset Red Firm C P V XR Drum

Made as a 4kg Cheddar and coloured orange with annatto before being matured for 3 months then smoked.

Variants :

Notes :

Oakwood Firm C P V XR Drum

Made as a 4kg traditional Cheddar matured for 12 months before being oak smoked.

Variants :

Notes :

Truffler Firm C P V XR Drum

Made as a 4kg traditional Cheddar flavoured with black truffle.

Variants :

Notes :

Wookey Hole Cheddar Firm C P V NR Cylinder

Made as a 27kg cheese, clothbound and matured in the caves at Wookey Hole in Somerset.

Variants :

Notes :

Wookey Hole Goat Cheese Firm G P V NR Cylinder

Made as a large cheese, clothbound and matured in the caves at Wookey Hole in Somerset.

Variants :

Notes :

FOWLER'S OF EARLSWOOD
Warwickshire

Cheesemaker : Adrian Fowler

The oldest cheesemaking family in Britain, going back to 1670 using milk from a local Montbeliarde herd.

Clarabel Firm C P V NR Drum

Made as a 3kg cheese.

Variants : Original, Cranberry, Apricot

Notes :

Earl of Arden Hard S P V XR Drum

Made as a 3kg cheese.

Variants :

Notes :

Forest Blue Blue C P V NR Drum

Made as a 3kg cheese and matured for 3 months.

Variants :

Notes :

Fowlers Firm C P V XR Block

Made as a 5kg cheese and matured for 3 months.

Variants : Mature, Mild, Extra Mature, XXX Mature

Notes :

Fowlers Flavour Added Firm C P V XR Drum

Made as a 3kg cheese and matured for 3 months.

Variants : Black Pepper, Chilli, Garlic & Parsley, Onion & Chive

Notes :

Fowlers Sage Derby Firm C P V FR Drum

Made as a 3kg cheese.

Variants :

Notes :

Little Derby   Firm   C   P   V   NR   Drum

Made as a 3kg cheese and matured for 3 months.

Variants :

Notes :

Red Lakes   Firm   C   P   V   XR   Drum

Made as a 3kg cheese.

Variants :

Notes :

Soft Bard   Soft   C   P   V   BR   Disc

Made as a 1.1kg cheese.

Variants :

Notes :

Warwickshire   Firm   C   P   V   NR   Cylinder

Made as a 6kg cheese and smoked.

Variants : Original, Vintage Clothbound, Oak Smoked

Notes :

FFYNNON WEN FARM
Carmarthenshire

Cheesemaker : Harriet Cooke

Started in 2021 when the family bought a second-hand milking parlour and a flock of sheep.

Great White   Semisoft   S   P   V   NR   Drum

Made as a 2kg cheese based on Tomme and matured for 2 - 12 months.

Variants :

Notes :

Soft Joyce   Soft   S   P   V   WR   Disc

Made as a 200g cheese and washed in cider.

Variants :

Notes :

GALLOWAY FARMHOUSE CHEESE
Dumfries & Galloway

Cheesemakers : Alan & Helen Brown

Started cheesemaking in 1980s using milk from own herd of mainly Friesian and Viking Red crosses.

Cairnsmore Cow   Firm   C   U   V   O   NR   Drum

Made as a 2kg & 1 kg cheese and matured for 12 months.

Variants : Original, Smoked, Green Peppercorns

Notes :

Cairnsmore Ewe   Firm   S   U   V   NR   Drum

Made as a 2kg & 1kg cheese, clothbound and matured for 9 - 12 months.

Variants : Original, Smoked, Green Peppercorns

Notes :

Cairnsmore Goat   Firm   G   U   V   NR   Drum

Made as a 2kg & 1kg cheese, clothbound and matured for 6 months.

Variants : Original, Smoked

Notes :

GODMINSTER CHEESE
Somerset

Commercial Cheesemaker

Godminster Farm organic milk used to make a range of cheddars at neighbouring Wyke Farm.

Bruton Beauty   Firm   C   P   V   O   WC   Drum, Heart, Star

Made as a 2kg, 1kg, 400g & 200g vintage Cheddar.

Variants :

Notes :

Cheyney's Fortune   Firm   C   P   V   O   WC   Drum

Made as a 1kg & 200g oak smoked Cheddar.

Variants :

Notes :

Devil's Dance   Firm   C   P   V   O   WC   Drum

Made as a 200g Cheddar infused with a secret chilli sauce.

Variants :

Notes :

Howling Hound   Firm   C   P   V   O   WC Drum, Heart

Made as a 1kg & 200g Cheddar flavoured with real black truffle.

Variants :

Notes :

GODSELLS CHEESE
Gloucestershire
Cheesemaker : Liz Godsell

Family farm making a range of cheeses with their own and local milk named after local places and legends.

Cockadilly Chilli   Firm   C   P   V   XR Disc

Made as a 3.5kg cheese based on Godsell's Single Gloucester, blended with chilli and matured for 3 months.

Variants :

Notes :

Godsells Double Gloucester   Firm   C   P   V   NR Drum

Made as a 4 kg cheese, clothbound and matured for 5 months.

Variants :

Notes :

Godsells Single Gloucester PDO   Firm   C   P   V   NR Drum

Made as a 4kg clothbound cheese.

Variants :

Notes :

Holy Smoked   Firm   C   P   V   NR Drum

Made as a 4kg Single Gloucester and smoked over oak and beech.

Variants :

Notes :

Hooded Monk   Firm   C   P   V   WC Drum

Made as a 4kg Double Gloucester coated in wax.

Variants :

Notes :

Leonard Stanley   Firm   C   P   V   NR Drum

Made as a 10kg cheese based on Cheddar, clothbound and matured for 7 months.

Variants : Original, Waxed

Notes :

Singing Granny   Firm   C   P   V   NR   Drum

Made as a 4kg Single Gloucester and clothbound.

Variants :

Notes :

Three Virgins   Crumbly   C   P   V   XR   Drum

Made as a 3.5kg cheese based on Cheshire and matured for 3 months while vacuum packed.

Variants :

Notes :

Village Gossip   Firm   C   P   V   XR   Drum

Originally made as a Single Gloucester but now made as a 4kg Cheddar blended with chives.

Variants :

Notes :

GOLDEN CROSS CHEESE COMPANY

East Sussex

Cheesemakers : Kevin & Alison Blunt

Originally goat farmers supplying to a cheesemaker but took over in 1989 and started with Golden Cross.

Chabis   Soft   G   U   V   BR   Flat Cone

Made using Golden Cross curd as a 90g cheese to be eaten young or matured for deeper complex tastes.

Variants :

Notes :

Flower Marie   Soft   S   U   V   BR   Cube

Made with a long overnight curd set as a 600g & 200g cheese and matured for 4 weeks.

Variants :

Notes :

Golden Cross   Soft   G   U   V   BR   Log

Made as a 250g cheese based on Sainte-Maure, hand-ladled, ash coated and matured for 3 weeks.

Variants :

Notes :

Laughton Log   Soft   G   U   V   BR   Log

A larger cutting version of Golden Cross made infrequently as a 1kg cheese and matured for 3 weeks.

Variants :

Notes :

GOODWOOD HOME FARM
West Sussex
Cheesemaker : Bruce Rowan

Cheese dairy located on the 12,000 acre Goodwood Estate owned by the Duke of Richmond.

Charlton	Firm	C	P	V	O	NR	Drum

Made as a 10kg cheese and matured for 12 months.

Variants :

Notes :

Levin Down	Soft	C	P	V	O	BR	Disc

Made as a 250g cheese based on Brie.

Variants :

Notes :

Molecomb Blue	Blue	C	P	V	O	NR	Disc

Made as a 250g cheese.

Variants :

Notes :

THE GREAT BRITISH CHEESE COMPANY
Cheshire
Commercial Cheesemaker

Cheeses made by Belton Farm, processed, flavoured, blended and waxed by David Williams Cheese.

Great British Flavoured Cheddar	Firm	C	P	V	WC	Drum

Mature Cheddar blended with various flavours and coated in coloured wax as a 200g cheese.

Variants : Flagship, Drunken Monk, Chilli & Lime, Peri Peri, Smokey Pepper & Garlic, Smokey Redwood, Peaky Blinder, Sticky Toffee Tastic, Ploughman's Choice, Horseradish & Parsley

Notes :

Great British Flavoured Cheshire	Firm	C	P	V	WC	Drum

Creamy Cheshire blended with various flavours and coated in coloured wax as a 200g cheese.

Variants : Garlic & Black Pepper

Notes :

Great British Flavoured Red Leicester	Firm	C	P	V	WC	Drum

Creamy Red Leicester blended with various flavours and coated in coloured wax as a 200g cheese.

Variants : Red Arrow

Notes :

Great British Flavoured Wensleydale Firm C P V WC Drum
Creamy Wensleydale blended with various flavours and coated in coloured wax as a 200g cheese.
Variants : Hot Cross Bun, Italian Job
Notes :

Great British Lancaster Bomber Firm C P V WC Drum
Creamy Lancashire coated in coloured wax as a 200g cheese.
Variants :
Notes :

GREEN'S OF GLASTONBURY (LONGMAN'S)
Somerset
Cheesemaker : Lloyd Green
Fourth generation Cheddar maker, now part of Longman's, on the Somerset levels close to Glastonbury Tor.

Green's Cheddar Firm C U/P V (O) XR Block
Made as a 20kg cheese.
Variants : Mild, Mature, Vintage, Smoked, Organic, Farmhouse
Notes :

Green's Double Gloucester Firm C P V (O) XR Block
Made as a 12kg cheese before being matured and portioned into smaller blocks.
Variants : Original, Organic
Notes :

Green's Sheep Firm S P V (O) XR Block
Made as a 20kg block before being matured and portioned into smaller blocks.
Variants : Regular, Organic
Notes :

Green's Traditional Cheddar Firm C U/P A (O) NR Cylinder
Made as a 27kg traditional Cheddar..
Variants : Mild, Mature, Vintage, Smoked, Organic, Farmhouse
Notes :

Green's Traditional Goat Firm G P A (O) XR Cylinder
Made as a 27kg cheese before being matured and portioned into smaller blocks.
Variants : Regular, Organic
Notes :

Green's Twanger	Firm	C	P	V		XR	Block

Made as a 5kg cheese and matured for 24 months before being portioned into smaller blocks.

Variants :

Notes :

GREENFIELDS DAIRY PRODUCTS
Lancashire
Cheesemaker : Steven Procter

Family owned cheesemakers in the Trough of Bowland using local farms' milk to make a range of cheeses.

Blackjack Vintage Charcoal	Firm	C	P	V		XR	Block

Made as a 20kg extra mature vintage Cheddar and blended with charcoal.

Variants :

Notes :

Chilli con Cheddar	Firm	C	P	V		XR	Block, Cylinder

Made as a 20kg block & 10kg cylinder of mature Cheddar blended with mixed peppers, garlic and chilli.

Variants :

Notes :

Grace's Goats Cheese	Semisoft	G	P	V		XR	Cylinder

Made as a 10kg cheese.

Variants :

Notes :

Greenfields Cheddar	Firm	C	P	V		XR	Block, Cylinder

Made as a 20kg block & 10kg cylinder.

Variants : Mild, Mature, White, Coloured, Smoked

Notes :

Greenfields Cheshire	Crumbly	C	P	V		XR	Block, Cylinder

Made as a 20kg block & 10kg cylinder.

Variants : White, Coloured

Notes :

Greenfields Double Gloucester	Firm	C	P	V		XR	Block, Cylinder

Made as a 20kg block & 10kg cylinder coloured orange with annatto.

Variants : Original, Chive & Onion

Notes :

Greenfields Crumbly Lancashire Crumbly C P V XR Block, Cylinder
Made as a 20kg & 10kg cheese and matured for 5 weeks.
Variants :
Notes :

Greenfields Lancashire Firm C P V WC Block, Cylinder
Made as a 20kg & 10kg cheese, clothbound and then waxed.
Variants : Creamy (2 - 4 months), Tasty (6 - 12 months), Firm, Smoked, Garlic, Black Pepper
Notes :

Greenfields Red Leicester Firm C P V XR Block, Cylinder
Made as a 20kg block & 10kg cylinder coloured orange with annatto.
Variants :
Notes :

Greenfields Wensleydale Crumbly C P V XR Block, Cylinder
Made as a 20kg block & 10kg cylinder with flavour added variants.
Variants : Original, Cranberry, Apricot
Notes :

Stripey Firm C P V XR Drum
Layers of White Cheddar, Red Leicester, Wensleydale, Double Gloucester and Creamy Lancashire.
Variants :
Notes :

Sykes Fell Semisoft S P V XR Cylinder
Named after a fell in the Ribble valley and made as a 10kg cheese.
Variants :
Notes :

GRIMBISTER FARM CHEESE
Orkney
Cheesemaker : Anne Seator
Second generation cheesemaker on family farm.

Grimbister Crumbly C U V XR Drum
Made as a 700g cheese in a similar style to Dales cheeses.
Variants :
Notes :

GUERNSLEIGH CHEESE
Staffordshire
Cheesemaker : Ernie Durose

Guernsey herd established in 1955 and cheesemaking started in 2008 by third generation.

Golden Brie | Soft | C | P | V | | BR | Drum

Made as a 180g cheese.

Variants : Original, Smoked, Peppered

Notes :

Guernsleigh Blue | Blue | C | P | V | | NR | Drum

Made as a 300g cheese in a blue Brie style.

Variants :

Notes :

Guernsleigh Buffalo Cheddar | Firm | B | P | V | | PC | Drum

Made as a 4.5kg cheese.

Variants :

Notes :

Guernsleigh Goat Cheddar | Firm | G | P | V | | PC | Block

Made as a 2.5kg cheese.

Variants :

Notes :

Guernsleigh Original | Firm | C | P | V | | PC | Drum

Made as a 15kg & 4.5kg cheese based on Cheddar.

Variants : Original, Pepper

Notes :

Guernsleigh Soft | Soft | C | P | V | | NR | Pot

Sold in a 170g pot.

Variants : Garlic & Herb, Black Pepper, Harissa

Notes :

Hallernie | Semisoft | C | P | V | | XR | Block

Made as a 4.5kg cheese.

Variants : Original, Garlic, Pepper

Notes :

HAMM TUN FINE FOODS
Northamptonshire
Cheesemaker : Gary Bradshaw
Founded on a farm in 2013 and now in a purpose built cheese dairy using rich Jersey milk from a local herd.

Cobblers Nibble   Firm   C   U   V   NR   Drum
With the recipe having improved over the years it is now made as a 3kg cheese using Jersey milk.
Variants :
Notes :

Little Bertie   Blue   C   U   V   NR   Disc
Made as a 200g cheese.
Variants :
Notes :

Northamptonshire Blue   Blue   C   U   V   NR   Drum
Made as a 3.5kg cheese and matured for 2 months.
Variants :
Notes :

Shoetown Blue   Blue   C   U   V   NR   Drum
Made as a 250g soft creamy blue cheese.
Variants :
Notes :

St Crispin   Soft   C   U   V   BR   Drum
Limited edition version of Shoetown but with bloomy rind and no blue.
Variants :
Notes :

===

HAMPSHIRE CHEESES
Hampshire
Cheesemakers : Stacey Hedges, Charlotte Spruce
Started in 2005 after experimenting with home cheesemaking and guidance from Neals Yard founder.

Tunworth   Soft   C   P   A   BR   Disc
'The World's Best Camembert' says Raymond Blanc, it is made as a 250g cheese and matured for 6 weeks.
Variants :
Notes :

Winslade   Soft   C   P   A   WR   Disc

A 250g cross between Camembert and Vacherin, wrapped in a spruce collar and matured for 8 weeks.

Variants :

Notes :

HANCOCKS MEADOW FARM
Herefordshire
Cheesemaker : Pauline Healey

Family farm making cheese and cider on the banks of the River Wye with their own flock of Friesland ewes.

Valley Drover   Hard   S   U   A   NR   Drum

Based on Tomme and pressed in a 100 year old cast iron cheese press before being matured for 4 months.

Variants :

Notes :

HAND STRETCHED CHEESE
Carmarthenshire
Cheesemaker : Holly Bull

Using 100% Jersey milk from a nearby pasture for life organic farm which only milks once a day.

Leno   Soft   C   P   V   O   XR   Ball

Made as a Fior di Latte which is the name given to a cow's milk Mozzarella.

Variants :

Notes :

HARTINGTON CREAMERY
Derbyshire
Cheesemaker : Diana Alcock

The only Derbyshire based and smallest of the Stilton makers makes mainly blue cheeses in the Peak District.

Devonshire Gold   Blue   C   P   V   WR   Drum

Made as a 2.2kg cheese coloured orange with annatto for the Duke of Devonshire's Chatsworth Estate.

Variants :

Notes :

Hartington Dovedale Blue PDO   Blue   C   P   V   WR   Drum

Must be made within 50 miles of the River Dove, it is made as a 2.2kg cheese and matured for 4 weeks.

Variants :

Notes :

Hartington Shropshire Blue Blue C P V NR Cylinder

Similar to a Stilton, it is made as an 8kg cheese, coloured orange with annatto and matured for 10 weeks.

Variants :

Notes :

Hartington Stilton PDO Blue C P V NR Cylinder

Using the same recipe since 1900 it is made as an 8kg & 2.2kg cheese and matured for 6 weeks.

Variants : Original, Smoked, White

Notes :

King's Blue Blue C P V NR Drum

Developed for Charles III's Coronation as a 2.2kg cheese, it is coloured orange with annatto.

Variants :

Notes :

Peakland Blue Blue C P V NR Cylinder

Created at Hartington it is made as a 8kg cheese, coloured orange with annatto then matured for 10 weeks.

Variants :

Notes :

Peakland White Crumbly C P V XR Cylinder

Created at Hartington it is made as a 8kg cheese similar to Cheshire or Feta then matured for 2 weeks.

Variants : Cranberry & Orange, Tomato & Garlic, Black Pepper, Chilli, Lemon & Lime, Chocolate & Chilli

Notes :

HAYFIELDS DAIRY
Cheshire

Cheesemaker : Rob Huntbach

Third generation dairy farmers, started cheesemaking in 1957 and now using milk from local farms.

Effin Hot Firm C P V XR Block

Made as a 20kg block Cheddar and flavoured with chilli, jalapeño and garlic.

Variants : Original, Not So Effin Hot

Notes :

Hayfields Cheddar Firm C P V XR Block

Made as a 20kg block and matured before being cut into retail blocks.

Variants : Mild, Mature, Extra Mature, Black Pepper, Caramelised Onion, Garlic & Herb

Notes :

Hayfields Cheshire | Crumbly | C | P | V | | XR | Block

Made as a 20kg block and matured before being cut into retail blocks.

Variants :

Notes :

Hayfields Crunch | Firm | C | P | V | | XR | Drum

Made as a 2kg extra mature Cheddar.

Variants :

Notes :

Hayfields Double Gloucester & Chive | Firm | C | P | V | | XR | Block

Made as a 20kg block coloured orange with annatto and matured before being cut into retail blocks.

Variants :

Notes :

Hayfields Red Leicester | Firm | C | P | V | | XR | Block

Made as a 20kg block coloured orange with annatto and matured before being cut into retail blocks.

Variants :

Notes :

Reggie Red Crunch | Firm | C | P | V | | XR | Drum

Named after the dairy dog, made as a 2kg cheese coloured orange with annatto and matured.

Variants :

Notes :

HIGH WEALD DAIRY
West Sussex
Cheesemakers : Mark & Sarah Hardy

Started milking sheep to supply a cheesemaker but now making a range of cheeses on the family dairy farm.

Ashdown Foresters | Firm | C | P | V | O | NR | Ammonite

Made as a 2kg cheese and matured for 3 months.

Variants : Original, Smoked

Notes :

Brighton Blue | Blue | C | P | V | (O) | NR | Drum

Made as a 3kg cheese and matured for 3 months.

Variants : Original, Organic

Notes :

Brighton Ewe   Blue   S   P   V   NR   Drum

Made as a 2kg sheep's milk version of Brighton Blue.

Variants :

Notes :

Brother Michael   Semisoft   C   P   V   O   WR   Drum

Made as a 3kg cheese based on Saint Giles and matured for 10 weeks.

Variants :

Notes :

Chilli Marble   Semisoft   C   P   V   (O)   XR   Drum

Made as a 3kg cheese based on Saint Giles and infused with chilli.

Variants : Original, Organic

Notes :

Duddleswell   Firm   S   P   V   NR   Cylinder

Made as a 3kg cheese and matured for 3 months.

Variants : Original, Smoked

Notes :

High Weald Halloumi   Semisoft   SC   P   V   O   XR   Block

Made as a 1kg & 150g cheese and matured for 7 days.

Variants : Original Sheep, Blended Sheep & Cow

Notes :

High Weald Ricotta   Fresh   S   P   V   O   XR   Block

Made as a 1kg & 125g cheese.

Variants : Original, Salata

Notes :

Little Sussex   Soft   S   P   V   O   BR   Button

Made as an 80g cheese based on Sussex Slipcote and matured for 10 days.

Variants :

Notes :

Medita   Fresh   S   P   V   O   XR   Block

Made as a 1kg & 125g cheese based on Feta and matured for 3 months.

Variants :

Notes :

Saint Giles Semisoft C P V (O) XR Drum
Made as a 3kg cheese coated with organic carrot juice to make it bright orange.
Variants : Original, Organic
Notes :

Seven Sisters Semisoft S P V (O) FR Drum
Made as a 3kg cheese coated in Hebridean seaweed.
Variants : Original, Organic
Notes :

Sister Sarah Semisoft G P V XR Drum
Made as a 3kg cheese coated with annatto to make it bright orange and matured for 8 weeks.
Variants :
Notes :

Sussex Blossom Firm S P V O XR Drum
Made as a 3kg cheese for King Charles III's coronation coated in edible flowers and matured for 4 months.
Variants :
Notes :

Sussex Marble Firm C P V (O) XR Drum
Made as a 3.4kg cheese based on Saint Giles and infused with garlic and parsley.
Variants : Original, Organic
Notes :

Sussex Slipcote Fresh S P V O XR Button, Log
Made as a 100g cheese and matured for 7 days.
Variants : Original, Dill, Garlic & Parsley
Notes :

Sussex Velvet Firm C P V O NR Drum
Made as a 3kg cheese based on Saint Giles and matured for 3 months.
Variants :
Notes :

Tremains Firm C P V O NR Drum
Made as a 4kg cheese based on Cheddar and matured for 6 months.
Variants :
Notes :

Truffle Ewe Firm S P V XR Drum

Made as a 3.2kg cheese and matured for 4 months before being split and layered with truffle.

Variants :

Notes :

HIGHLAND FINE CHEESES
Ross-shire

Cheesemaker : Rory Stone

A descendant of the 15th century creator of Caboc is now making a range of cheeses covering every style.

Black Crowdie (Gruth Dhu) Fresh C P V BR Log

Made as a 500g & 110g dry curd cheese rolled in cracked black pepper and oatmeal.

Variants :

Notes :

Blue Murder Blue C P V NR Cube

Made as a 650g soft creamy cheese and believed to be the only square blue cheese in the world.

Variants :

Notes :

Caboc Fresh C P V FR Log

Made as a 110g curd cheese rolled in pinhead oatmeal, this is the 15th century 'chieftain's cheese'.

Variants :

Notes :

Fat Cow Firm C P V WR Wheel

Made as a 6kg Alpine style cheese with Emmental like holes or eyes.

Variants :

Notes :

Highland Brie Soft C P V BR Disc

Made as a 1kg & 250g cheese based on Brie.

Variants :

Notes :

Highland Camembert Soft C P V BR Disc

Made as a 250g cheese.

Variants :

Notes :

Minger Soft C P V WR Square

Made as a 250g cheese and washed in annatto to give a sticky pungent orange rind.

Variants :

Notes :

Morangie Brie Soft C P V BR Disc

Named after the Glen of Tranquility famed for its whisky and made as a 1kg & 250g cheese based on Brie.

Variants :

Notes :

Skinny Crowdie Soft C P V FR Pot

Made as a 140g cheese.

Variants :

Notes :

Strathdon Blue Blue C P V NR Drum

Made as a 3kg cheese and matured for 10 weeks.

Variants :

Notes :

Tain Cheddar Firm C P V NR Cylinder

Made as a 20kg clothbound cheese.

Variants :

Notes :

===

HILL FARM REAL FOOD
Cheshire

Cheesemakers : Elaine Aidley

Fourth generation family farm using milk from their own pasture fed herd in the restored cheese cellar.

Pagewood Firm C U A NR Cylinder

Made as a 6kg Cheddar, previously called 'Classic', matured for up to 6 months with some sold very young.

Variants : Original, Unsalted

Notes :

===

HINXDEN FARM DAIRY
Kent

Farmers : Richard & Dee Manford

Third generation family whose Guernsey milk is used to make a range of dairy products.

Tam's Tipple Firm C U V NR Drum

Made as a 2.5kg Cheddar by Cheesemakers of Canterbury using Hinxden Guernsey milk.

Variants :

Notes :

☐

Winnie's Wheel Soft C P V BR Disc

Made as a 1kg & 250g by Cheesemakers of Canterbury based on Camembert using Hinxden Guernsey milk.

Variants :

Notes :

☐

===

HOLDEN FARM DAIRY
Ceredigion

Cheesemakers : Patrick & Becky Holden

Registered organic farm since the early 70s using milk from their own herd of Ayrshires.

Hafod Firm C U/P A O NR Cylinder

The Welsh name for 'pasture', it is made as a 10kg Cheddar and matured for 14 months.

Variants :

Notes :

☐

===

HOLLIS MEAD ORGANIC DAIRY
Dorset

Cheesemaker : Oliver Hemsley

Family owned organic farm with pasture fed cows milked once daily to promote land and animal welfare.

Benville Soft C P V O BR Disc

Made as a 250g cheese based on Brie.

Variants : Original, Truffled

Notes :

☐

Corscombe Soft C P V O BR Disc

Made as a 250g cheese based on Camembert.

Variants :

Notes :

☐

Marvel   Soft   C   P   V   O   WR   Disc

Made as a 250g cheese washed rind cheese based on Camembert.

Variants :

Notes :

HOMEWOOD CHEESES

Somerset

Cheesemaker : Tim Homewood, Angela Morris

Located in the Chew Valley, south of Bristol, cheeses are handmade using milk from two local flocks.

Aveline   Soft   S   T   V   BR   Millstone

Made as an unusual millstone shaped 150g cheese based on Brie and matured for 3 - 4 weeks.

Variants :

Notes :

Bristol Button   Soft   S   T   V   BR   Disc

Made as a 70g cheese and matured for 2 - 3 weeks.

Variants :

Notes :

Chattox   Firm   S   T   V   WR Block

Made as a 3kg lightly pressed version of Old Demdike in limited quantities during the summer months.

Variants :

Notes :

Fresh Ewe's Cheese   Fresh   S   T   V   XR ʳ Pot

Simple strained curd cheese filled into various sized pots.

Variants :

Notes :

Hello Ewe   Semisoft S   T   V   XR   Block

Based on Halloumi and sold in 700g & 200g blocks.

Variants :

Notes :

Homewood Ricotta   Fresh   S   T   V   XR   Pot

Made using the whey from making Halloumi and has a very short shelf life due to being unsalted.

Variants :

Notes :

Lamb Leer   Crumbly   S   T   V   BR   Drum

Made as a 300g cheese it is both crumbly and soft at the same time after being matured for 3 - 4 weeks.

Variants :

Notes :   ☐

Old Demdike   Firm   S   T   V   WR   Drum

Made as a 900g washed curd cheese which is then rind washed and matured for 2 - 4 months.

Variants :

Notes :   ☐

Pickled Ewe's Cheese   Semisoft   S   T   V   XR   Block

Baaed on Feta and matured in brine for at least one month before being cut into 1kg & 200g blocks.

Variants :

Notes :   ☐

Tibb   Firm   S   T   V   WR   Drum

Smaller version of Old Demdike, made as a 300g cheese.

Variants :

Notes :   ☐

HONOUR NATURAL FOODS
Kent

Cheesemaker : Hannah Loades

Made next to the milking parlour on Silcocks Farm and only sold in their own farm shop.

Boresisle   Soft   C   P   V   O   BR   Disc

Made as a 250g cheese and matured for 3 weeks.

Variants :

Notes :   ☐

St Michael's   Fresh   C   P   V   O   XR   Disc

Made as a 250g cheese and matured for 3 days.

Variants :

Notes :   ☐

St Michael's Blue   Blue   C   P   V   O   NR   Disc

Made as a 250g cheese and matured for 3 weeks.

Variants :

Notes :   ☐

INVERLOCH CHEESE COMPANY
Argyll & Bute
Cheesemakers : David & Grace Eaton

Began making goat's milk Cheddar at home for the family 25 years ago now making a wide range of cheeses.

Campbeltown Loch Firm C P V WR Drum

Made as a 1.5kg cheese and washed in local whisky.

Variants :

Notes :

Christmas Pudding Firm C P V WC Christmas Pudding

Mature Scottish Cheddar shaped and coated in wax to resemble a festive pudding.

Variants :

Notes :

Howgate Kintyre Blue Blue C P A NR Drum

Made as a 1.5kg cheese using milk from a local Ayrshire herd and matured for 2 months.

Variants :

Notes :

Howgate Kintyre Brie Soft C P V BR Wheel

Made as a 1.3kg cheese using milk from a local Ayrshire herd.

Variants :

Notes :

Inverloch Goats Cheese Firm G P V WC Drum

Made as a 3kg cheese.

Variants :

Notes :

Isle of Kintyre Gigha Fruit Cheese Firm C P V WC Fruits

Mature Scottish Cheddar blended with different flavours and shaped as fruits coated in relevant colour wax.

Variants : Pear, Orange, Apple, Whisky Apple, Garlic Apple

Notes :

Isle of Kintyre Magnus' Hammer Firm C P V WC Disc

Vintage Cheddar moulded as a 200g cheese and coated in black wax.

Variants :

Notes :

Isle of Kintyre Wax Cheddar   Firm   C   P   V   WC   Disc

Range of 200g mature Cheddar blended with various flavours and coated in coloured wax.

Variants : Plain Jane, Island Herb, Gin & Tonic, Truffler, Warbonnet, Applesmoke, Ben Gunn, Mild Madras, Captain's Claret, Highland Chief, Chilli & Tomato, Laird's Mustard, Lazy Ploughman, Poacher's Choice, Old Smokey, Laphroaig Whisky, Springbank Whisky, Glen Scotia 15, Glen Scotia Double Cask

Notes :

THE ISLAND SMOKERY
Orkney
Cheesemaker : Callum & Fiona MacInnes

Deli owners who took over smoking Cheddar after the local dairy moved and ceased smoking cheeses.

Orkney Flavoured Mature Cheddar   Firm   C   P   V   XR   Block

Cheddar made by Orkney Cheese Company is smoked and flavoured using a blend of local wood shavings.

Variants : Dark Smoked, Light Smoked, Smokey Red, Garlic, Red Onion, Ploughman's Pickle, Highland Whisky, Christmas Spice, Cracked Pepper, Sweet Chilli, Cranberry, Dark Island Reserve Ale

Notes :

ISLE OF MULL CHEESE
Argyll & Bute
Cheesemaker : Brendan Reade

Sustainable farm using wind and water power and a single herd used to produce cheese and a whey spirit.

Hebridean Blue   Blue   C   U   A   NR   Drum

Made as a 7kg cheese and matured for 2 - 3 months to produce a rich creamy blue cheese.

Variants :

Notes :

Isle of Mull Cheddar   Firm   C   U   A   NR   Cylinder

A 25kg clothbound cheese aged for 12 - 18 months using milk from grain-fed cows to give a boozy flavour.

Variants : Original, Smoked

Notes :

ISLE OF WIGHT CHEESE COMPANY
Isle of Wight
Cheesemaker : Richard Hodgson

Based on the farm where they originally sourced their milk from, a new dairy was built in 2017.

Gallybagger	Firm	C	U	V		NR	Rounded Drum

Made as a 5kg cheese in a Gouda mould and matured for 5 months on Lawson Cypress wooden shelves.

Variants :

Notes :

Isle of Wight Blue	Blue	C	P	V		NR	Disc

Made as a 200g cheese and matured for 4 weeks.

Variants :

Notes :

Isle of Wight Soft	Soft	C	P	V		BR	Disc

Made as a 200g cheese and matured for 4 weeks.

Variants :

Notes :

J J SANDHAM
Lancashire
Commercial Cheesemaker

Third generation family owned cheesemakers using milk from local farms to make and smoke cheeses.

Sandham Cheddar	Firm	C	P	V		WC	Drum

Made as a Cheddar and blended with various flavours before forming as 200g cheeses and coating in wax.

Variants : Original, Smoked, Sticky Toffee, Pizza, Flamin 'Eck, Chilli & Lime, Horseradish & Parsley, Caramelised Onion & Red Wine, Ploughman's Pickle, Ale & Mustard, Roasted Onion & Garlic

Notes :

Sandham Coverdale	Firm	C	P	V		WC	Drum

Made as a traditional dales style cheese and formed as a 200g cheese coated in wax.

Variants : Original, Smoked

Notes :

Sandham Lancashire	Crumbly	C	P	V		WC	Drum

Made as a Lancashire and blended with various flavours before forming as 200g cheeses and coating in wax.

Variants : Creamy, Tasty, Firm, Smoked, Lemon, Black Pepper

Notes :

Sandham Lancashire Bomb Firm C P V WC Bomb
Made as a Lancashire formed as 454g & 225g bomb shaped cheeses and coated in black wax.
Variants :

Notes :

Sandham Ogden Original Firm C P V WC Drum
Made as a mature Cheddar and formed as a 200g cheese coated in wax.
Variants : Original, Smoked

Notes :

Sandham Old King Coal Firm C P V WC Drum
Made as a mature Cheddar blended with charcoal and formed as a 200g cheese coated in wax.
Variants :

Notes :

Sandham Red Crunch Firm C P V WC Drum
Made as a vintage Red Leicester and formed as a 200g cheese coated in wax.
Variants :

Notes :

Sandham Wensleydale Crumbly C P V WC Drum
Made as an open textured Wensleydale some of which is smoked and some blended with fruit.
Variants : Original, Smoked, Cranberry

Notes :

===

JAMES'S CHEESE
Dorset
Cheesemaker : James McCall
Trained with famed cheesemonger James Aldridge, worked with many dairies and now creates own cheeses.

Chardown Hill Soft C P V XR Ball
Made as a 120g soft cheese flavoured with cracked black pepper and parsley and sprinkled with parsley.
Variants :

Notes :

Francis Semisoft C P V WR Drum
Made as a 1kg cheese by Lyburn Cheesemakers and matured for 3 - 4 months by James's Cheese.
Variants :

Notes :

Hambledon Hill Soft C P V XR Ball

Made as a 120g soft cheese flavoured with garlic and chives.

Variants :

Notes :

Hod Hill Soft C P V XR Ball

Made as a 120g soft cheese flavoured with cracked black pepper and dusted with pepper.

Variants :

Notes :

Little Colonel Semisoft C P V WR Drum

Made as a 200g cheese by Lyburn Cheesemakers, a smaller version of Francis matured for 7 weeks.

Variants :

Notes :

Okeford Beacon Soft C P V XR Ball

Made as a 120g soft cheese flavoured with chilli flakes.

Variants :

Notes :

===

JONATHAN CRUMP'S GLOUCESTER CHEESES
Gloucestershire

Cheesemaker : Jonathan Crump

The only dairy in the world using only 100% Gloucester cow milk to make traditional Gloucester cheeses.

Crump's Double Gloucester Firm C U V NR Drum

Made as a 2kg cheese, coloured orange with annatto and matured for 4 months.

Variants :

Notes :

Crump's Single Gloucester PDO Firm C U V NR Drum

Made as a 2kg cheese and matured for 2 months.

Variants :

Notes :

===

JONES' CHEESE COMPANY
Ceredigion
Cheesemaker : Mark Jones

After working for Welsh cheesemakers, now teaches and makes his own cheese at Food Centre Wales.

| **Tysul Blue** | Blue | C | P | V | NR | Drum |

Using milk from a local co-operative it is made as a 2kg sweet creamy blue cheese and matured for 5 weeks.

Variants :

Notes :

===

JOSEPH HELER CHEESE
Cheshire
Commercial Cheesemaker

Fifth generation Heler family owned Laurel Farm near Nantwich remains the home of this handmade cheese.

| **Blackstone** | Firm | C | P | V | XR | Block |

Made as a vintage Cheddar in 1kg & 200g blocks.

Variants :

Notes :

| **Hatherton Smoked** | Firm | C | P | V | XR | Block |

Made as a 400g mature Cheddar which has been naturally smoked over woodchips.

Variants :

Notes :

| **Joseph Heler Cheddar** | Firm | C | P | V | XR | Block |

Made as a 1kg & 200g Cheddar at two different levels of maturity up to 9 months.

Variants : Mild, Mature

Notes :

| **Joseph Heler Cheshire** | Crumbly | C | P | V | XR | Block |

Made as a 1kg & 200g handmade Cheshire.

Variants : White, Coloured

Notes :

| **Joseph Heler Gloucester** | Firm | C | P | V | XR | Block |

Made as a 1kg & 200g handmade Gloucester.

Variants :

Notes :

Joseph Heler Leicester   Firm   C   P   V   XR   Block

Made as a 1kg & 200g Leicester which is coloured orange with annatto and matured for 9 months.

Variants :

Notes :

KAPPACASEIN
London
Cheesemaker : Bill Oglethorpe

After working as at Neal's Yard Dairy, Swiss trained cheesemaker who collects organic milk from Kent daily.

Bermondsey Frier   Semisoft   C   U   A   O   XR   Block

Based on Halloumi and perfect for cooking.

Variants :

Notes :

Bermondsey Hard Pressed   Firm   C   U   A   O   WR   Wheel

Made as a 24kg cheese based on Gruyère and matured for up to 12 months.

Variants :

Notes :

Kappacasein Ricotta   Fresh   C   U   A   O   XR   Basket

Made fresh using the left over whey after regular cheesemaking.

Variants :

Notes :

London Raclette   Firm   C   U   A   O   WR   Wheel

Made in the same way as a typical Alpine cheese and matured for 3 months.

Variants :

Notes :

THE KEDAR CHEESE COMPANY
Dumfries & Galloway
Cheesemakers : Gavin & Jane Lochhead

Third generation dairy farmers with own herd of award winning Brown Swiss cows known as the Kedar Herd.

Kedar Halloumi Style Cheese   Semisoft   C   P   V   XR   Block

Based on Halloumi.

Variants : Original, Smoked, Honey, Mint, Chilli Flakes

Notes :

Kedar Mozzarella	Fresh	C	P	V	XR	Ball, Log

Made as a 110g individual cheese and as a 1kg pizza version, both original and smoked.

Variants : Original, Smoked

Notes :

Kedar Ricotta	Fresh	C	P	V	XR	Pot

Made using whey left after making other cheeses to be eaten after just a few days.

Variants :

Notes :

Kedar Tomme	Firm	C	P	V	NR	Drum

Made as a 4.5kg cheese based on Tomme.

Variants :

Notes :

Solway Mountain	Firm	C	P	V	NR	Drum

Made as a 4.5kg cheese based on an Alpine style.

Variants :

Notes :

KEEN'S CHEDDAR
Somerset
Cheesemakers : George & James Keen

Fifth generation cheesemakers at Moorhayes Farm alongside Wincanton Racecourse since 1899.

Keen's Cheddar	Firm	C	U	A	NR	Cylinder

Made as a 25kg, 3kg & 1.5kg cheese, clothbound and matured for 12 - 18 months.

Variants : Mature, Extra Mature

Notes :

KING STONE DAIRY
Gloucestershire
Cheesemaker : David Jowett

Based on a Cotswold regenerative organic farm and using milk from the farm's single herd to make cheeses.

Ashcombe	Firm	C	P	A	O	WR	Wheel

Based on Morbier with a line of ash in the middle.Made as a 6kg cheese and matured for 3 months.

Variants :

Notes :

| **Evenlode** | Semisoft | C | P | A | O | WR | Disc |

Made as a 250g cheese and matured for 8 weeks.

Variants :

Notes :

| **Moreton** | Firm | C | P | A | O | NR | Drum |

Made as a 1.8kg cheese based on Tomme and matured for 4 months.

Variants :

Notes :

| **Rollright** | Semisoft | C | P | A | O | WR | Disc |

Made as a 1kg & 205g cheese, wrapped in wood and matured for 6 weeks.

Variants :

Notes :

| **Yarlington** | Semisoft | C | P | A | O | WR | Disc |

Made as a 220g cheese and matured for 7 weeks.

Variants :

Notes :

KINGCOTT DAIRY
Kent

Cheesemakers : Karen, Steve, Frank Reynolds

Family farm with their own herd of Viking Red cows.

| **Kentish Blue** | Blue | C | U | V | | NR | Drum |

Made as a 2.5kg cheese and matured for 8 weeks.

Variants :

Notes :

| **Kingcott Blue** | Blue | C | U | V | | NR | Flying Saucer |

Softer continental style blue created by son Frank and made as a 900g cheese matured for 6 weeks.

Variants :

Notes :

126

LA LATTERIA
London
Cheesemaker : Simona di Vietri

Italian ex-banker making cheese the old fashioned way based on her family's recipes.

La Latteria Fior di Latte Fresh C P A XR Ball
Made as a 400g cheese and matured for 3 days.
Variants : Campagnola, Bocconcini, Nodini, Perline, Ciliegine, Treccia

Notes :

LACEY'S CHEESE
North Yorkshire
Cheesemaker : Simon Lacey

Located in the heart of Swaledale making their own versions of traditional Yorkshire cheeses.

Fallen Monk Firm S U V NR Drum
Made as a 3.0 - 3.5kg cheese and matured for 4 months.
Variants :

Notes :

Kisdon Ewe Firm S U V NR Drum
Made as a 3.0 - 3.5kg cheese and matured for 5 months.
Variants :

Notes :

Lacey's Brie Soft C P V BR Disc
Made as a 1kg cheese.
Variants :

Notes :

Lacey's Mature Cheddar Firm C P V NR Drum
Made as a 2.5kg cheese and matured for 12 months.
Variants :

Notes :

Lacey's Wensleydale Firm C P V NR Drum
Softer version of traditional Wensleydale with flavours added to the curd to mature in the traditional method.
Variants : Original, Garlic & Chive, Cracked Black Pepper, Olive Mescolate, Fresh Chilli, Smoked

Notes :

Richmond Blue	Blue	C	P	V		NR	Cylinder

Made as a 2.5kg cheese and matured for 5 months.

Variants :

Notes :

St Benedict	Firm	S	U	V		NR	Drum

Made as a 3.0 - 3.5kg sheep's milk version of Wensleydale and matured for 12 months.

Variants :

Notes :

LARKTON HALL CHEESE
Cheshire

Cheesemaker : Anne Clayton

Italian Alpine style cheeses made on family farm after returning from living in Italy and enjoying the cheeses.

Crabtree	Firm	C	U	A		NR	Drum

Young unpressed Alpine style cheese matured for 5 - 6 weeks.

Variants : Original, Oregano, Chill, Chive, Cumin, Sage

Notes :

Federia	Firm	C	U	A		NR	Drum

Pressed Alpine style cheese matured for 5 months.

Variants :

Notes :

The Cheese with no Name	Firm	CG	U	A		NR	Drum

Made with cows milk plus 10% goat's milk, pressed and matured for 12 months.

Variants :

Notes :

LAVERSTOKE PARK FARM
Hampshire

Cheesemaker : Martin McCallum

Founded by Formula 1 champion Jodie Scheckter, introducing an organic buffalo herd in 2003.

Buffaloumi	Semisoft	B	P	V	O	XR	Block

Made as a 250g cheese based on Halloumi.

Variants :

Notes :

Laverstoke Park Mozzarella   Fresh   B   P   V   O   XR   Ball

Made as a 250g & 125g cheese and matured for 3 days.

Variants :

Notes :

LEICESTERSHIRE HANDMADE CHEESE COMPANY

Leicestershire

Cheesemakers : Jo, David, Will Clarke

Third generation dairy farmers who started cheesemaking using an 18th century recipe and their own milk.

Bosworth Field   Firm   C   U   A   NR   Drum

Made as a 5kg cheese and matured for 2 months.

Variants :

Notes :

Sparkenhoe Blue   Blue   C   U   A   NR   Cylinder

Made as a 6kg cheese and matured for 5 months.

Variants :

Notes :

Sparkenhoe Red Leicester   Firm   C   U   A   NR   Wheel

The only raw milk version made in the county, made as a 10kg cheese, clothbound and aged for 12 months.

Variants : Original, Vintage (14 months)

Notes :

Sparkenhoe Shropshire Blue   Blue   C   U   A   NR   Cylinder

Made as a 6kg cheese, coloured orange with annatto and matured for 5 months.

Variants :

Notes :

LIGHTWOOD CHEESE

Worcestershire

Cheesemaker : Haydn Roberts

Trained as a cheesemaker with Charlie Westhead at Neal's Yard Creamery before setting up his own dairy.

Amalthea   Soft   G   U   A   BR   Disc

Originally developed in collaboration with Courtyard Dairy and made as a 150g cheese.

Variants :

Notes :

Elgar Mature Firm C U V NR Drum
Based on a 19th century recipe and made as a 3.5kg cheese, clothbound and matured for 6 months.
Variants :
Notes :

Lightwood Chaser Soft C P V BR Disc, Heart
Made as a Brie style cheese with extra cream added.
Variants :
Notes :

St Thom Soft G U A BR Brick
Made as a 200g cheese with a wrinkled rind.
Variants :
Notes :

Worcester Blue Blue C P A NR Drum
Made as a 1.8kg soft blue cheese.
Variants :
Notes :

===

LINCOLNSHIRE POACHER CHEESE
Lincolnshire
Cheesemaker : Simon & Tim Jones, Richard Tagg
Sustainable family farm owned by two brothers that started as dairy in 1970s and making cheeses in 1990s.

Double Barrel Hard C U A PC Cylinder
Made as a 20kg cheese, and matured for 2 - 3 years.
Variants :
Notes :

Knuckleduster Hard C U A PC Cylinder
Selected Poacher cheeses that have developed 'wild' flavours after 12 months and and matured for 3 years.
Variants :
Notes :

Lincolnshire Poacher Firm C U A PC Cylinder
Described as cross between Cheddar and Alpine, made as a 20kg cheese and matured for 14 - 16 months.
Variants : Original, Vintage (18 - 22 months), Poacher 50 (50 months), Smoked
Notes :

Lincolnshire Red   Firm   C   U   V   PC   Cylinder

Based on a Red Leicester coloured orange with annatto and matured for 6 months.

Variants :

Notes :

LLAETH Y BONT

Powys

Cheesemaker : Llewelyn Williams

Third generation family farm started selling produce direct to the public in 2020 including their own cheeses.

Llaeth y Bont Blue Cheese   Soft   C   P   V   NR   Drum

Yet to be properly named, it is made as a 2kg cheese.

Variants :

Notes :

Llaeth y Bont Brie Type Cheese   Soft   C   P   V   BR   Drum

Yet to be properly named, it is made as a 1.5kg & 400g cheese.

Variants :

Notes :

Llaeth y Bont Caerphilly Style Cheese   Style   C   P   V   NR   Drum

Yet to be properly named, it is made as a 2kg cheese.

Variants :

Notes :

LOCH ARTHUR CREAMERY (CAMPHILL COMMUNITY)

Dumfries & Galloway

Cheesemaker : Barry Graham

Part of a working community for adults with learning difficulties using milk from their cows to make cheese.

Loch Arthur Farmhouse   Firm   C   U   V   O   NR   Cylinder

Made as an 8 - 9kg cheese, clothbound and matured for 6 months

Variants : Original, Herbs, Caraway, Mature (12 months)

Notes :

LOCKERBIE CREAMERY (ARLA)
Dumfries & Galloway
Commercial Cheesemaker
Built by Northern Wholesale Dairies, now part of the Arla farmers' co-operative making mainly Cheddar.

| Lockerbie Cheddar | Firm | C | P | V | | XR | Block |

Made as a 20kg mature Cheddar and matured for varying times before being cut into retail blocks.
Variants :

Notes :

LONG CLAWSON DAIRY
Leicestershire
Commercial Cheesemaker
Farming co-operative founded in 1911 using milk from 32 member farms, all within 30 miles of the dairy.

| Blueberry Fayre | Crumbly | C | P | V | | XR | Half Drum |

White Stilton blended with blueberries.
Variants :

Notes :

| Carnival | Crumbly | C | P | V | | XR | Half Drum |

White Stilton blended with sweet mango and fiery crystallised ginger.
Variants :

Notes :

| Charnwood | Firm | C | P | V | | FR | Half Drum |

Cheddar flavoured with natural smoke and coated in paprika.
Variants :

Notes :

| Clawson Reserve Shropshire Blue | Blue | C | P | V | | NR | Cylinder |

Mellow blue cheese coloured orange with annatto.
Variants :

Notes :

| Clawson Reserve Blue Stilton PDO | Blue | C | P | V | | NR | Cylinder |

Made as a 8kg & 2.2kg cheese.
Variants : Original, Mature, 1912 Artisan

Notes :

Clawson Reserve White Stilton PDO   Crumbly   C   P   V   XR   Cylinder

Made as a 8kg cheese with a fresh, clean flavour.

Variants :

Notes :

Clawson Reserve Rutland Red   Firm   C   P   V   XR   Drum

Made as a 3.6kg Leicestershire Red, coloured orange with annatto, clothbound and matured for 6 months.

Variants :

Notes :

Cotswold   Firm   C   P   V   XR   Half Drum

Creamy Double Gloucester blended with chive and onion.

Variants :

Notes :

Crimson   Crumbly   C   P   V   XR   Half Drum

Crumbly, milky Wensleydale blended with sweet, juicy cranberries.

Variants :

Notes :

Flaming Pepper   Firm   C   P   V   XR   Half Drum

Red Leicester blended with diced chilli and roasted red pepper coloured orange with annatto.

Variants :

Notes :

Huntsman   Firm/Blue   C   P   V   XR   Drum

Layers of Double Gloucester with layers of blue Stilton between.

Variants :

Notes :

Innkeepers Choice   Firm   C   P   V   XR   Half Drum

Mature Cheddar blended with pickled onion and chives.

Variants :

Notes :

Lemon Zest   Crumbly   C   P   V   XR   Half Drum

White Stilton blended with sweet and sharp candied lemon peel.

Variants :

Notes :

Scarlet	Crumbly	C	P	V		XR	Half Drum

White Stilton blended with sweet, juicy cranberries.

Variants :

Notes :

⬚

Sunburst	Crumbly	C	P	V		XR	Half Drum

White Stilton blended with sweet apricots.

Variants :

Notes :

⬚

Windsor Red	Firm	C	P	V		XR	Half Drum

Cheddar blended with port, brandy and carmine colouring to produce a marbled appearance.

Variants :

Notes :

⬚

LONG LANE DAIRY
Herefordshire
Cheesemaker : Katie Cordle

Micro-dairy set up during lockdown building on experience gained working with other cheesemakers.

Herefordshire Frier	Semisoft	S	P	V		XR	Brick

Made as a 175g cheese based on Halloumi using cardoon thistle rennet.

Variants :

Notes :

⬚

Long Lane Ricotta	Fresh	S	P	V		XR	Pot

Made using the whey left over from Halloumi making.

Variants :

Notes :

⬚

LONGMAN'S
Somerset
Commercial Cheesemonger

Two centuries of Vale of Camelot farmers and cheesemakers who expanded into a wider business in 1930s.

Bruton Brie	Soft	C	P	V	O	BR	Disc

Made by White Lake Cheeses as a 1kg & 180g cheese exclusively for Longman's.

Variants :

Notes :

⬚

| Longman's Cheddar | Firm | C | P | V | | NR | Block |

Made as a 20kg block Cheddar before being matured for different times and portioned.

Variants : Youngman (6 months), Matureman (12 months), Strongman (18 months), Vintage (24 months)

Notes :

| Vale of Camelot Blue | Blue | C | P | V | | NR | Drum |

Made by Tuxford & Tebbutt as an 8kg Longman's exclusive cheese and matured for 9 weeks.

Variants :

Notes :

| Yarlington Blue | Blue | C | P | V | | NR | Drum |

Made by Tuxford & Tebbutt as an 8kg cheese exclusively for Longman's.

Variants :

Notes :

===

LUBBORN CREAMERY (LACTALIS)
Somerset
Commercial Cheesemaker

Creamery built in 2002 and now owned by the world's largest dairy company, Lactalis.

| Capricorn Goat | Firm | G | P | V | | BR | Square, Drum |

Made using milk from local goat farms as a 1.1kg & 100g cheese.

Variants :

Notes :

| Cricket St Thomas Brie | Soft | C | P | V | | BR | Disc |

Made as a 2.3kg & 1.1kg cheese.

Variants :

Notes :

| Cricket St Thomas Camembert | Soft | C | P | V | | BR | Disc |

Made as a 220g & 140g cheese.

Variants :

Notes :

===

LUDLOW FARM SHOP
Shropshire
Cheesemaker : Paul Bedford

Dairy alongside farm shop on the Earl of Plymouth's estate using milk from the estate farm.

Bringewood   Firm   C   P   V   WR   Drum

Made as a slightly salted cheese, washed in cider brandy and matured for 7 - 12 weeks.

Variants :

Notes :

Lady Halton Smoked   Firm   C   P   V   XR   Drum

Smoked over beechwood chips and matured for 7 - 15 weeks.

Variants :

Notes :

Ludlow Red   Firm   C   U   A   NR   Cylinder

Made as a Cheddar, using kefir as a starter and kid rennet, clothbound and matured for at least 5 months.

Variants :

Notes :

Oakly Park   Firm   C   P   A/V   NR   Cylinder

Made as a vegetarian or traditional Cheddar and matured for at least 5 months.

Variants : Traditional, Vegetarian

Notes :

Remembered Hills   Blue   C   P   V   NR   Cylinder

Made as a British style blue cheese and matured for 9 - 14 weeks.

Variants :

Notes :

LYBURN FARMHOUSE CHEESEMAKERS
Wiltshire
Cheesemaker : Mike Smales

Family dairy farm on the northern edge of the New Forest, making washed curd cheeses since 1999.

Lyburn Gold   Firm   C   P   V   PC   Drum

Made as a 5.5kg cheese in a young Gouda style, coated and matured for 10 weeks.

Variants : Original, Smoked, Garlic & Nettle

Notes :

Old Winchester   Hard   C   P   V   PC   Drum

Made as a 4kg Gouda/Cheddar/Parmesan style cheese, coated and matured for 18 months.

Variants :

Notes :

Stoney Cross   Semisoft   C   P   V   NR   Drum

Made as a 2.5kg cheese in a style similar to a Tomme de Savoie and matured for 2 months.

Variants :

Notes :

Winchester   Firm   C   P   V   PC   Drum

Made as a 5kg cheese in a medium aged Gouda style, coated and matured for 9 months.

Variants :

Notes :

LYE CROSS FARM
Somerset

Cheesemakers : Alvis Family

Fourth generation cheesemakers who farm and produce cheese both traditionally and organically.

Lye Cross Cheddar   Firm   C   P   V   XR   Block

Made as a 20kg block and matured before being cut into smaller blocks.

Variants : Mild, Medium, Mature, Extra Mature, Vintage, Smoked

Notes :

Lye Cross Double Gloucester   Firm   C   P   V   (O)   XR   Block

Made as a 20kg block coloured orange with annatto and matured before being cut into smaller blocks.

Variants : Original, Organic

Notes :

Lye Cross Grass-Fed Organic Cheddar   Firm   C   P   V   O   XR   Block

Made as a 20kg block and matured before being cut into smaller blocks.

Variants :

Notes :

Lye Cross Organic Cheddar   Firm   C   P   V   O   XR   Block

Made as a 20kg block and matured before being cut into smaller blocks.

Variants : Mild, Medium, Mature, Extra Mature, Vintage, Smoked

Notes :

Lye Cross Red Leicester   Firm   C   P   V   (O)   XR   Block

Made as a 20kg block coloured orange with annatto and matured before being cut into smaller blocks.

Variants : Original, Organic

Notes :

LYMN BANK FARM CHEESE COMPANY (JOSEPH HELER)
Lincolnshire
Commercial Cheesemonger

Founded by the Grinstead family, now part of Heler, flavouring, shaping and waxing a range of cheeses.

Just Jane to Fly Again   Firm   C   P   V   WC   Disc

Made as a 200g Cheddar in aid of the appeal to get a Lancaster bomber flying again at a nearby airfield.

Variants : Mature, Vintage, Smoked

Notes :

Lymn Bank Flavoured Cheddar   Firm   C   P   V   WC   Drum

Made as a 200g Cheddar and flavoured before being wax coated.

Variants : Smoked, Garlic & Chive, Chilli, Caramelised Onion

Notes :

Lymn Bank Signature Barrels   Firm   C   P   V   XR   Barrel

Made as a 145g cheese unrinded barrel with added flavours.

Variants : Strongest, Smoked, Applesmoked, Two Barrels, Caramelised Onion, Tomato & Basil, Hot Spicy, Black Pepper, Garlic Herb, Horseradish, Ginger, Garlic, Brewer's Choice, Cranberry, Limoncello, Hot Garlic

Notes :

Mouse House Flavoured Cheddar   Firm   C   P   V   WC   Drum, Heart

Made as a 200g mature Cheddar, flavoured and coated in coloured waxes.

Variants : Black as Coal, Ale & Mustard, Lemon Cheesecake, Orange & Whisky, Cranberry, Truffle Tracker, Heart of Lincoln (heart shaped)

Notes :

LYNHER DAIRIES CHEESE COMPANY
Cornwall
Cheesemaker : Catherine Mead

Yarg was first made in 1984 by Alan Gray using an old recipe but is now made at Pengeep Farm near Truro.

Cornish Kern   Hard   C   P   A   WC   Drum

Made as a 4kg Gouda / Alpine style cheese, coated in a breathable wax and matured for 24 months.

Variants :

Notes :

Cornish Yarg   Crumbly   C   P   V   FR   Drum

The name is 'Gray' backwards, made as a 3kg & 1.7kg cheese, wrapped in nettles and matured for 2 months.

Variants :

Notes :

Stithians   Firm   C   P   A   NR   Drum

Originally developed as an unwrapped Cornish Yarg and made as a 1.7kg & 350g cheese.

Variants : Original, Vintage

Notes :

Wild Garlic Yarg   Crumbly   C   P   V   FR   Drum

Made as a 1.7kg cheese, wrapped in wild garlic leaves and matured for 5 weeks.

Variants :

Notes :

===

MARLOW CHEESE COMPANY
Buckinghamshire
Cheesemaker : James Hill

Started as a home cheesemaker, built a dairy at a local farm, getting Guernsey milk from another local farm.

Bisham   Soft   C   P   V   BR   Disc

Made using Guernsey milk as a 240g golden Brie style cheese and matured for 2 weeks.

Variants :

Notes :

Bucks Blue   Blue   C   P   V   NR   Cylinder

A blue version of Cygnet, made using Guernsey milk as a 120g cheese and matured for 4 weeks.

Variants :

Notes :

Chiltern Cloud   Hard   S   P   V   O   PC   Drum

Made in the style of a Manchego as a 4kg cheese and matured for 9 months with a black rind.

Variants :

Notes :

Cygnet   Soft   C   P   V   BR   Drum

Their first cheese made, a lactic set cheese using Guernsey milk as a 120g cheese and matured for 2 weeks.

Variants :

Notes :

Father Thames	Blue	C	P	V	NR	Cylinder

Made with locally sourced Holstein-Friesian milk and based on a Stilton style recipe.

Variants :

Notes :

Regatta	Hard	C	P	V	PC	Drum

Made as an Alpine style 6kg cheese using Guernsey milk.

Variants :

Notes :

MIKE'S FANCY CHEESE
Down
Cheesemaker : Michael Thomson

Having learned alongside many top British cheesemakers, Mike set up in 2013 in his native Northern Ireland.

Young Buck	Blue	C	U	A	NR	Cylinder

Made as a 8kg cheese based on Stilton style recipe and matured for 3 months.

Variants :

Notes :

MILLBROOK DAIRY
Devon
Cheesemongers : David Evans, Kevin Beer

Started in 2018 to source and supply bulk cheese and butter and have created their own Cheddar brand.

1057 Extra Mature Scottish Cheddar	Firm	C	P	V	XR	Block

Made using Scottish milk as a large block cheese and matured for 14 months before portioning.

Variants :

Notes :

MONKEY CHOP CHEESE
Dorset
Cheesemaker : Jason Barber

Seaborough Dairy's own herd of mixed breed dual-purpose cows provide milk for the dairy.

Lovable Rogue	Soft	C	P	V	BR	Disc

Using morning milk this cheese is made as a 200g rustic Camembert.

Variants :

Notes :

MONKLAND CHEESE DAIRY
Herefordshire
Cheesemaker : Dean Storey

Ex-chef took over cheesemaking in 2023 from founders Mark & Karen Hindle using milk from local farms.

Blue Monk   Blue   C   U   V   NR   Drum
Made as a 250g cheese and matured for 4 weeks.
Variants :
Notes :

Hereford Sage   Firm   C   U   V   NR   Drum
Made as a 5kg cheese based on Little Hereford blended with sage and matured for 8 weeks.
Variants :
Notes :

Little Hereford   Firm   C   U   V   NR   Drum
Made using a 1918 recipe as a 5kg cheese and matured for 4 months.
Variants : Original, Smoked
Notes :

Monkland   Firm   C   U   V   NR   Drum
Made as a 2.5kg almost crumbly cheese and matured for 6 weeks.
Variants : Original, Garlic & Chive
Notes :

The Other Monk   Soft   C   U   V   BR   Disc
Made as a 230g cheese based on Camembert and matured for 4 weeks.
Variants :
Notes :

MONKTON WYLD COURT
Dorset
Cheesemaker : Simon Fairlie

A resident workers' co-operative in an old rectory with its own herd Jersey cows and micro dairy.

Cobbett   Firm   C   U   A   XR   Jar, Block
Based on Halloumi and packed in 500g jar or as a 1kg block.
Variants :
Notes :

MONMOUTH SHEPHERD
Monmouthshire
Cheesemaker : Isabel Coates

Family farm making cheese and soap using sheep's milk from their own flock.

Hollywell | Firm | S | P | V | | XR | Drum
Made as a 1.5kg cheese.
Variants :
Notes :

Parkapella | Hard | S | P | V | | NR | Drum
Made as a 3kg cheese based on Manchego.
Variants :
Notes :

Trothy | Semisoft | S | P | V | | XR | Block
Based on Feta.
Variants :
Notes :

Whitehill | Semisoft | S | P | V | | XR | Block
Based on Halloumi mixed with herbs.
Variants :
Notes :

===

MONTGOMERY'S CHEESES
Somerset
Cheesemaker : Jamie Montgomery

Third generation cheesemaker on family farm since 1911 using milk from their ownFriesian and Jersey herds.

Montgomery's Cheddar | Firm | C | U | A | | NR | Cylinder
Friesian milk, 100 year old starters and made as a 26kg cheese, clothbound and matured for 12 - 18 months.
Variants : Original, Extra Mature, Smoked
Notes :

Ogleshield | Firm | C | U | A | | WR | Wheel
Made as a 5kg Raclette style cheese using Jersey milk and matured for 5 months.
Variants :
Notes :

===

MOYDEN'S HANDMADE CHEESE
Shropshire
Cheesemakers : Martin & Beth Moyden

Established 2005 making a range of hand crafted cheeses capturing the essence of Shropshire.

Caer Caradoc   Firm   C   U   V   NR   Drum

Made as a 4.5kg Caerphilly style cheese and matured for 2 - 3 months to produce a crumbly texture.

Variants :

Notes :

Ironbridge   Blue   C   U   V   BR   Disc

Made as a 200g individual cheese and matured for 6 weeks.

Variants :

Notes :

Newport   Hard   C   U   V   NR   Drum

Made as a 4.5kg cheese and matured for 3 -4 months and the 1665 version cold smoked over oak chips.

Variants : Original, 1665

Notes :

Shrewsbury Fretta   Fresh   C   U   V   XR   Square

Based on Feta and meaning 'quick' in Italian acknowledging that this cheese is best less that a week old.

Variants :

Notes :

Wrekin Blue   Blue   C   U   V   NR   Drum

Named after a local hill and made as 1.8kg cheese and matured for 2 months.

Variants :

Notes :

Wrekin White   Firm   C   U   V   NR   Drum

Brushed with local rapeseed oil and matured for 3 months.

Variants :

Notes :

MRS BOURNE'S CHESHIRE CHEESE
Cheshire
Cheesemaker : Hugo Bourne

Family cheesemaking since 1752 with third generation cheesemaker at the current farm.

Clothbound Cheshire   Crumbly   C   U/P   V   NR   Cylinder
Made as an 8kg - 10kg cheese, clothbound and matured in the farmhouse cellar.
Variants :
Notes :

John Bourne's Blue Cheshire   Blue   C   P   V   NR   Cylinder
The only Blue Cheshire made in Cheshire itself, it is made as an 8kg - 10kg cheese, clothbound and matured.
Variants :
Notes :

Jubilee Blue   Blue   C   P   V   NR   Cylinder
Limited edition cheese made for Queen Elizabeth II's Platinum Jubilee.
Variants :
Notes :

Mrs Bourne's Mature Cheshire   Crumbly   C   P   V   WC   Cylinder
Made as an 8kg - 10kg cheese and matured for 5 months, described as being like a 'Cheshire cheese of old'.
Variants : Original, Smoked
Notes :

MRS KIRKHAM'S LANCASHIRE
Lancashire
Cheesemaker : Graham Kirkham

Third generation cheesemaker making the only raw milk traditional Lancashire in the world.

Mrs Kirkham's Lancashire   Crumbly   C   U   A   NR   Cylinder
Made as a 20kg & 10kg cheese, clothbound, buttered and matured to a buttery crumble for min. 3 months.
Variants : Mild & Creamy (3 months), Tasty (4 months), Smoked (6 months), Mature (10 months),
Garlic & Parsley, Ruby (Coloured with annatto)
Notes :

MRS TEMPLE'S CHEESE
Norfolk

Cheesemaker : Catherine Temple

Low input regenerative family farm producing green energy using milk from their Brown Swiss herd.

Binham Blue   Blue   C   P   V   NR   Drum
Made as a 1kg and 500g cheese and matured for at least 6 weeks.
Variants :

Notes :

Copys Cloud   Soft   C   P   V   BR   Disc
Made as a 650g & 200g cheese and matured for 6 weeks.
Variants :

Notes :

Gurney's Gold   Semisoft   C   P   V   WR   Square, Disc
Made as a 1.2kg square and 300g disc cheese.
Variants :

Notes :

Walsingham   Crumbly   C   P   V   XR   Drum
Described as a cross between Wensleydale and Cheddar made as a 5kg cheese matured for 4 - 18 months.
Variants : Original, Oak Smoked

Notes :

Wells Alpine   Firm   C   P   V   PC   Rounded Drum
Made as a 4kg Alpine style cheese and matured for 6 months.
Variants :

Notes :

Wighton   Fresh   C   P   V   XR   Disc
Based on a 1930 local recipe and made as a 200g cheese similar in style to Feta with a distinctive pattern.
Variants :

Notes :

NAKED WHITE CHEESE CO (BRADBURY'S)
Nottinghamshire
Commercial Cheesemaker

Based in Cropwell Bishop, previously called Shirevale, the only non-blue Stilton maker, part of Bradbury's.

Naked White Stilton PDO   Crumbly   C   P   V   XR   Cylinder

Made as a traditional PDO cheese using milk from local farms before being blended with various fruits.

Variants : Original, Apricot, Cranberry, Mango & Ginger

Notes :

===

NEAL'S YARD CREAMERY
Herefordshire
Cheesemaker : Charlie Westhead

Started as part of Neal's Yard Dairy, now independent with on site green energy making them sustainable.

Dorstone   Soft   G   P   A   BR   Cylinder

Made as a 180g cheese with long overnight setting, hand ladling, rolling is ash and maturing for 3 weeks.

Variants :

Notes :

Finn   Soft   C   P   V   O   BR   Drum

Made as a 200g double-cream lactic-set cheese and matured for 3 weeks.

Variants :

Notes :

Hay-on-Wye   Soft   G   P   A   BR   Disc

Made as a 70g cheese based on Selles-sur-Cher, slow-drained, ash coated and matured for 2 weeks.

Variants :

Notes :

Perroche   Soft   G   P   V   XR   Cylinder

Made as a 700g & 150g cheese using cardoon rennet and matured for 3 weeks.

Variants : Original, Fresh Herbs

Notes :

Ragstone   Soft   G   P   A   BR   Log

Made as a 600g & 200g cheese using kid rennet and matured for 3 weeks.

Variants :

Notes :

===

NETTLEBED CREAMERY
Oxfordshire

Cheesemaker : Rose Grimond

Fourth generation family farm who built a dairy in 1950, became organic in 2001 and made cheese in 2005.

Bix   Soft   C   P   A   O   BR   Drum

Made as a 100g triple-cream cheese in a Brillat Savarin style with a meltingly soft creamy interior.

Variants :

Notes :

Highmoor   Semisoft   C   P   A   O   WR   Square

Made as a 300g cheese, rind washed and matured for 4 weeks.

Variants :

Notes :

Leckford   Semisoft   C   P   A   O   WR   Disc

Made as a 150g cheese washed in Leckford Estate Sparkling White Wine exclusively for Waitrose.

Variants :

Notes :

Witheridge   Firm   C   P   A   O   NR   Drum

Made as a 2kg cheese and matured in dried hay for 6 months.

Variants :

Notes :

===

NORBURY PARK FARM CHEESE COMPANY
Surrey

Cheesemakers : Michaela & Neil Allam

Using milk from a closed British Friesian herd at a small dairy on their farm on the edge of the Surrey Hills.

Dirty Vicar   Crumbly   C   U   V   BR   Drum

Made as a 2kg Caerphilly style cheese and matured for 4 weeks.

Variants :

Notes :

Dorking Cock   Firm   C   U   V   NR   Drum

Made as a 20kg cheese based on Cheddar and matured for 6 months.

Variants :

Notes :

Norbury Blue	Blue	C	U	V		NR	Drum

Made as a 2.5kg cheese and matured for 4 - 6 weeks.

Variants :

Notes :

NORSELAND
Somerset
Commercial Cheesemaker

Owned by Norway's largest dairy co-operative specialising in blended own label and branded cheeses.

Applewood	Firm	C	P	V		FR	Block, Half Drum

Made as a Cheddar in a 4.2kg block and 1.5kg Half Drum, flavoured with smoke and rolled in paprika.

Variants : Original, Vintage

Notes :

Ilchester Cheddar	Firm	C	P	V		VR	Stick, Half Drum

Made as a Cheddar and moulded into half drum or portioned into small 20g snacking sticks.

Variants : Original (Stick), Vintage (Stick), Truffle

Notes :

Marmite Cheddar	Firm	C	P	V		XR	Block

Made as a large block Cheddar flavoured with Marmite, before being portioned into retail blocks.

Variants :

Notes :

Mexicana	Firm	C	P	V		XR	Block, Half Drum

Made as a Cheddar in a 4.2kg block and 1.5kg Half Drum, blended with spices, chillis and peppers.

Variants : Original, Extra Hot

Notes :

NORSWORTHY DAIRY GOATS
Devon
Cheesemaker : Dave & Marilyn Johnson

Established in 1999 to provide milk to local dairies, before building their own cheese room in 2006.

Chelwood	Soft	G	U	V		XR	Drum

Made as a 100g cheese designed to be eaten young and fresh.

Variants : Original, Mixed Herbs, Ash

Notes :

Gunstone	Firm	G	U	V		NR	Rounded Drum

Made as a 2kg washed curd cheese and matured for 1 - 6 months.

Variants :

Notes :

Norsworthy	Semisoft	G	U	V		NR	Rounded Drum

Made as a 2kg cheese and matured for 1 - 6 months, with nutty caramel flavours developing with age.

Variants :

Notes :

Posbury	Semisoft	G	U	V		NR	Rounded Drum

Made as a 2kg Norsworthy cheese blended with various flavours.

Variants : Garlic, Ginger, Horseradish, Onion, Paprika

Notes :

Tillerton	Soft	G	U	V		BR	Log

Made as a 100g cheese matured for 2 weeks.

Variants :

Notes :

NORTHAMPTON CHEESE COMPANY
Northamptonshire

Cheesemakers : Steve Reid, Mark Rogers

Starting by making charcuterie and chutney led to learning cheesemaking and launching own range in 2021.

Beckets Brie	Soft	C	P	V	O	BR	Drum

Made as a 450g cheese with double cream added and matured for 4 weeks.

Variants :

Notes :

Clickers	Firm	C	P	V	O	PC	Rounded Drum

Made as a 5.5kg Cheddar, matured for at least 3 months and cut into 150g retail packs.

Variants :

Notes :

Hobnail	Blue	C	P	V	O	PC	Rounded Drum

Made as a 5.5kg cheese coloured orange with annatto and cut into 150g retail packs.

Variants :

Notes :

Phipps Firkin   Firm   C   P   V   O   PC   Rounded Drum

Made as a 5.5kg cheese infused with Phipps ale, matured for 4 months and cut into 150g retail packs.

Variants :

Notes :

☐

Skyver   Firm   C   P   V   O   PC   Rounded Drum

Made as a 5.5kg cheese coloured orange with annatto, matured for 2 month and cut into 150g retail packs.

Variants :

Notes :

☐

Togglers   Firm   C   P   V   O   XR   Rounded Drum

Made as a 5.5kg mild flavoured cheese matured for 30 days and portioned into 150g retail packs.

Variants :

Notes :

☐

Tongue Taster   Firm   C   P   V   O   PC   Rounded Drum

Made as a 5.5kg Clickers matured for 5 month then smoked over oak chips and cut into 150g retail packs.

Variants :

Notes :

☐

NORTHUMBERLAND CHEESE COMPANY (BRADBURY'S)
Northumberland

Cheesemaker : Martin Atkinson

Founded in 1984, now cheesemaking in a converted granary using milk from Northern farms.

Chesterwood   Firm   G   P   V   XR   Drum

Made as Elsdon, the firm goat's cheese is smoked over oak chippings.

Variants :

Notes :

☐

Elsdon   Firm   G   P   V   XR   Drum

Using milk from a single herd in Yorkshire, it is made as a 2.5kg cheese and matured for 3 months.

Variants : Original, Nettle

Notes :

☐

Hadston   Firm   C   P   V   WC   Block

Made as a 200g extra mature Cheddar.

Variants :

Notes :

☐

Northumberland	Firm	C	P	V		XR	Drum

Made as a 2.5kg Gouda style cheese and matured for 3 months.

Variants : Original, Oak Smoked, Chilli, Nettle

Notes :

Redesdale	Firm	S	P	V		XR	Drum

The first cheese made in 1984 originally using their own sheep's milk.

Variants :

Notes :

Tynedale	Firm	C	P	V		XR	Block

Made as an extra mature Cheddar.

Variants :

Notes :

NORTON & YARROW CHEESE
Oxfordshire

Cheesemakers : Fraser Norton, Rachel Yarrow

Started in 2016 and now milking a large herd of Anglo-Nubian goats to make their cheeses.

Brightwell Ash	Fresh	G	U	A		BR	Disc

Made as a 140g cheese, ash coated and matured for 1 week as it develops a wrinkled rind.

Variants :

Notes :

Sinodun Hill	Fresh	G	U	A		BR	Flat Pyramid

Gently made over several days as a 200g cheese using cardoon thistle rennet and matured for up to 3 weeks.

Variants :

Notes :

NORTONS DAIRY
Norfolk

Cheesemakers : Ruth Norton

Third and fourth generation dairy farmers of the Norton family producing a full range of dairy products.

Nortons Soft Cheese	Soft	C	P	V		XR	Pot

Made as a 200g cheese using milk from their own herd of Brown Swiss.

Variants : Original, Lavender, Apricot, Chilli, Black Pepper & Chive, Limited Editions

Notes :

NUT KNOWLE FARM
East Sussex
Cheesemakers : Lyn & Jenny Jenner
Established in 1979 and still making a wide range of goat's cheese styles using milk from their own herd.

Aspire	Semisoft	G	P	V	NR	Cone

Made as a 100g ash coated cheese.
Variants :
Notes :

Black Jack	Soft	G	P	V	BR	Log

Wealdway cut in half and matured for longer.
Variants :
Notes :

Blue Knowle	Blue	G	P	V	BR	Cylinder

Made as a 140g cheese.
Variants :
Notes :

Caprini	Soft	G	P	V	XR	Slices

Wealdway cut into slices and marinated in vegetable oil with herbs and spices.
Variants :
Notes :

Gun Hill	Firm	G	P	V	NR	Drum

Made as a 1kg cheese based on Sussex Yeoman and smoked in wedges over pine.
Variants :
Notes :

Little Truffle	Soft	G	P	V	BR	Disc

Made as a 110g cheese.
Variants :
Notes :

Martlet Gold	Semisoft	G	P	V	WR	Sunken Disc

Made as a 120g cheese similar to Langres.
Variants :
Notes :

Pyramid   Semisoft   G   P   V   BR   Flat Pyramid

Made as a 140g cheese and ash coated.

Variants :

Notes :

Saint George   Soft   G   P   V   BR   Disc

Made as a 180g cheese based on Camembert.

Variants :

Notes :

Sussex Squire   Semisoft   G   P   V   XR   Square

Made as a 170g cheese coloured with annatto and layered with smoked garlic.

Variants :

Notes :

Sussex Yeoman   Firm   G   P   V   NR   Drum

Made as a 2kg cheese, hard pressed and matured for 2 months.

Variants :

Notes :

Wealden   Soft   G   P   V   BR   Cylinder

Made as an 80g cheese and matured for 4 weeks.

Variants :

Notes :

Wealden Hard   Firm   G   P   V   BR   Cylinder

Made as a 50g matured version of Wealden.

Variants :

Notes :

Wealdway   Soft   G   P   V   XR   Log

Made as a 220g & 150g cheese coated in herbs and spices.

Variants : Original, Mature Ash, Chilli, Black Pepper, Lemon Pepper, Chive, Garlic Herb

Notes :

Wealdway Mature   Soft   G   P   V   XR   Log

Made as a 220g cheese rolled in ash and matured for 2 - 3 weeks.

Variants :

Notes :

NUTFIELD DAIRY
Surrey
Cheesemakers : Bessie Edge, Matthew Elphick

Regenerative farmers in the Surrey Hills with their own herd of pasture fed Dairy Shorthorns.

Nutfield Cheddar Firm C P V NR Cylinder

Made as a 12kg cheese and clothbound with butter soaked cloth and matured for 6 months.

Variants :

Notes :

Surrey Red Firm C P V NR Drum

Made as a 1.8kg cheese based on an Alpine Tomme recipe, unpressed and matured for 2 months.

Variants :

Notes :

THE OLD CHEESE ROOM
Wiltshire
Cheesemaker : Julianna Sedli

Hungarian cheesemaker working in the old dairy at Neston Park using organic Jersey milk from the farm.

Baronet Semisoft C P V O WR Disc

Made as an 800g & 200g cheese and matured for 4 weeks.

Variants : Original (800g), Mini (280g)

Notes :

Bybrook Firm C P V O WR Drum

Made as a 4kg cheese and matured for 3 months.

Variants :

Notes :

Lypiatt Soft C P V O BR Disc

Made as a 220g cheese, ash coated and matured for 2 weeks.

Variants :

Notes :

Medleys Semisoft C P V O WR Disc

Made as a 280g cheese, a lightly smoked young unripened Baronet.

Variants :

Notes :

THE OPEN AIR DAIRY
Dorset
Cheesemongers : Tom Foot, Neil Grigg

Their own cows are milked in the fields as they graze and the milk made into cheese by nearby Ford Farm.

West Country Mature Cheddar Firm C P V NR Cylinder

Made as a 27kg cheese, clothbound and matured for 15 - 24 months.

Variants :

Notes :

===

ORKNEY CHEESE COMPANY
Orkney
Cheesemaker : John Bruce

A joint venture owned by an Orkney farmers' co-operative and Lactalis the French dairy giant.

Orkney Cheddar PGI Firm C P V XR Block

Made using only Orkney milk as a 2.5kg white and coloured cheese and matured for 6 - 12 months.

Variants : Medium Coloured (6 month), Mature White & Coloured (12 month), Extra Mature (15 month)

Notes :

===

OTTINGE COURT DAIRY
Kent
Cheesemaker : Judy Wilson

Third generation family farm for over 100 years with own herd of pedigree Holstein-Friesians.

Ottinge Bramshill Firm C U A WR Drum

Made as a 6kg Alpine style cheese and matured between 6 - 30 months with a different name at each age.

Variants : Original (6), Mature (12), Hopel (30)

Notes :

Ottinge Mutschli Firm C U A WR Drum

Made as a 1kg cheese and matured for 6 - 8 weeks.

Variants :

Notes :

Ottinge Oaxaca Fresh C U A XR Rope

Made as a fresh Mexican style cheese in ropes wrapped into balls exclusively Kol restaurant in London.

Variants :

Notes :

===

OXFORD CHEESE COMPANY
Oxfordshire
Affineur & Cheesemonger : Baron Robert Pouget
Based in Oxford market with a range of unique cheeses made by various dairies for maturing in Oxford.

Cerne Abbas Cheddar   Firm   C   P   V   WC   Drum
Made by Ford Farm in blocks, formed as 150g cheeses and matured for 18 months.
Variants :
Notes :

College White   Soft   C   P   V   BR   Disc
Made by Butlers then sliced and filled with truffle to produce this 600g Coulommiers style cheese.
Variants :
Notes :

Oxford Blue   Blue   C   P   V   NR   Drum
Made by Butlers as a 2.7kg cheese and matured for 3 months at Oxford Cheese Company.
Variants :
Notes :

Oxford Dolce   Blue   C   P   V   NR   Drum
Made by Butlers as a 2.7kg cheese based on a Gorgonzola style.
Variants :
Notes :

Oxford Isis   Soft   C   P   V   WR   Disc
Made in France as a 900g & 200g cheese, then brought to Oxford to be washed in honey mead for 6 weeks.
Variants :
Notes :

Spitfire   Firm   C   P   A   WC   Drum, Half Drum
Made by Croome Cuisine as a Cheddar blended with garlic & chilli as 1.2kg half drum & smaller drums.
Variants :
Notes :

PADSTOW CHEESE COMPANY
Cornwall
Cheesemakers : Lawrence & Rosea Reynolds

Known for making Cornish Jack but milk supply problems have led to launching a new soft cheese range.

Cornish Jack Firm C P A NR Drum

Made as a 12kg Emmental style cheese and matured for 4 months.

Variants :

Notes :

Ele, The Original Fresh C P V NR Pot

Lactic cheese made with Himalayan salt, in rapeseed oil, peppercorns, chipotle and garlic flakes.

Variants :

Notes :

Little Herbert Fresh C P V NR Cube

Made as a 100g triple cream cheese blended with garlic, parsley and chives and matured for 7 - 10 days.

Variants :

Notes :

Rokke Fresh/Hard C P V FR Ball

Flavoured 150g cheese matured for 7 - 10 days as fresh cheese or 2 - 3 months as a hard cheese for shaving.

Variants : Black Rokke (Black Garlic), Chilli Rokke (Chipotle), Herb Rokke (Garlic, Chive & Parsley)

Notes :

===

PANT MAWR FARMHOUSE CHEESES
Pembrokeshire
Cheesemakers : David, Cynthia, Jason Jennings

Family owned small-holding making cheese using Welsh milk from local farmer's co-operative.

Caws Cerwyn Firm C P V NR Disc

Made as a 1.2kg and 200g cheese and matured for 2 weeks.

Variants : Original, Oak Smoked, Mature (6 months)

Notes :

Caws Preseli Soft C P V BR Disc

Made as Brie style 1kg cheese matured for 2 weeks.

Variants : Original, Smoked

Notes :

Drewi Sant   Soft   C   P   V   FR   Disc

Made as a 1.1kg cheese sprayed with Welsh honey mead and matured for 3 weeks.

Variants :

Notes :

PAXTON & WHITFIELD
London
Commercial Affineur & Cheesemonger

Trading since 1742 and royal warrant holder, they work with cheesemakers to develop their own cheeses.

Barrel Aged   Semisoft   S   P   V   XR   Block

Made in Somerset and barrel aged in brine by Paxton & Whitfield before being portioned into 200g blocks.

Variants :

Notes :

Corinium   Firm   C   P   A   O   WR   Drum

Made by King Stone Dairy exclusively for Paxton & Whitfield based on a Tomme style cheese.

Variants :

Notes :

Cullum   Firm   S   P   V   WR   Drum

Developed with and made by St James Cheese only in summer months and matured at Paxton & Whitfield.

Variants :

Notes :

Dorset Goat   Firm   G   P   V   WC   Disc

Made in Dorset as a 200g cheese before being waxed.

Variants :

Notes :

Paxton & Whitfield Cave Aged Cheddar Firm   C   P   V   NR   Cylinder, Truckle

Made in Dorset as a 26kg, 1.8kg & 550g cheese, clothbound and matured in Wookey Hole caves.

Variants : Original, XO (20 month)

Notes :

Paxton & Whitfield Smoked Ceodre   Firm   C   P   V   WC   Disc

Made in Dorset as a 200g Cheddar matured for 12 months before being smoked and wax coated.

Variants :

Notes :

PEVENSEY CHEESE COMPANY
East Sussex
Cheesemakers : Martin & Hazel Tkalez
After working for Neal's Yard Dairy, set up the new dairy in 2020 on family farm using neighbours milk.

Pevensey Blue   Blue   C   P   A   NR   Drum
Made as a 2.4kg cheese based on Gorgonzola and matured for 9 weeks.
Variants :

Notes :

PEXTENEMENT CHEESE COMPANY
West Yorkshire
Cheesemakers : Sandra Evans, Carl Warburton
Organic family farm using milk from their herd of Meuse Rhine Issel to make cheese in a 17th century barn.

Bertha   Blue   C   P   V   O   NR   Disc
Made as a 170g & 110g cheese the same as Devil's Rock Blue but unpierced so only the rind is blue.
Variants :

Notes :

Chapelhouse   Semisoft   C   P   V   O   WR   Disc
Made as an individual Reblochon style cheese.
Variants :

Notes :

Devil's Rock Blue   Blue   C   P   V   O   NR   Drum
Made as a 250g & 140g individual cheese.
Variants :

Notes :

East Lee   Semisoft   C   P   V   O   WC   Drum
Made as a 170g & 110g individual cheese to a 1920s recipe similar to a creamy Cheshire / Lancashire style.
Variants : Original, Garlic

Notes :

Nattercrop   Soft   C   P   V   O   BR   Disc
Made as an 850g Brie style cheese.
Variants :

Notes :

Organic Monterey Jack   Firm   C   P   V   O   WR   Drum
Made as a 4kg cheese and matured for 90 days.
Variants :
Notes :

Pexo Blanco   Fresh   C   P   O   XR   Block
Made as a 200g block using vinegar as a setting agent to make a cheese similar to a Halloumi or Paneer.
Variants :
Notes :

Pexommier   Soft   C   P   V   O   BR   Disc
Made as a 170g & 110g cheese as a Coulommier style to an old family recipe found in the barn.
Variants :
Notes :

Pike's Delight   Firm   C   P   V   O   WR   Dum
Made as a 4kg cheese washed and matured for 9 months with an unwashed version matured for 5 months.
Variants :
Notes :

PLAW HATCH FARM
West Sussex

Cheesemaker : Dom Lawrance

Biodynamic farm with a closed herd of mainly Meuse Rhine Issel cows whose milk is used to make cheeses.

Dutchman   Firm   C   U   V   O   NR   Rounded Wheel
Made as a 5kg Gouda style cheese, rubbed with olive oil and matured for 4 weeks.
Variants : Original, Chilli, Cumin, Peppercorn
Notes :

Plaw Hatch Cheddar   Firm   C   U   V   O   NR   Drum
Made as a 20kg & 10kg cheese, clothbound and matured for 3 - 18 months.
Variants : Mild (3m), Mature (6m), Extra Mature (12m), Vintage (18m), Smoked
Notes :

Sizzler   Semisoft   C   U   V   O   XR   Block
Made as a 1kg & 200g Halloumi style cheese.
Variants :
Notes :

POLMARKYN DAIRY
Cornwall
Cheesemaker : Katie Wood
Family goat farm using milk from their own herd to make cheese and other dairy and non-dairy products.

Alpine Goat's Salad Cheese	Fresh	G	U	V	XR	Square, Heart

Made as a 200g cheese.
Variants :
Notes :

Cornish Blue Goat's Cheese	Blue	G	U	V	BR	Square

Made as a 200g cheese.
Variants :
Notes :

Cornish Grey Goat's Cheese	Semisoft	G	U	V	BR	Drum

Made as a 200g ash coated cheese.
Variants :
Notes :

Cornish White Goat's Cheese	Soft	G	U	V	BR	Drum

Made as a 200g cheese.
Variants :
Notes :

Goatlloumi	Semisoft	G	U	V	XR	Block

Made as a 200g cheese based on Halloumi.
Variants :
Notes :

QUICKE'S TRADITIONAL
Devon
Cheesemaker : Mary Quicke
Family owned farm since 1540 and making cheese for five generations using milk from their hybrid herd.

Devonshire Red	Firm	C	P	V	NR	Cylinder

Made as a 27kg cheese as a Devon take on Red Leicester, coloured, clothbound and matured for 6 months.
Variants :
Notes :

Double Devonshire   Firm   C   P   V   NR   Cylinder

Made as a 27kg cheese as a Devon take on Double Gloucester, clothbound and matured for 3 months.

Variants : Original, Smoked

Notes :

Lady Prue   Firm   CG   P   V   NR   Cylinder

Made as an 8kg mixed milk cheese, clothbound and matured for 6 months.

Variants :

Notes :

Quicke's Cheddar   Firm   C   P   A/V   NR   Cylinder

Made as a 27kg, 8kg & 1.8kg cheese, clothbound and matured for 3 - 24 months.

Variants : Buttery (3m), Smoked (9m - 12m), Mature (12m - 15m), Extra Mature (18 m), Vintage (24 m)

Notes :

Quicke's Elderflower   Firm   C   P   V   NR   Cylinder

Made as a 27kg cheese, clothbound and matured for 3 months.

Variants :

Notes :

Quicke's Ewe Cheddar   Firm   S   P   A   NR   Cylinder

Made as an 8kg cheese and matured for 6 - 12 months.

Variants :

Notes :

Quicke's Goat Cheddar   Firm   G   P   V   NR   Cylinder

Made as a 27kg & 1.8kg cheese, clothbound and matured for 3 - 6 months.

Variants : Original, Smoked

Notes :

===

RENNET AND RIND

Cambridgeshire

Affineurs & Cheesemongers : Perry Wakeman, Mark Hulme

Cheesemonger and multiple award winning affineur who has two cheeses made exclusively for them.

The Duchess   Firm   C   U   V   WR   Drum

Made as an Alpine style cheese for Rennet & Rind and washed in local Saffron Grange Sparkling Rosé wine.

Variants :

Notes :

The Duke   Blue   C   U   V   NR   Drum

Creamy, sweet and salty blue made using milk from a local herd of Red Poll cattle and matured for 12 weeks.

Variants :

Notes :

RIBBLESDALE CHEESE COMPANY (CARRON LODGE)
North Yorkshire
Commercial Cheesemaker

Originally in Ribblesdale before moving to Hawes, with the cheese now made by new owners Carron Lodge.

Blue Goat   Blue   G   P   V   WC   Half Drum

One of only a few blue goat's cheeses made in Britain, it is made as a 1.8kg cheese.

Variants :

Notes :

Goatisan   Firm   G   P   V   NR   Drum

Made as an aged version of Superior Goat, it is clothbound and matured for 3 - 5 months.

Variants :

Notes :

Gouda Gold   Firm   G   P   V   NR   Ammonite

Made as a 1kg cheese with a distinctive ammonite shape and matured for 2 - 4 months.

Variants :

Notes :

Groovy Goat   Firm   G   P   V   NR   Drum

Clothbound and matured for 3 - 5 months.

Variants :

Notes :

Mature Goat   Firm   G   P   V   WC   Half Drum

Made as a 1.8kg cheese matured for 2 - 3 months and coated in white wax.

Variants : Original, Smoked

Notes :

Original Goat   Firm   G   P   V   WC   Drum

Made as a 2kg cheese based on Cheddar and matured for 2 - 3 months.

Variants : Original, Smoked

Notes :

| **Original Sheep** | Firm | S | P | V | | WC | Drum |

Made as a 2kg cheese and matured for 4 months.

Variants : Original, Smoked

Notes :

| **Owd Ewe** | Firm | S | P | V | | NR | Drum |

Made as a 2kg cheese, clothbound and matured for 4 months .

Variants :

Notes :

| **Superior Goat** | Firm | G | P | V | | WC | Drum |

Made as a 2kg Gouda style cheese matured for 3 months.

Variants :

Notes :

===

ROSARY GOAT'S CHEESE
Wiltshire

Cheesemakers : Chris & Claire Moody

Making fresh and aged goat's cheese since 1988 on the edge of the New Forest using local Saanen milk.

| **Dazel Ash** | Soft | G | P | V | | BR | Log |

Made as a 200g cheese, ash coated and matured for 3 weeks to develop a wrinkled black and white rind.

Variants :

Notes :

| **Little Lepe** | Soft | G | P | V | | BR | Disc |

Made as a 70g ash coated version of St Ella matured for 3 weeks.

Variants :

Notes :

| **Rosary** | Fresh | G | P | V | | XR | Cylinder |

Made as a 1kg, 275g & 100g cheese and matured for 3 days either as plain version or rolled in coating.

Variants : Original, Ash, Garlic & Herb, Pepper

Notes :

| **St Ella** | Soft | G | P | V | | BR | Disc |

Made as a 70g cheese matured for 3 weeks to develop a wrinkled cream coloured rind.

Variants :

Notes :

===

ROWCLIFFE
Kent
Cheesemonger

Cheese wholesaler who has a Cheddar made exclusively for them by Lye Cross Farm in Somerset.

Holmbury Vintage Cheddar	Firm	C	P	V		XR	Block

Made as a 5kg block and matured for 12 months.

Variants :

Notes :

SHARPHAM DAIRY
Devon
Cheesemakers : Greg Parsons, Peter Haworth

Established in the Dart Valley for over 40 years, with new owners achieving the first UK dairy B-Corp status.

Cremet	Soft	GC	P	V		BR	Disc

Made as a 480g cheese using goat's milk with cow's double-cream added to give a soft rich mousse.

Variants :

Notes :

Elmhirst	Soft	C	T	V		BR	Disc

Made as an 800g & 160g triple-cream cheese using Jersey milk and matured for 4 - 6 weeks.

Variants :

Notes :

Rushmore	Semisoft	CG	T	V		BR	Flying Saucer

Made as a 1.6kg & 450g mixed milk cheese originally created by an accidental mixing of milks.

Variants :

Notes :

Savour	Firm	CG	T	V		NR	Curved Drum

Made as a 900g mixed milk cheese based on a Savoie style.

Variants :

Notes :

Sharpham Brie	Soft	C	T	V		BR	Disc, Square, Heart

Made as a 1.2kg & 300g Coulommier style cheese with a golden yellow paste from Jersey milk.

Variants :

Notes :

Sharpham Camembert	Soft	C	T	V		BR	Disc

Made as a 260g cheese with a golden yellow paste due to the rich Jersey milk.

Variants :

Notes :

Sharpham Rustic	Crumbly	C	T	V		BR	Flying Saucer

Made as a 1.6kg & 500g cheese using rich Jersey milk that gives a golden colour and rich crumbly texture.

Variants : Original, Chive & Garlic, Dulse & Sea Lettuce

Notes :

Ticklemore	Semisoft	G	P	V		BR	Flying Saucer

Made as a 1.6kg & 550g cheese in a distinctive shape and matured for 2 months.

Variants :

Notes :

Washbourne	Firm	S	P	V		NR	Curved Drum

Made as a 1.6kg washed curd cheese and matured for 8 - 10 weeks.

Variants :

Notes :

SHEPHERDS PURSE CHEESES
North Yorkshire

Cheesemaker : Katie Matten

Founded in 1989 by Judy Bell on family farm making sheep' alternatives for people with cow's milk allergies.

Bluemin White	Blue	C	P	V		BR	Drum

Made as 170g blue but it is not pierced so only develops blue on the outside.

Variants :

Notes :

Buffalo Blue	Blue	B	P	V		NR	Drum

Made as a 1.4kg cheese and matured for 8 weeks to give a fresh delicate tangy flavour.

Variants :

Notes :

Harrogate Blue	Blue	C	P	V		NR	Drum

Launched in 2012 and made as a 1.4kg cheese matured for 10 weeks.

Variants :

Notes :

Katy's White Lavender   Firm   S   P   V   FR   Drum

Made as a 1.4kg cheese rolled in dried lavender which infuses into the cheese during maturing.

Variants :

Notes :

Mrs Bell's Blue   Blue   S   P   V   NR   Drum

Tangy sheep's milk version of Yorkshire Blue made as a 1.4kg cheese and matured for 10 weeks.

Variants :

Notes :

Mrs Bell's Salad Cheese   Semisoft   S   P   V   XR   Block

Based on Feta, originally called Fettle, now renamed and made as a 1.4kg cheese and matured for 4 weeks.

Variants :

Notes :

Northern Blue   Blue   C   P   V   NR   Drum

Made as a 1.4g cheese with a stronger flavoured strain of blue mould and matured for 10 weeks.

Variants :

Notes :

Olde York   Semisoft   S   P   V   WC   Drum

Made as an 800g cheese using the Coulommier method of settling under its own weight.

Variants :

Notes :

Yorkshire Blue   Blue   C   P   V   NR   Drum

The first blue cheese made at Shepherds Purse and made as a 1.4kg cheese, matured for 8 weeks.

Variants :

Notes :

====

SHORROCKS CHEESE
Lancashire
Cheesemaker : Andrew Shorrock

Lancashire cheesemaking family for over 100 years until 25 years ago when they created the famous 'bomb'.

Lancashire Bomb   Crumbly   C   P   V   WC   Bomb

Made as a 460g & 230g Lancashire Creamy and matured for 2 or 3 years in black wax.

Variants : Original, Vintage (3 years), Onion, Black Pepper, Garlic Herb, Chilli, Whisky, Home Smoked

Notes :

====

SIMON WEAVER ORGANIC
Gloucestershire
Cheesemaker : Simon Weaver

Third generation organic Cotswold dairy farmer with forage fed closed herd.

Cotswold Blue Veined Brie | Blue | C | P | V | O | BR | Square

Made as a 1kg, 300g & 140g cheese.

Variants :

Notes :

Cotswold Brie | Soft | C | P | V | O | BR | Disc

Made as a 1kg, 240g & 140g cheese.

Variants : Original, Herb, Smoked

Notes :

Greystones Single Gloucester PDO | Firm | C | P | V | O | NR | Drum

Made as a 4kg cheese.

Variants :

Notes :

Truffle Gloucester | Firm | C | P | V | O | NR | Drum

Made as a 4kg cheese.

Variants :

Notes :

===

SLACK HOUSE FARM
Cumbria
Cheesemakers : Eric & Dianne Horn

Making cheese at family farm on Hadrian's Wall using organic milk from their own herd of Ayrshires.

Birdoswald | Firm | C | P | V | O | NR | Cylinder

A traditional farmhouse cheese, made as a 9kg cheese based on Dunlop and matured for 6 months.

Variants :

Notes :

===

SMART'S TRADITIONAL
Gloucestershire
Cheesemaker : Rod Smart

Family farm using old recipes handed down with milk from own herd which includes Old Gloucester cows.

Harefield   Hard   C   U   V   NR   Drum

Made as a 3.5kg cheese and matured for 2 years.

Variants :

Notes :

Smart's Double Gloucester   Firm   C   U   V   NR   Drum

Made as a 3.5kg cheese, coloured orange with annatto and matured for 6 months.

Variants : Original, Aged

Notes :

Smart's Single Gloucester PDO   Firm   C   U   V   NR   Drum

Made with part full milk and part skimmed milk as a 3.5kg cheese and matured for 10 - 16 weeks.

Variants :

Notes :

===

SNOWDONIA CHEESE COMPANY
Denbighshire
Commercial Cheesemaker

Range of plain and flavoured cheeses blended and shaped in North Wales using block mature Cheddar.

Black Bomber Extra Mature   Firm   C   P   V   WC   Drum

Made as a 2kg, 400g & 200g Cheddar matured for 14 months.

Variants : Original, Truffle Trove

Notes :

Red Storm   Firm   C   P   V   WC   Drum

Made as a 2kg & 200g Red Leicester matured for 18 months.

Variants : Original, Red Devil

Notes :

Rock Star Cave-Aged Cheddar   Firm   C   P   V   WC   Drum

Made as a 1.5kg & 150g Cheddar matured for 18 months is sealed slate chambers.

Variants :

Notes :

Snowdonia Flavoured Cheddar Firm C P V WC Drum

Made as a 2kg & 200g cheese in a range of flavours each in a different coloured wax coating.

Variants : Green Thunder, Beechwood Smoked, Pickle Power, Amber Mist, Ginger Spice, Bouncing Berry, Ruby Mist

Notes :

SOMERSET CHEESE COMPANY

Somerset

Cheesemakers : Philip Rainbow, Anita Robinson

Former large dairy cheesemakers joined forces to make their own cheeses adapting traditional styles.

Fosse Way Fleece Firm S P V NR Drum

Made as a 3.5kg & 2kg cheese and matured for 6 - 12 months.

Variants :

Notes :

Guinevere Firm B P V PC Drum

Made as a 2kg cheese and matured for 3 - 9 months.

Variants :

Notes :

Pendragon Firm B P V NR Drum

Made as a 3.5kg & 2kg cheese and matured for 8 months.

Variants : Original, Smoked

Notes :

Pennard Red Firm G P V NR Drum

Made as a 2kg cheese and coloured orange with annatto.

Variants :

Notes :

Pennard Ridge Crumbly G P V NR Drum

Based on Caerphilly and made as a 2kg cheese.

Variants :

Notes :

Pennard Vale Firm G P V NR Drum

Made as a 3.5kg cheese.

Variants : Original, Oak Smoked

Notes :

Rainbow's Gold   Firm   C   P   V   WR   Drum

Made as a 2kg cheese and washed in Golden Chalice Ale from Glastonbury Brewing Company.

Variants :

Notes :

Six Spires   Firm   C   U   V   NR   Drum

Made as a 3.5kg cheese and matured for up to 15 months.

Variants : Original

Notes :

Somerset Chilli   Firm   C   P   V   XR   Drum

Made as a 3.5kg cheese and blended with fresh chilli and cracked black pepper.

Variants :

Notes :

Somerset Herb & Cider   Firm   C   P   V   XR   Drum

Made as a 3.5kg cheese and blended with herbs, garlic and Somerset cider.

Variants :

Notes :

Truffler   Firm   C   P   V   XR   Drum

Made as a 3.5kg cheese and infused with minced black truffles and truffle oil.

Variants :

Notes :

===

SOUTH CAERNARFON CREAMERIES
Gwynedd

Cheesemaker : Mark Edwards

Family owned farmer's co-operative which started in 1930s and started making cheese in 1959.

Dragon Welsh Caerphilly   Crumbly   C   P   V   XR   Block

Made to an authentic local Caerphilly recipe.

Variants :

Notes :

Dragon Welsh Cheddar   Firm   C   P   V   XR   Block

Made in large blocks and matured before being cut into 350g & 180g blocks.

Variants : Mild, Mature, Vintage

Notes :

Slate Cavern Aged Cheddar   Firm   C   P   V   XR   Block

Made in large blocks and matured in Llanfair slate caverns before being cut into 200g blocks.

Variants : Cavern Platinum (Original), Cavern Emerald (Leek), Cavern Onyx (Penderyn Whisky)

Notes :

Slate Cavern Aged Red Leicester   Firm   C   P   V   XR   Block

Made in large blocks and matured in Llanfair slate caverns before being cut into 200g blocks.

Variants :

Notes :

South Caernarfon Caerphilly   Crumbly   C   P   V   XR   Block

Made, matured and packed for sale as an own label product.

Variants :

Notes :

South Caernarfon Cheddar   Firm   C   P   V   XR   Block

Made, matured and packed for sale as a own label product.

Variants : White : Mild, Mature, Extra Mature, Vintage. Coloured : Mild, Mature

Notes :

South Caernarfon Double Gloucester   Firm   C   P   V   XR   Block

Made, matured and packed for sale as an own label product.

Variants :

Notes :

South Caernarfon Monterey Jack   Firm   C   P   V   XR   Block

Made, matured and packed for sale as an own label product.

Variants :

Notes :

South Caernarfon Red Leicester   Firm   C   P   V   XR   Block

Made, matured and packed for sale as an own label product.

Variants :

Notes :

South Caernarfon Wensleydale   Crumbly   C   P   V   XR   Block

Made, matured and packed for sale as an own label product.

Variants :

Notes :

ST ANDREWS FARMHOUSE CHEESE COMPANY
Fife

Cheesemaker : Jane Stewart

Family farm since 1930s and turned to using own milk to make cheese in 2008 to make territorial cheeses.

Anster   Crumbly   C   U   A   NR   Drum

The old name for nearby Anstruther, their first cheese is made as a 13kg cheese and matured for 3 months.

Variants : Original, Mature, Red, Smoked

Notes :

St Andrews Cheddar   Firm   C   U   A   NR   Cylinder

Made as a 24kg cheese using traditional starter cultures, clothbound and matured for 9 - 18 months.

Variants :

Notes :

===

ST IVES CHEESE
Cambridgeshire

Cheesemaker : John Sugden

Set up a micro dairy using sheep's milk from nearby Bevistan Dairy after working with local cheesemakers.

St Ivo   Soft   S   P   V   BR   Log

Made as a 120g - 150g lactic cheese matured for 3 weeks when it has developed a soft wrinkled rind.

Variants :

Notes :

===

ST JAMES CHEESE
Cumbria

Cheesemakers : Martin Gott, Nicola Robinson

Learned at other cheesemakers, then began sheep farming and cheesemaking with own homemade starters.

Apatha   Semisoft   G   U   A   WR   Disc

Named after an adjoining wood, made as a 1kg cheese and matured for 3 weeks giving complex flavours.

Variants :

Notes :

Castlerigg   Soft   S   U   A   BR   Flat Pyramid

Made as a 180g as a two day set cheese in August and September only, ash coated and matured for 2 weeks.

Variants :

Notes :

Crookwheel   Firm   S   U   A   NR   Drum

Made as a 2kg cheese in the same way as St James, but pressed, not rind washed and matured for 4 weeks.

Variants :

Notes :

Holbrook   Firm   G   U   A   NR   Drum

Made as a 1.5kg cheese based on an aged Lancashire, similar to a Tomme style, matured for 3 - 6 months.

Variants :

Notes :

Ingot   Semisoft   G   U   A   BR   Ingot

Made as a 190g cheese using their own Golden Guernsey goat's milk and matured for 2 weeks.

Variants :

Notes :

Lady Grey   Soft   G   U   A   BR   Disc

Unusually for an ash coated goat's cheese to be made so large, it is made as a 1.6kg cutting cheese.

Variants :

Notes :

St James   Semisoft   S   U   A   WR   Square

One of the few washed rind sheep's cheeses, made as a 1.4kg cheese and matured for 3 months.

Variants :

Notes :

St Sunday   Semisoft   C   P   V   WR   Disc

St James's first cow's milk cheese, made as a 250g cheese based on Reblochon and matured for 3 weeks.

Variants :

Notes :

ST JUDE CHEESE
Suffolk

Cheesemakers : Julie Cheyney, Blake Bowden

White Wood Dairy is located at Fen Farm Dairy and uses their Montbeliarde milk for cheesemaking.

St Cera   Soft   C   U   A   WR   Disc

Made the same as a St Jude as a 120g cheese, washed in brine and matured for 3 weeks.

Variants :

Notes :

St Helena   Semisoft   C   U   A   WR   Disc

Made as a 1kg cheese, washed in brine and matured for 4 weeks.

Variants :

Notes :

St Jude   Soft   C   U   A   BR   Disc

Made as a 100g cheese and matured for 2 - 3 weeks.

Variants :

Notes :

===

STAFFORDSHIRE CHEESE CO.

Staffordshire

Cheesemaker : Mary Button, Vitali Bespalovs

Founded in 1994 to re-establish long-lost Staffordshire cheeses using milk from a single grass-fed local herd.

Black and Blue   Blue   C   P   V   NR   Drum

Made as a 2.5kg Dovedale Blue with cracked black peppercorns added.

Variants :

Notes :

Buxton Blue PDO   Blue   C   P   V   NR   Cylinder

Made as an 8.5kg cheese and coloured orange with annatto.

Variants :

Notes :

Cheddleton   Firm   C   P   V   NR   Cylinder

Made as a young Staffordshire 4kg cheese matured for just few weeks.

Variants : Original, Oak Smoked, Beer & Garlic, Chilli, Chives, Honey Mustard, Chutney, Sage

Notes :

Dovedale Blue PDO   Blue   C   P   V   NR   Drum

Made as a 2.5kg cheese as a continental style blue.

Variants :

Notes :

Staffordshire PDO   Firm   C   P   V   NR   Cylinder

Made as an 8.5kg cheese, clothbound and matured for 3 months.

Variants : Original, Vintage Staffordshire Sage

Notes :

===

STAMFORD ARTISAN CHEESE
Cambridgeshire
Cheesemaker : Alison Williamson

Based in a small dairy in an artisan courtyard, the only traditional cheesemaker in Cambridgeshire.

Whyte Wytch   Soft   C   U   A   BR   Disc
Made as a 250g cheese using milk from a predominantly Brown Swiss local herd and matured for 4 weeks.
Variants :

Notes :

STICHELTON DAIRY
Nottinghamshire
Cheesemaker : Joe Schneider

Formed in 2006 as a three way partnership on the Welbeck Estate using its raw Holstein-Friesian milk.

Stichelton   Blue   C   U   A   NR   Cylinder
Made using a 24 hour make as a 8kg cheese which is hand-ladled, hand-milled and matured for 3 months.
Variants :

Notes :

STONEBECK CHEESE
North Yorkshire
Cheesemakers : Andrew & Sally Hattan

Family hill farm making cheese with Northern Dairy Shorthorn milk based on old dales recipes.

Stonebeck   Firm   C   U   A   NR   Drum
Made slowly and traditionally using grass fed milk, clothbound using local calico and matured for 3 months.
Variants :

Notes :

STRATHEARN CHEESE CO.
Perthshire
Cheesemakers : Drew Watson, Pierre Leger

Founded by two friends in 2016 in a former prisoner of war camp using local sourced milk.

Lady Mary's Bairn   Soft   C   P   V   FR   Cylinder
Made as a small 60g version of The Lady Mary, sprinkled with different flavours.
Variants : Sweet Paprika, Truffle, Wild Garlic,

Notes :

The Lady Mary   Soft   C   P   V   FR   Disc

Made as a 200g lactic cheese, sprinkled with local wild garlic and rapeseed truffle oil, matured for 10 days.

Variants : Original, Truffle Mary

Notes :

The Strathearn   Semisoft   C   P   V   WR   Square

Made as a 250g cheese, washed in local Glenturret single malt whisky and brine and matured for 4 weeks.

Variants :

Notes :

Wee Comrie   Soft   C   P   V   NR   Disc

Made as a 200g cheese matured for 3 weeks with a soft buttery flavour and a soft delicate rind.

Variants :

Notes :

===

SUFFOLK FARMHOUSE CHEESES
Suffolk

Cheesemaker : James Salisbury

Family owned dairy farm with own herd of Guernsey cows giving a rich golden colour to their cheeses.

Suffolk Blue   Blue   C   P   V   NR   Drum

Made as a lightly blue veined 700g cheese and matured for 3 weeks.

Variants :

Notes :

Suffolk Blue Brie   Soft   C   P   V   BR   Disc

Made as a 500g cheese and matured for 3 weeks.

Variants :

Notes :

Suffolk Brie   Soft   C   P   V   BR   Disc

Made as a 1kg cheese and matured for 3 weeks.

Variants :

Notes :

Suffolk Gold   Firm   C   P   V   NR   Drum

Made as a 3kg cheese and matured for 3 months.

Variants :

Notes :

SWALEDALE CHEESE COMPANY
North Yorkshire
Cheesemaker : Richard Darbishire

Swaledale cheese goes back to 11th century monks and was restarted in 1987 using a traditional recipe.

Swaledale   Crumbly   C   P   V   NR   Cylinder
Made as a Wensleydale style 3kg original & 1.7kg smoked cheese, matured for 6 - 8 weeks.
Variants : Original, Smoked

Notes :

Swaledale Blue   Blue   C   P   V   NR   Cylinder
Made as a 7.5kg Stilton style cheese.
Variants :

Notes :

Yorkshire   Firm   C   P   V   WC   Disc
Made as a 200g individual waxed truckle.
Variants : Original, Smoked

Notes :

TAW VALLEY CREAMERY (ARLA)
Devon
Commercial Cheesemaker

Built by Express Dairies in 1974, now part of the Arla farmers' co-operative making hard and firm cheeses.

Castello Tickler   Firm   C   P   V   XR   Block
Made as a 20kg cheese and matured for 12 - 21 months.
Variants : Mature (12 months), Extra Mature (17 months), Vintage (21 months)

Notes :

Taw Valley Cheddar   Firm   C   P   V   XR   Block
Made as a 20kg mature Cheddar and matured for varying times before being cut into retail blocks.
Variants :

Notes :

Taw Valley Churnton   Firm   C   P   V   XR   Block
Made as a 20kg medium Cheddar and matured for 6 months to give a creamy sweet finish.
Variants :

Notes :

Taw Valley Double Gloucester   Firm   C   P   V   XR   Block

Made as a 20kg cheese and matured for 12 months before being cut into retail blocks.

Variants :

Notes :

Taw Valley Red Leicester   Firm   C   P   V   XR   Block

Made as a 20kg cheese and matured for 12 months before being cut into retail blocks.

Variants :

Notes :

Taw Valley Tasty   Firm   C   P   V   XR   Block

Made as a 20kg extra mature Cheddar and matured for 22 months before being cut into retail blocks.

Variants :

Notes :

TEESDALE CHEESEMAKERS
Durham

Cheesemakers : Allison & Jonathan Raper

Family owned farm using own milk to make cheese with rare breed pigs fed with whey from cheesemaking.

Allison's Garlic Special   Semisoft   C   P   V   XR   Disc

Inspired by a Maltese recipe as a nod to Allison's roots infused with wild garlic from the farm.

Variants :

Notes :

Barney Brie   Soft   C   P   V   BR   Disc

Made as a robust farmhouse Brie with wild Teesdale cultures rather than the more usual soft white mould.

Variants :

Notes :

Doris   Semisoft   C   P   V   BR   Drum

Named after grandmother and made as a dales style cheese, crumbly in the centre and soft under the rind.

Variants :

Notes :

Durham Blue   Blue   C   P   V   NR   Drum

Created during lockdown in 2020 as a tribute to the local community and coloured orange with annatto.

Variants :

Notes :

Nanny Blue   Blue   G   P   V   NR   Drum
Rich creamy blue goat's cheese with a mild tang.
Variants :
Notes :

Ronnie   Firm   C   P   V   WC   Drum
Named after grandfather and similar to Doris but cut, waxed and matured to produce a tangier flavour.
Variants :
Notes :

Teesdale Blue   Blue   C   P   V   NR   Drum
One of the first cheeses made at the farm, a mild creamy blue.
Variants :
Notes :

Teesdale Goat   Semisoft   G   P   V   NR   Disc
Mild mellow goat's cheese with the distinctive Teesdale rind.
Variants :
Notes :

White Hilton   Semisoft   C   P   V   NR   Disc
Named after the village where the family farm is located, a complex creamy cheese with a distinctive rind.
Variants :
Notes :

TENACRES CHEESE
West Yorkshire
Cheesemaker : Gillian Clough
Home dairy in the hills above Hebden Bridge with a small herd of hand milked Anglo-Nubian goats.

Hebden Goat   Soft   G   U   A   BR   Disc
Made as a 100g cheese and matured for 3 weeks to develop a wrinkled rind with a meltingly soft centre.
Variants :
Notes :

THORNBY MOOR DAIRY
Cumbria

Cheesemakers : Carolyn & Leonie Fairbairn

Started kitchen cheesemaking in 1979 with own goat's milk, now sourcing local milk for cheesemaking.

Allerdale Firm G U A NR Cylinder

First cheese made by Carolyn 40 years ago, made as a 2kg cheese, clothbound and matured for 5 months.

Variants : Original, Smoked

Notes :

Blue Whinnow Blue C U A NR Rounded Drum

Made as a unpressed 1kg & 450g cheese using Dairy Shorthorn milk matured for 2 months.

Variants :

Notes :

Crofton Semisoft CG U A NR Drum

Made as a 800g & 300g mixed milk cheese matured for 4 weeks developing a soft rind.

Variants :

Notes :

Cumberland Farmhouse Firm C U A NR Cylinder

Made as a 9kg, 2.5kg & 850g cheese, clothbound and matured for 6 months.

Variants : Original, Oak Smoked

Notes :

Curthwaite Fresh G U V XR Pot

Made as a 1kg, 500g & 120g soft creamy curd cheese using cardoon thistle rennet.

Variants :

Notes :

St Bees Fresh G U V XR Cylinder

Formerly known as Stumpies and made as a 120g cheese using cardoon thistle rennet.

Variants :

Notes :

Thornby Moor Fresh C U V XR Pot

Made as a 1kg, 500g & 120g soft creamy curd cheese using cardoon thistle rennet.

Variants :

Notes :

Tovey	Semisoft	G	U	A		BR	Drum

Made as a 600g & 250g cheese and matured for 3 - 6 weeks.

Variants :

Notes :

TICKLEMORE CHEESE DAIRY
Devon

Cheesemaker : Ben Harris

Founded by sheep's cheese pioneer, Robin Congdon and now specialising solely in blue cheeses.

Beenleigh Blue	Blue	S	P	V		XR	Cylinder

Using sheep's milk from a Devon based flock and made as a 3.5kg cheese then matured for 5 months.

Variants :

Notes :

Brunswick Blue	Blue	S	P	V		NR	Cylinder

Made as a 3.5kg cheese based on Beenleigh Blue, matured at Neal's Yard Dairy to form a dry natural rind.

Variants :

Notes :

Devon Blue	Blue	C	P	V		XR	Cylinder

Using cow's milk from a local farmer's co-operative and made as a 3.5kg cheese then matured for 5 months.

Variants :

Notes :

Harbourne Blue	Blue	G	P	V		XR	Cylinder

Using goat's milk from a single herd and made as a 3.5kg cheese then matured for 6 months.

Variants :

Notes :

TIMES PAST CHEESE DAIRY
Somerset

Cheesemakers : Stephen, Janice, Kate, Emma Webber

Family dairy established in 1987 close to Cheddar Gorge making traditional and flavoured cheeses.

Draycott Blue	Blue	C	P	V		NR	Drum

Made as a 2kg cheese and matured for longer than most blue cheeses to give a creamier flavour.

Variants :

Notes :

Times Past Farmhouse Cheddar Firm C P V XR Block
Made as a traditional Cheddar and matured for up to 18 months.
Variants : Mature, Extra Mature

Notes :

Times Past Mature Cheddar Firm C P V XR Block
Made as a mature Cheddar and blended with a range of flavours before maturing.
Variants : Smoked, Whisky, Horseradish, Sage & Onion, Cider Apple, Garlic & Parsley, Caramelised Onion, Chilli Apple, Mexican, Marmite, Mustard Seed, Pepper & Garlic, Tomato & Basil

Notes :

Times Past Traditional Cheddar Firm C P V NR Drum
Made as a a traditional Cheddar and matured for up to 24 months.
Variants : Mature, Extra Mature

Notes :

TORPENHOW FARMHOUSE DAIRY
Cumbria

Cheesemakers : Jenny & Mark Lee
Family owned farm on the northern edge of the Lake District producing organic Jersey-Friesian milk.

Binsey Red Firm C P V O NR Drum
Made as a 12kg cheese based on Red Leicester, coloured orange with annatto and matured for 8 weeks.
Variants :

Notes :

Darling Howe Soft C P V O BR Disc
Made as a 1.2kg, 230g & 120g (Little Darling) Brie style cheese and matured for 3 weeks.
Variants :

Notes :

Park House Cheddar Firm C P V O NR Drum
Made as a 12kg cheese and matured for 6 months.
Variants : Original, Smoked

Notes :

Trusmadoor Crumbly C P V O NR Drum
Made as a 12kg cheese similar to a crumbly Lancashire style and matured for 6 weeks.
Variants :

Notes :

THE TRADITIONAL CHEESE DAIRY
East Sussex
Cheesemaker : Ben Cottingham, Andy Delves
Third generation traditional dairy farmers acquired this local cheese dairy and relocated it to the family farm.

Burwash Rose | Semisoft | C | P | V | | WR | Disc
Made as a 700g cheese and washed to produce a pungent sticky rind.
Variants :
Notes :

Goodweald Smoked | Firm | C | U | V | | XR | Drum
Smoked over oak chippings and matured for 3 months.
Variants :
Notes :

Lord of The Hundreds | Hard | S | U | V | | NR | Rounded Square
Made as a 4kg cheese and matured for 9 months.
Variants :
Notes :

Olde Sussex | Firm | C | U | V | | NR | Drum
Made as a 4kg Cheddar style cheese and matured for 4 months.
Variants :
Notes :

Scrumpy Sussex | Firm | C | U | V | | XR | Drum
Based on Cheddar, blended with garlic, cider and herbs and matured for 3 months.
Variants :
Notes :

===

TREFALDWYN CHEESE
Powys
Cheesemaker : Clare Jones
Named after the ancient Welsh for Montgomery where it was created but moving to Caersws in Powys.

Trefaldwyn Blue | Blue | C | P | V | | NR | Drum
Made as a 2.5kg cheese coloured orange with annatto with a bold flavour and creamy texture.
Variants :
Notes :

===

TRETHOWAN BROTHERS
Somerset

Cheesemakers : Todd, Maugan, Kim Trethowan

For over 25 years the cheesemaking brothers have been making organic small batch award-winning cheeses.

Gorwydd Caerphilly   Crumbly   C   U   A   O   NR   Drum
Created originally in Wales as a 4kg cheese and matured for 3 months developing a soft mushroomy rind.
Variants :

Notes :

Pitchfork Cheddar   Firm   C   U   A   O   NR   Cylinder
Made as a 25kg cheese, clothbound and matured for 12 months, the 'Aston Martin of Cheddar' Jamie Oliver.
Variants :

Notes :

TREVEADOR FARM DAIRY
Cornwall

Cheesemakers : Alastair & Bernadette Rogers

Family farm on the the Helford river with their own mixed breed herd who started cheesemaking in 2006.

Helford Blue   Blue   C   P   V   NR   Rounded Disc
Made as a 1kg, 250g cheese matured for 9 weeks.
Variants :

Notes :

Helford Camembert   Soft   C   P   V   BR   Disc
Made as a 200g cheese and matured for 2 weeks.
Variants :

Notes :

Helford Sunrise   Semisoft   C   P   V   WR   Disc
Made as a 1kg & 200g cheese washed in cider, matured for 10 weeks and sprinkled with black pepper.
Variants :

Notes :

Helford White   Semisoft   C   P   V   WR   Rounded Disc
Based on a Reblochon, it is made as a 1kg & 200g cheese washed in brine and matured for 10 weeks.
Variants :

Notes :

TUXFORD & TEBBUTT (ARLA)
Leicestershire
Commercial Cheesemaker

Started as a Stilton creamery in 1780 in Melton Mowbray and now part of the Arla farmers' co-operative.

1780 Aged Reserve Stilton PDO Blue C P V NR Cylinder
1780 is when Stilton was first made at the creamery, made as a 8kg cheese matured for 15 weeks.
Variants :

Notes :

Tuxford & Tebbutt Shropshire Blue Blue C P V NR Cylinder
Made as an 8kg cheese similar to a Stilton but coloured orange with annatto.
Variants :

Notes :

Tuxford &Tebbutt Stilton PDO Blue C P V NR Cylinder
Made as a 8kg cheese matured for 9 - 11 weeks.
Variants :

Notes :

TWO HOOTS CHEESE
Berkshire
Cheesemakers : Sandy & Andy Rose

Started by making homemade simple goat's cheese but wanted to make cheeses using Channel Island milk.

Barkham Blue Blue C P V NR Ammonite
Made as a 750g cheese and matured for 10 weeks developing a rich butteriness and a grey blue rind.
Variants :

Notes :

TŶ CAWS
Cardiff
Cheesemonger : Owen Davies

Cardiff based cheesemonger who has developed and made his own cheeses at Food Centre Wales.

Crwys Crumbly CS P V NR Drum
Based upon a traditional farmhouse style, made as a 4kg cheese and matured for 6 months.
Variants :

Notes :

Hiraeth Soft S P V BR Drum
Made as a 1kg & 200g Brie style cheese matured for 6 - 8 weeks.
Variants :

Notes :

VELOCHEESE
Antrim

Cheesemaker : Davide Tani

Love for cheese and cycling reflected in the name, aiming to be a carbon neutral plastic feee cheesemaker.

Velocheese Burrata Fresh C P A O XR Ball
Made as a 125g stracciatella encased in mozzarella.
Variants :

Notes :

Velocheese Fior di Latte Fresh C P A O XR Ball
Made as a 125g Mozzarella & 20g Bocconcini but called Fior di Latte as it is made with cow's milk.
Variants :

Notes :

Velocheese Scamorza Semisoft C P A O XR Hourglass
Made as a 200g cheese similar to Mozzarella but tied and left to dry out, some being smoked over maple.
Variants : Original, Smoked

Notes :

Velocheese Stracciatella Fresh C P A O XR Pot
Blend of double cream and pieces left after mozzarella making, sometimes referred to as Naked Burrata.
Variants :

Notes :

VILLAGE MAID CHEESE
Berkshire

Cheesemakers : Anne, Andy, Jake Wigmore

Dairy scientist turned home cheesemaker turned award winning maker of a range of cheeses.

Farley Firm G T V NR Drum
New in 2023, a younger goat's milk version of Spenwood, matured for 4 - 6 months developing a sticky rind.
Variants :

Notes :

Heckfield   Firm   C   T   V   WR   Drum

Unusually a firm cheese made from Guernsey milk, made as a 2kg cheese and matured for 8 - 9 months

Variants :

Notes :

Maida Vale   Soft   C   T   V   WR   Drum

Made as a 350g cheese, washed in Siren Craft Brewery Soundwave IPA and matured for 3 months.

Variants :

Notes :

Riseley   Semisoft   S   T   V   WR   Disc

Made as a 750g cheese and matured for 6 weeks.

Variants :

Notes :

Spenwood   Hard   S   T   V   NR   Drum

Their first cheese based on Pecorino they had seen in Italy, made as a 2kg cheese and matured for 9 months.

Variants :

Notes :

Waterloo   Soft   C   T   V   BR   Disc

Made as a 750g, 350g & 180g cheese and matured for 8 weeks with a golden paste from the Guernsey milk.

Variants : Original, Baby

Notes :

Wigmore   Soft   S   T   V   BR   Disc

Made as a 750g, 350g & 180g cheese and matured for 6 weeks.

Variants :

Notes :

WACKY WEDGE CHEESE COMPANY
Gwynedd
Cheesemakers : Brad & Beth Cunningham

Lancashire based cheesemakers relocated to Snowdonia to farm their own herd of goats and make cheese.

Gafr Goch (Red Goat)   Soft   G   U   A   XR   Pot

Made as a 90g lactic set cheese blended with paprika and packed in a small pot.

Variants :

Notes :

Gafr Wen (White Goat)   Soft   G   U   A   XR   Pot

Made as a 90g lactic set cheese packed in a small pot.

Variants :

Notes :

Yr Afr (The Goat)   Soft   G   U   A   NR   Cylinder

Made as a 100g lactic set cheese matured for 2 weeks developing a wrinkled rind.

Variants :

Notes :

WANDERING EWE DAIRY
Somerset

Cheesemakers : Hugh & Pippa Stables

Farmhouse cheese from their own certified pasture fed flock.

Wandering Ewe   Firm   S   U   A   PC   Rounded Drum

Made as a 3kg Alpine style cheese between April and August and matured for 9 months.

Variants :

Notes :

WEARDALE CHEESE
Durham

Cheesemaker : Simon Raine

Dairy is located in a converted 1943 prisoner of war hut at Harperley Camp in Weardale using local milk.

Brie a Dale   Soft   C   P   V   BR   Disc

Made as a 2kg & 800g traditional Brie style cheese and matured for 4 -10 weeks.

Variants :

Notes :

Prince Bishop   Blue   C   P   V   NR   Drum

Made as a 3.0 - 3.5kg cheese and matured for 10 - 16 weeks.

Variants :

Notes :

St Cuthbert   Blue   C   P   V   NR   Drum

Made as a 3.0 - 3.5kg cheese and matured for 8 - 12 weeks.

Variants :

Notes :

Weardale   Firm   C   P   V   NR   Drum
Made as a 2.0 - 2.5kg Dales style cheese and matured for 3 - 8 weeks.
Variants : Original, Nettle, Pimenton (with paprika), Bonny Moor Hen (cherry wood smoked)
Notes :

WENSLEYDALE CREAMERY / THE YORKSHIRE CREAMERY (SAPUTO)
North Yorkshire
Commercial Cheesemaker
Opened in 1897, avoided two closures by management buyouts and now owned by Canadian dairy Saputo.

Abbot's Gold   Firm   C   P   V   XR   Half Drum
Made as a a creamy style Cheddar infused with caramelised onions.
Variants :
Notes :

Double Yorkshire   Firm   , C   P   V   XR   Block
Made as a large block based on Double Gloucester and matured for 7 months then cut into smaller blocks.
Variants :
Notes :

Fountains Gold Cheddar   Firm   C   P   V   XR   Half Drum, Disc
Made as a creamy style Cheddar matured for 6 months then moulded into half drums and waxed discs.
Variants : Original, Smoked, Garlic & Herb, Black Sheep Riggwelter, Caramelised Onions
Notes :

Kit Calvert Wensleydale PGI   Crumbly   C   P   V   NR   Cylinder
Made as a a 4kg traditional farmhouse Wensleydale which is clothbound and matured for 3 months.
Variants :
Notes :

Wensleydale Double Gloucester Firm   C   P   V   XR   Block
Made as a large block, blended with onion and chive and matured for 3 months then cut into smaller blocks.
Variants :
Notes :

Yorkshire Extra Mature Cheddar Firm   C   P   V   XR   Block
Made as a large block and matured for 15 months for full flavour then cut into smaller blocks.
Variants :
Notes :

Yorkshire Red   Firm   C   P   V   XR   Block
Made as a large block based on Red Leicester and matured for 10 months then cut into smaller blocks.
Variants :

Notes :

Yorkshire Wensleydale PGI   Crumbly   C   P   V   NR   Cylinder, Disc
Made as a 4.3kg traditional cheese and matured for 5 months, some of which is blended with fruit.
Variants : Special Reserve, Oak Smoked, Cranberry, Apricot, Pineapple, Ginger, Blueberry, Figs & Honey, Mango & Ginger

Notes :

Yorkshire Wensleydale Blue   Blue   C   P   V   NR   Cylinder
Wensleydale was originally a blue cheese in the past, now made as a 4.8kg cheese and matured for 8 weeks.
Variants :

Notes :

===

WEST COUNTRY WATER BUFFALO
Somerset
Cheesemaker : Jonathan Corpe
Having farmed buffalo for 20 years, started importing milking buffalo to make cheese and ice cream in 2019.

Buffalicious Mozzarella   Fresh   B   U   V   XR   Ball
Made as a 100g - 100g traditional Mozzarella ball.
Variants : Original, Bocconcini

Notes :

===

WESTCOMBE DAIRY
Somerset
Cheesemakers : Tom Calver, Rob Howard, Jason Coles
Family farm with historical connections back to late 19th century and a sustainable farming philosophy.

Duckett's Caerphilly   Crumbly   C   U   A   NR   Drum
Made as a 4kg cheese and matured for 6 - 12 months.
Variants :

Notes :

Lamyatt   Firm   C   U/P   A   NR   Drum
Made as a 30kg Alpine style cheese and matured for 4 months, only sold at the dairy.
Variants :

Notes :

Oxonlees Firm C U/P A NR Cylinder

Selected 24kg clothbound Cheddars are chosen for maturing for 18 months.

Variants :

Notes : □

Wedmore Firm C U A NR Cylinder

Made as a 2kg cheese based on Duckett's Caerphilly with chives added and matured for 6 - 12 weeks.

Variants : Original, Smoked

Notes : □

Westcombe Cheddar Firm C U A NR Cylinder

Made as a 24kg cheese, clothbound and matured for 12 months.

Variants : Original, Smoked

Notes : □

Westcombe Red Firm C U A NR Drum

Made as a 10kg Red Leicester style, coloured orange with annatto, clothbound and matured for 5 months.

Variants :

Notes : □

Westcombe Ricotta Fresh C U A XR Pot

Made as a 1.2kg & 250g cheese and sold freshly made.

Variants :

Notes : □

===

WHALESBOROUGH CHEESE
Cornwall

Cheesemaker : James Smith, Lucy Jones

Founded by Sue Proudfoot and now made in the dairy at Norton Barton Artisan Food Village.

Cornish Crumbly Crumbly C P V NR Drum

Made as a 1.3kg & 350g cheese based on Lancashire and clothbound.

Variants :

Notes : □

Cornish Herbert Soft C P V XR Pot

Cream cheese style sold in 1kg Pots.

Variants :

Notes : □

Cornish Smuggler Firm C P V NR Drum
Made as a 1.3kg &350g cheese Based on Cheddar with orange marbling.
Variants :
Notes :

Coronation Gold Semisoft C P V WR Brick
Made as a 1kg cheese washed in Cornish spiced rum made on the same site.
Variants :
Notes :

Heligan Gold Firm C P V WR Drum
Made as a 1.3kg cheese washed in Skinners Hops 'n' Honey Ale.
Variants :
Notes :

Keltic Gold Semisoft C P V WR Cylinder
Made as a 1.3kg & 350g cheese, washed in Cornish cider and matured for 4 - 6 weeks.
Variants :
Notes :

Little Wheal Semisoft C P V BR Disc
Made as a 350g cheese and matured for 4 weeks.
Variants :
Notes :

Miss Muffet Semisoft C P V NR Drum
Made as a 1.3kg & 350g washed curd cheese.
Variants :
Notes :

Miss Thymed Semisoft C P V NR Drum
Made as a 1.3kg & 350g cheese blended with lemongrass, thyme, garlic and Cornish sea salt.
Variants :
Notes :

Nanny Muffet Semisoft G P V NR Drum
Made as a 1.3kg & 350g washed curd cheese.
Variants :
Notes :

Sergeant Pepper   Crumbly   C   P   V   NR   Drum
Made as a 1.3kg cheese based on Lancashire with orange and green peppercorn marbling.
Variants :
Notes :

Vintage Trelawny   Firm   C   P   V   NR   Drum
Made as a 2kg cheese and matured for 6 - 8 weeks.
Variants :
Notes :

WHIN YEATS DAIRY
Cumbria
Cheesemakers : Tom & Clare Noblett
Started cheesemaking in 2015 on a farm with cheesemaking history using milk from their own herd.

Fellstone   Crumbly   C   U   A   NR   Drum
Based on a from 1933 recipe Wensleydale, made as a 3.3kg cheese, clothbound and matured for 3 months.
Variants :
Notes :

Wash Stone   Firm   C   U   A   WR   Drum
Made in a similar way to Fellstone but washed and matured for 8 weeks to develop a Tomme like character.
Variants :
Notes :

Whin Yeats Farmhouse   Firm   C   U   A   NR   Drum
Made as a 3.3kg cheese, clothbound and matured for 4 months.
Variants :
Notes :

WHITE LAKE CHEESE
Somerset
Cheesemaker : Roger Longman
Third generation farmer and cheesemaker who switched from Cheddar making to be a goat's milk specialist.

Bagborough Brie   Soft   C   P   V   O   BR   Disc
Made as a 200g cheese using organic Guernsey milk.
Variants :
Notes :

Burrow Mump   Firm   S   T   V   WR   Drum
Made as a 250g cheese which is washed in Somerset Cider Brandy and matured for 8 weeks.
Variants :
Notes :

Driftwood   Fresh   G   T   V   BR   Log
Made as a 200g cheese which is coated in ash and develops a wrinkled rind as it matures.
Variants :
Notes :

Equinox   Semisoft   G   T   V   WR   Disc
Made as a 140g cheese and washed in locally made Glastonbury Brewing Company Equinox ale.
Variants :
Notes :

Eve   Soft   G   T   V   WR   Disc
Made as an individual 140g cheese which is washed in Somerset Cider Brandy and wrapped in a vine leaf.
Variants :
Notes :

Fetish   Fresh   S   T   V   XR   Block
Made as a 200g cheese based on Feta and matured for 3 months.
Variants :
Notes :

Glaston Tile   Semisoft   G   T   V   XR   Brick
Made as a 150g cheese designed to be cut into slices or cubes.
Variants :
Notes :

Hamstone   Semisoft   C   P   V   O   XR   Flat Pyramid
Made with rich creamy Guernsey milk as a 1kg cheese.
Variants :
Notes :

Katherine   Firm   G   U   A   WR   Drum
Made as a 1.5kg & 250g cheese which is washed in Somerset Cider Brandy and matured for 3 months.
Variants :
Notes :

King of the Castle   Crumbly G T V   XR Drum

Made as a 3.2kg cheese based on an old family Caerphilly recipe.

Variants :

Notes :

Limestone   Soft   G T V   BR Brick

Made as a soft lactic 700g cheese with a thin delicate rind.

Variants :

Notes :

Little Lilly   Soft   G T V   BR Disc

Made as an individual 140g cheese based on Brie.

Variants :

Notes :

Little She   Soft   S T V   BR Disc

Made as a 140g cheese made in the style of a Camembert.

Variants :

Notes :

Longbow   Semisoft G T V   BR Log

Made as a 1kg cheese using White Nancy curds but has a more condensed texture and more citric flavour.

Variants :

Notes :

Michael's Mount   Soft   G T V   BR Cylinder

Made as an individual 140g soft lactic cheese.

Variants :

Notes :

Morn Dew   Firm   C P V   WR Drum

Made as a 1.2kg cheese using rich Guernsey milk.

Variants :

Notes :

Pavé Cobble   Soft   S T V   BR Flat Pyramid

Made as a 200g cheese and coated in ash with a wrinkled rind as it ages.

Variants :

Notes :

Rachael Reserva   Firm   G   T   V   NR   Wheel

Made as an Alpine style 12kg cheese which is brine washed and matured for at least 12 months.

Variants :

Notes :

Rachel   Firm   G   T   V   WR   Ammonite

Made as a 2.2kg cheese which is brine washed and matured for 3 months.

Variants :

Notes :

Sheep Rustler   Semisoft   S   T   V   WR   Drum

Sheep's milk version of Rachel which is made as a 750g cheese and matured for 3 months.

Variants :

Notes :

Solstice   Semisoft   C   P   V   WR   Drum

Made as a 200g cheese using Guernsey milk washed in Somerset Cider Brandy and matured for 4 weeks.

Variants :

Notes :

Somerset Goat Halloumi   Semisoft   G   T   V   XR   Block

Made as a 130g cheese designed to be grilled.

Variants :

Notes :

The English Pecorino   Hard   S   T   V   NR   Drum

Made as a 1.8kg cheese and matured for 5 months.

Variants :

Notes :

Tor   Soft   G   T   V   BR   Pyramid

Made as a 200g cheese which is coated in ash and develops a wrinkled rind as it matures.

Variants :

Notes :

White Heart   Soft   G   T   V   BR   Heart

Made as a 220g shaped version of White Nancy.

Variants :

Notes :

White Nancy	Soft	G	T	V	BR	Drum

Made as a 500g mild flavoured slightly crumbly cheese.

Variants :

Notes :

White Wood	Soft	G	T	V	BR	Log

Made as a 215g traditional log shaped goat's cheese.

Variants :

Notes :

===

WILDCROFT DAIRY
Surrey
Cheesemakers : Tracey & Graham Longhurst

Home to one fifth of the world's population of English Goats and producing a range of goat's milk products.

Demeter	Semisoft	G	U	A	XR	Block

Based on Feta using a kefir starter and kid rennet and aged in whey brine for 3 months.

Variants :

Notes :

Frowsbury Hill	Fresh	G	U	A	XR	Pot

Made as a creamy crumbly cheese with some flavour variants and packed into 100g pots.

Variants : Original, Puttenham Oak (Garlic & Herb), Pilgrim's Bell (Paprika), Smokey Doe (Smoked)

Notes :

===

WILTON FARM
Norfolk
Cheesemaker : Becky Enefer

Fourth generation family farm since 1930 who took over an existing Norfolk cheese business in 2021.

Norfolk White Lady	Soft	S	P	V	BR	Disc

Made as a 1kg & 180g cheese based on a Brie style and matured for 9 days.

Variants :

Notes :

Wissington	Firm	S	P	V	NR	Drum

Made as a 2.5kg cheese in a style similar to a young Manchego and matured for 6 - 8 weeks.

Variants :

Notes :

===

WINDRUSH VALLEY GOAT DAIRY
Gloucestershire
Cheesemakers : Renee & Richard Loveridge
Using milk from their own herd of British Saanen goats to make cheese and other dairy products.

Windrush Fresh G P V XR Disc
Made as a 130g cheese and matured for 1 - 3 days.
Variants : Original, Herb & Garlic, Black Pepper, Ripened (Natural Rind - 2 - 4 weeks matured)
Notes :

Windrush Greek Style Semisoft G P V XR Block
Based on a Feta and matured for 1 - 2 weeks.
Variants : Original, Herb & Garlic
Notes :

===

WINTERDALE CHEESEMAKERS
Kent
Cheesemaker : Robin Betts
Third generation carbon neutral family farm with the dairy in a traditional oak barn using their own milk.

Winterdale Shaw Firm C U A NR Cylinder
Made as a Cheddar, clothbound and cellar matured for 10 months.
Variants : Original, Oak Smoked
Notes :

===

WOODBRIDGE FARM
Dorset
Cheesemakers : Mike & Emily Davies
Home to the Davies family dairy since 1980 when they resurrected a 300 year old Dorset cheese recipe.

Dorset Blue Vinny PDO Blue C P V NR Cylinder
The first PGI food in Britain, it is made over 24 hours as a 7kg cheese and matured for 3 months.
Variants :
Notes :

===

WOODLANDS DAIRY

Dorset

Cheesemakers : Shane Herbert

Family owned sheep farm believed to have the country's largest organic flock making yogurt and cheese.

Melbury   Firm   S   P   V   O   NR   Rounded Drum

Named after the location of the sheep farm and made as a 1.5kg cheese and matured for 4 - 6 months.

Variants :

Notes :

===

WOOKEY FARM

Somerset

Cheesemakers : Sarah Davies

Family owned goat farm close to the famous caves with their own herd of mainly British Toggenburg goats.

Burcott   Firm   G   U   V   NR   Drum

Made as a 3kg cheese and matured for 4 - 12 months.

Variants : Mild (4 months), Mature (9 -12 months)

Notes :

Ebbor Gorge   Soft   G   P   V   BR   Disc

Made as an individual 100g Brie style cheese matured for 3 - 6 weeks.

Variants :

Notes :

Wookey Soft Goats Cheese   Fresh   G   P   V   XR   Pot

Made as a soft spreadable cheese in a 100g pot which can be used immediately.

Variants : Plain, Garlic & Herb

Notes :

Wookey Salad Cheese   Semisoft   G   P   V   XR   Block

Made as a Feta style cheese in a 1kg block before being cut into smaller 200g blocks.

Variants :

Notes :

Yarley   Semisoft   G   P   V   XR   Block

Made as a Halloumi style in a 1kg block before being cut into smaller 200g blocks.

Variants :

Notes :

===

WYKE FARMS
Somerset
Cheesemakers : Clothier Family

Family owned farm which is run on 100% green energy who have been making Cheddar since 1861.

Ivy's Reserve Vintage Cheddar   Firm   C   P   V   XR   Block

The world's first carbon neutral Cheddar, matured for 18 months in wood to give a sweet nutty flavour.

Variants :

Notes :

Worthy Farm Reserve Cheddar   Firm   C   P   V   XR   Block

Using milk from herds grazing on the Glastonbury Festival site and matured for 6 months.

Variants :

Notes :

Wyke Farms Cheddar   Firm   C   P   V   XR   Block

Made to the same secret family recipe for 160 years and matured for 6 - 15 months.

Variants : Mature, Extra Mature, Vintage

Notes :

Y CWT CAWS
Anglesey
Cheesemakers : Nigel, Rhian, Ffion Jefferies

Welsh for 'the cheese hut', they have been making cheese since 2006 using milk from their own goats.

Cybi Melyn   Firm   G   P   V   WC   Drum

Made as a 2kg cheese coloured orange with annatto and matured for at least 6 months in blue wax.

Variants : Original, Chilli Flakes

Notes :

Ffetys   Fresh   G   P   V   XR   Block

Made as a 1.2kg Feta style cheese and brined before being cut into 150g blocks.

Variants :

Notes :

Mon Wen   Soft   G   P   V   BR   Disc

Made as a 140g cheese based on Camembert

Variants :

Notes :

Parys   Firm   G   P   V   WC   Drum

Made as a 2kg cheese coated in smoked paprika, wax coated and matured for at least 6 months.

Variants :

Notes :

Seriol Wyn   Firm   G   P   V   XR   Drum

Made as a 2kg cheese and matured for at least 6 months.

Variants : Original, Cracked Black Pepper

Notes :

Taid   Firm   G   P   V   WC   Drum

Made as a 2kg cheese, the name means 'grandfather' and it is matured for at least 9 months.

Variants :

Notes :

Tysilio   Fresh   G   P   V   XR   Disc

Named after a prince who founded a hermitage on Anglesey, made as a distinctive pure white dimpled disc.

Variants :

Notes :

Y Cwt Caws Goat Curd   Fresh   G   P   V   XR   Rock

Made as a very young fresh curd cheese in sealed packets.

Variants :

Notes :

===

YELLISON FARM
North Yorkshire

Cheesemakers : Sharron & Edward Parker

Originally made at Yellison Farm until it moved to Sire Bank Farm where they milk their own herd of goats.

Carlton Crowdie   Soft   G   P   L   XR   Pot

Unusual to make crowdie using goat's milk, made in 500g & 150g pots.

Variants :

Notes :

Yellison Soft Goat's Cheese   Soft   G   P   V   XR   Log

Made as an 800g & 150g cheese.

Variants :

Notes :

YESTER FARM DAIRIES
East Lothian
Cheesemakers : Simon & Jacky McCreery
Family run dairy located alongside family farm and making wide range of different dairy products.

Yester Mozzarella Fior di Latte   Soft   C   P   V   XR   Block
Made as a 250g cheese.
Variants :

Notes :

===

YORKSHIRE DAMA CHEESE
West Yorkshire
Cheesemaker : Razan Alsous
Pharmacist and refugee from Syria who in 2014 started making her Syrian style Yorkshire 'squeaky cheese'.

Queso Fresco   Fresh   C   P   V   XR   Disc
Simple Spanish style fresh cheese.
Variants :

Notes :

Squeaky Goat's Cheese   Semisoft   G   P   V   XR   Block
Made as a 220g cheese based on Halloumi.
Variants :

Notes :

Squeaky Sheep's Cheese   Semisoft   S   P   V   XR   Block
Made as a 220g cheese based on Halloumi.
Variants :

Notes :

Yorkshire Ricotta   Fresh   C   P   V   XR   Disc
Made using the whey protein left after making squeaky cheese.
Variants :

Notes :

Yorkshire Squeaky Cheese   Semisoft   C   P   V   XR   Block
Made as a 1kg & 220g cheese based on Halloumi.
Variants : Original, Smoked, Chilli, Nabulsi, Cool Mint, Rosemary, Za'atar

Notes :

YORKSHIRE FINE CHEESE
West Yorkshire
Cheesemakers : Ruth Baker

Made by a former teacher using milk from a local herd of Meuse-Rhine-Issel cows in small 45kg batches.

Barncliffe Blue	Blue	C	P	V		NR	Disc

Made as a 1.2kg & 175g cheese and matured for 3 weeks.
Variants :

Notes :

Barncliffe Brie	Soft	C	P	V		BR	Disc

Made as a 1kg & 200g cheese and matured for 2 weeks.
Variants :

Notes :

Barncliffe Truffled	Soft	C	P	V		BR	Disc

Made as a 200g cheese with a layer of Barncliffe made Mascarpone and truffle through the middle.
Variants :

Notes :

YORKSHIRE ORGANIC CHEESEMAKERS
North Yorkshire
Cheesemaker : Andrew Foley

Professional food consultant and food enthusiast turned cheesemaker using organic milk from Acorn Dairy.

Shorthorn Blue	Blue	C	P	V	O	NR	Drum

Mild blue cheese made using organic milk from Dairy Shorthorn cows.
Variants :

Notes :

YORKSHIRE PECORINO
West Yorkshire
Cheesemaker : Mario Olianas

Having been brought up in Sardinia with a love of food, started cooking and cheesemaking in Yorkshire.

Ewe-mi	Semisoft	S	P	V		XR	Block

Made as a 220g cheese based on Halloumi.
Variants :

Notes :

Leeds Blue   Blue   S   P   A   NR   Drum

Made as a 1kg cheese and matured for 4 weeks.

Variants :

Notes :

Yorkshire Pecorino Fiore   Firm   S   P   A   NR   Drum

Made as a 1kg cheese and matured for 6 months.

Variants :

Notes :

Yorkshire Pecorino Fresco   Hard   S   P   A   XR   Drum

Made as a 1kg cheese and matured for 4 weeks.

Variants :

Notes :

Yorkshire Ricotta   Fresh   S   P   A   XR   Pot

Made as a 1kg cheese and matured for 3 days.

Variants :

Notes :

Montbeliarde Cows

ACKNOWLEDGEMENTS

I am not sure where to start as there are so many people whose help has been invaluable in bringing this book to life, but I will try and acknowledge as many of them as possible.

On a personal level, I have to thank my wife, Amanda, for tolerating my often lengthy road trips visiting cheesemakers and for the long hours at my desk researching, writing and editing.

Olive, my mother, to whom this book is dedicated, knew that I was writing it but didn't really understand what it was all about. Suffice to say, she was always positive about it and thought it would be wonderful, no matter what. Sadly, she didn't live long enough to see its publication.

My daughters Selina, Holly and Felicity and daughter-in-law, Laura for being so enthusiastic and sampling so many different cheeses as part of the research.

Graham Pannett, a good friend and fellow writer, who has dedicated many evenings of drinking beer in the pub with me as we talked through our literary endeavours.

Barry and Justine Walker of The Hampshire Deli for sourcing cheese samples for me and being all round cheese buddies.

The Cookbook Kitchen, a team of ladies who organise and run the brilliant Chiswick Cheese Market (Cheesewick) on the third Sunday of each month. They all give their time and expertise freely to put on this incredible market showcasing a wide variety of cheesemakers, cheesemongers and sellers of all cheese related food and drink with the proceeds all being donated to charitable causes. I go every month because it is one of the best places to continue to learn more about cheese.

There is one important group of people without whom this book would not be possible. The cheesemakers of Britain cannot be thanked enough for their tireless efforts and commitment to making the worlds best cheeses. Often working from the early hours of the morning, milking or tending to their herds and still working late into the night salting and turning cheeses.

In the course of the research for this book, I have visited over 120 cheesemakers across Britain, each of whom has been welcoming, helpful and in many cases very generous. It is impossible to thank everyone individually but particular thanks to Phil and Carol Stansfield of Cornish Cheese Company, Carolyn and Leonie Fairbairn of Thornby Moor Dairy and Greg and Nicky Parsons of Sharpham Dairy, who not only welcomed me to their dairies but also invited me to stay with them in their homes.

And finally to the cows, goats, sheep and buffalo - thank you all.

Gary Bradshaw (Hamm Tun Fine Foods) and John Sugden (St Ives Cheese)
at the Artisan Cheese Fair 2023

LEARNING MORE ABOUT CHEESE

Recommended Reading

As you have bought or been given this book, it is a reasonable assumption that you have more than a passing interest in cheese. Should you wish to take your interest further, there are a number of ways in which you can learn more and I have given brief details below.

ACADEMY OF CHEESE

Established by a panel of industry experts to promote cheese knowledge, education and careers. Their programme of courses is designed to educate both consumers and professionals through four levels of certification culminating in the prestigious Master of Cheese.

In addition to the programme of training, the Academy of Cheese has a range of cheese resources including a comprehensive Cheese Library, online learning tools, knowledge base , gifts and events including the Big Cheese Weekender held in October every year.

Why not take a look at www.academyofcheese.org

FURTHER READING

There are an ever growing number of books about British cheeses on the market, and I have listed a few below that I would highly recommend.

The Philosophy of Cheese   Patrick McGuigan

A Cheesemongers Compendium of British & Irish Cheese   Ned Palmer

A Cheesemonger's History of the British Isles   Ned Palmer

A Portrait of British Cheese   Angus D. Birditt

Gimblett's Guide to the Best of British Cheeses   Francis Gimblett

The Cheese Connoisseur's Handbook   Svetlana Kukharchuk

The Cheese Wheel   Emma Young

British Cheese on Toast   Steve Parker (of course I recommend this book!)

Green & Lovely

James Grant at No2 Pound Street

Cotswold Cheese Company

Funk

Cheesewick

RECOMMENDED CHEESE SHOPS

Having worked for many years in the cheese business, as a retailer, wholesaler, restauranteur, consultant, cheese judge and writer, I have had the privilege and pleasure of visiting many superb cheese shops throughout Britain.

Whilst not purporting to be a comprehensive list, these are some of the cheese shops that I would highly recommend for their range of British cheeses, their knowledge and experience. I am sure there are many more fine cheese shops which I haven't had the pleasure of visiting, but this is my personal list arranged in alphabetical order.

& Caws
www.andcaws.co.uk
🗋 1 Dale Street, Menai Bridge, Anglesey, LL59 5AL   01248 564056

Anderson & Hill
www.andersonandhill.co.uk
🗋 7 Great Western Arcade, Birmingham, West Midlands, B2 5HU   0121 236 2829

Arcadia Delicatessen
www.arcadiadeli.co.uk
🗋 378 Lisburn Road, Belfast, Antrim, BT9 6JL   02890 381779

Ashburton Delicatessen
www.ashburtondelicatessen.co.uk
🗋 16 North Street, Ashburton, Devon, TQ13 7QD   01364 652277

The Artisan Cheesemonger
www.theartisancheesemonger.com
🗋 40-42 High Street, Holywood, Down, BT18 9AD   02890 424281

Bakers and Larners of Holt
www.bakersandlarnersco.uk
🗋 8 Market Place, Holt, Norfolk, NR25 6BW   01263 712244

Bayley & Sage
www.bayley-sage.co.uk
🗋 141 Ebury Street, Belgravia, London   020 7199 7245
🗋 180-184 Fulham Road, Chelsea, London, SW10 9PN   020 7199 8485
🗋 835 Fulham Road, Fulham, London, SW6 5HQ   020 7952 5440
🗋 1-2 Lancer's Square, Kensington, London, W8 3EP   020 7199 3945

Bayley & Sage (cont)

⌐ 95 Northcote Road, Battersea, London, SW11 6PL   020 7199 6843

⌐ 43-45 Parkgate Road, Battersea, London, SW11 4NP   020 7199 2960

⌐ 30-34 New Kings Road, Parsons Green, London, SW6 4ST   020 7736 2826

⌐ 33 Turnham Green Terrace, Turnham Green, London, W4 1RG   020 8995 8632

⌐ 509 Old York Road, Wandsworth, London, SW18 1TF   020 8634 719

⌐ 660 High Street, Wimbledon Village, London, SW19 5EE   020 8946 9904

Birkdale Cheese Co

www.birkdalecheese.com

⌐ 42a Liverpool Road, Southport, Merseyside, PR8 4AY   01704 568822

The Bristol Cheesemonger

www.bristol-cheese.co.uk

⌐ Unit 8, Cargo 2, Museum Street, Bristol, BS1 6ZA   020 3441 8010

Buchanan's

www.buchananscheesemonger.com

⌐ 5a Porchester Place, Connaught Village, London, W2 2BS   0117 929 2320

The Cambridge Cheese Company

www.cambridgecheese.com

⌐ 4 All Saints Passage, Cambridge, Cambridgeshire, CB2 3LS   01223 328672

Cartmel Cheeses

www.cartmelcheeses.co.uk

⌐ 1 & 2 Unsworth's Yard, Cartmel, Cumbria, LA11 6PG   01539 534307

Cheddar Deli

www.cheddardeli.co.uk

⌐ 108 Northfield Avenue, Ealing, London, W13 9RT   020 8810 0690

Cheese at Leadenhall

www.cheeseatleadenhall.co.uk

⌐ 4–5 Leadenhall Market, London, EC3V 1LR   020 7929 1697

Cheeses of Muswell Hill

www.cheesesonline.co.uk

⌐ 13 Fortis Green Road, Muswell Hill, London, N10 3HP   020 8444 9141

Cheese Etc
www.cheese-etc.co.uk
🏠 17 Reading Road, Pangbourne, Berkshire, RG8 7LU   0118 984 3323

Cheesegeek
www.thecheesegeek.com
🏠 2 Station Approach, Raynes Park, London, SW20 0FT

The Cheese Hamlet
www.thecheesehamlet.co.uk
🏠 706 Wilmslow Road, Didsbury, Manchester, M20 2DW   0161 434 4781

The Cheese Hut
www.thecheesehutshop.co.uk
🏠 1 Basin Road South, Portslade, East Sussex, BN41 1WF   01273 789107

The Cheese Lady
www.thecheeselady.co.uk
🏠 3 Court Street, Haddington, East Lothian, EH41 3JD   01620 823729

The Cheese Locker
www.thecheeselocker.com
🏠 High Ash, Goose Lane, Abbotts Bromley, Staffordshire, WS15 3DF   07414 458666

Cheese on the Green
www.cheeseonthegreen.com
🏠 27 The Green, Bilton, Rugby, Warwickshire, CV22 7LZ   01788 522813

The Cheese Press
www.thecheesepressrichmond.co.uk
🏠 7 Victoria Road, Richmond, North Yorkshire, DL10 4DW   01748 829789

The Cheese Shed
www.thecheeseshed.com
🏠 41 Fore Street, Bovey Tracey, Newton Abbot, Devon, TQ13 9AD   01626 835599

The Cheese Shop (Nottingham)
www.cheeseshopnottingham.co.uk
🏠 6 Flying Horse Walk, Nottingham, NG1 2HN   0115 941 9114

The Cheese Shop (Canterbury)

www.thecheeseshopcanterbury.co.uk

55 Palace Street, Canterbury, Kent, CT1 2DY   01227 785535

The Cheese Shop (Tunbridge Wells)

www.thecheeseshoptw.co.uk

48b St Johns Road, Tunbridge Wells, Kent, TN4 9NY   01892 517905

The Cheese Society

www.thecheesesociety.co.uk

1 St Martin's Lane, Lincoln, LN2 1HY   01522 511003

The Cheeseboard of Harrogate

www.thecheeseboard.net

1 Commercial Street, Harrogate, North Yorkshire, HG1 1UB   01423 508837

The Cheeseworks

www.thecheeseworks.co.uk

5 Regent Street, Cheltenham, Gloucestershire, GL50 1HE   01242 255022

The Cheesery

www.thecheesery.co.uk

9 Exchange Street, Dundee, DD1 3DJ   01382 202160

Cheezelo

www.cheezelo.com

46 Chalton Street, Euston, London, NW1 1JB   020 7380 0099

Chiswick Cheese Market (Third Sunday of every month)

www.chiswickcheesemarket.uk

Old Market Place, Chiswick, London W4 2DR   07768 596019

Chorlton Cheesemongers

www.chorltoncheesemongers.co.uk

486 Wilbraham Road, Chorlton, Manchester, M21 9AS   0161 881 1100

The Cotswold Cheese Company

www.cotswoldcheese.com

5 High Street, Moreton-in-the-Marsh, Gloucestershire, GL56 0AH   01608 652862

Digbeth Street, Stow on the Wold, Gloucestershire, GL54 1BN   01451 870034

113 High Street, Burford, Oxfordshire, OX18 4RG   01993 823882

Country Cheeses
www.countrycheeses.co.uk

- Market Road, Tavistock, Devon, PL19 0BW — 01822 615035
- 26 Fore Street, Topsham, Devon, EX3 0HD — 01392 877746
- 1 Ticklemore Street, Totnes, Devon, TQ9 5EJ — 01803 865926

The Courtyard Dairy
www.thecourtyarddairy.co.uk

- Crows Nest Barn, Austwick, Settle, North Yorkshire, LA2 8A — 01729 823291

Cryer and Stott
www.cryerandstott.co.uk

- 20 Market Place, Pontefract, West Yorkshire, WF8 1AU — 01977 599744
- 31a Carlton Street, Castleford, West Yorkshire, WF10 1AL — 01977 518371
- 25 Station Road, Allerton Bywater, Castleford, WF10 2BP — 01977 511022

Darts Farm
www.dartsfarm.co.uk

- Darts Farm, Topsham, Devon, EX3 0QH — 01392 878200

The Deli at No.5
www.thedeliatno5.co.uk

- 73 Giffard Way, Long Crendon, Buckinghamshire, HP18 9DN — 01844 214229

The East Street Deli
www.theeaststreetdeli.co.uk

- 41b East Street, Wimborne, Dorset, BH21 1DX — 01202 900390

The Fine Cheese Company
www.finecheeseshops.co.uk

- 29 - 31 Walcot Street, Bath, BA1 5BN — 01225 448748
- 17 Motcomb Street, Belgravia, London, SW1 8LB — 01225 617953

Forest Deli
www.forest-deli.co.uk

- 4 Market Place, Coleford, Gloucestershire — 01594 833001

Friday Street Farm Shop
www.fridaystfarm.co.uk

- Friday Street Farm, Farnham, Suffolk, IP17 1JX — 01728 602783

Funk

www.thecheesebar.com

  142 Columbia Road, London, E2 7RG   0113 345 0203

George & Joseph

www.georgeandjoseph.co.uk

  140 Harrogate Road, Chapel Allerton, Leeds, LS7 4NZ   0113 345 0203

George Mewes

www.georgemewescheese.co.uk

  106 Byres Road, Glasgow, G12 8TB   0141 334 5900

  3 Dean Park Street, Stockbridge, Edinburgh, EH4 1JN   0131 332 5900

Godfrey C. Williams

www.godfreycwilliams.co.uk

  9/11 The Square, Sandbach, Cheshire, CW11 1AP   01270 762817

Goo Cheese

www.goo-cheese.co.uk

  252 Jesmond Road, Jesmond, Newcastle upon Tyne, NE2 1LD   0191 649 2828

Grate Newcastle

www.thecheeseboard.net

  1 Commercial Street, Harrogate, North Yorkshire, HG1 1UB   01423 508837

Green and Lovely

www.greenandlovely.co.uk

  8 Bridge Road, East Molesey, Surrey, KT8 9HA   020 3154 8638

Hamish Johnston

www.hamishjohnston.com

  48 Northcote Road, Battersea, London, SW11 1PA   020 7738 0741

Hampshire Deli

www.hampshire-deli.co.uk

  Wolverton Park, Ramsdell Road, Wolverton, RG26 5PU   01256 861372

Heritage Cheese

www.heritagecheese.uk

  1b Calton Avenue, Dulwich, London, SE21 7DE   020 7052 4483

House of Bruar
www.houseofbruar.com

📇 Blair Atholl, Perthshire, PH18 5TW — 01796 48323

I.J. Mellis
www.mellischeese.net

📇 30a Victoria Street, Edinburgh, EH1 2JW — 0131 226 6215
📇 330 Morningside Road, Edinburgh, EH10 4QJ — 0131 447 8889
📇 6 Bakers Place, Stockbridge, Edinburgh, EH3 6SY — 0131 225 6566
📇 492 Great Western Road, Glasgow, G12 8EW — 0141 339 8998
📇 149 South Street, St Andrews, KY16 9UN — 01334 471410

Jericho Cheese Company
www.jerichocheese.co.uk

📇 25 Little Clarendon Street, Oxford, Oxfordshire, OX1 2HU — 01865 516000
📇 7 St Michael's Mansions, Ship Street, Oxford, Oxfordshire, OX1 3DE — 01865 516000

Knowles Green
www.knowlesgreen.uk

📇 114 Wellington Road, Bollington, Cheshire, SK10 5HT — 01625 408661

La Fromagerie
www.lafromagerie.co.uk

📇 2-6 Moxon Street, Marylebone, London, W1U 4EW — 020 7935 0341
📇 30 Highbury Park, London, N5 2AA — 020 7359 7440
📇 52 Lamb's Conduit Street, London, WC1N 3LL — 020 7242 1044

Lewis & Cooper
www.lewisandcooper.co.uk

📇 92 High Street, Northallerton, North Yorkshire, DL7 8PT — 01609 777700

The Little Cheesemonger
www.thelittlecheesemonger.co.uk

📇 87 High Street, Prestatyn, Denbighshire, LL19 9AP — 01745 852954

Liverpool Cheese Company
www.liverpoolcheesecompany.com

📇 29a Woolton Street, Liverpool, Merseyside, L25 5NH — 0151 428 3942

Love Cheese
www.lovecheese.co.uk

📇 16 Gillygate, York, North Yorkshire, YO31 7EQ — 01904 622967

Macknade
www.macknade.com
🧀 Selling Road, Faversham, Kent, ME13 8XF   01795 534497

Madame Fromage
www.madamefromage.co.uk
🧀 16 Neville Street, Abergavenny, Monmouthshire, NP7 5AD   01873 856118

Magdalen Cheese & Provisions
www.magdalencheese.co.uk
🧀 71 Magdalen Road, Exeter, Devon, EX2 4TA   01392 259980

Mike's Fancy Cheese
www.mfcheese.com
🧀 41 Little Donegall Street, Belfast, BT1 2JD   07794 570420

The Mousetrap Cheeseshop
www.mousetrapcheese.co.uk
🧀 6 Church Street, Ludlow, Herefordshire, SY8 1AP   01584 879556
🧀 3 School Lane, Leominster, Herefordshire, HR6 8AA   01568 615512
🧀 30 Church Street, Hereford, Herefordshire, HR1 2LR   01432 353423

Neal's Yard Dairy
www.nealsyarddairy.co.uk
🧀 9 Park Street, Borough Market, London, SE1 9AB   020 7500 7520
🧀 Arch 8, Lucy Way, Bermondsey, London, SE16 3UF   020 7500 7654
🧀 17 Shorts Gardens, Seven Dials, London, WC2H 9AT   020 7500 7520

Newlyns Farm Shop
www.newlyns-farmshop.co.uk
🧀 Lodge Farm North, Warnborough, Hampshire, RG29 1HA   01256 704128

No2 Pound Street
www.2poundstreet.com
🧀 No.2 Pound Street, Wendover, HP22 6EJ   01296 585 022

The Norfolk Deli
www.norfolk-deli.co.uk
🧀 16 Greevegate, Hunstanton, Norfolk, PE36 6AA   01485 535540

Oxford Cheese Company

www.oxfordcheese.co.uk

The Covered Market, Market Street, Oxford, Oxfordshire, OX1 3DU — 01865 721420

Paxton & Whitfield

www.paxtonandwhitfield.co.uk

93 Jermyn Street, London, SW1Y 6JE — 020 7321 0621
22 Cale Street, Chelsea, London, SW3 3QU — 020 7584 0751
13 Wood Street, Stratford-upon-Avon, Warwickshire, CV37 6JF — 01789 415544
1 John Street, Bath, Somerset, BA1 2JL — 01225 466403

Pong Cheese

www.pongcheese.co.uk

Online only — 0843 837 2200

Provender Brown

www.provenderbrown.co.uk

23 George Street, Perth, PH1 5JY — 01738 587300

Rennet and Rind

www.rennetandrind.co.uk

62 - 64 Papworth Business Park, Papworth, Cambridgeshire, CB23 3GY — 01480 831112

Rippon Cheese Store

www.ripponcheeselondon.com

26 Upper Tachbrook Street, Pimlico, London, SW1V 1SW — 020 7931 0628

Teddington Cheese

www.teddingtoncheese.co.uk

42 Station Road, Teddington, Middlesex, TW11 9AA — 020 8977 6868
74 Hill Rise, Richmond, Surrey, TW10 6UB — 020 8948 5794

Tŷ Caws

www.tycaws.com

Online and Cardiff farmer's markets

Welbeck Farm Shop

www.welbeckfarmshop.co.uk

Welbeck Estate, Worksop, Nottinghamshire, S80 3LW — 01909 478725

The Welsh Cheese Company

www.welshcheesecompany.co.uk

Unit 13, Rombourne Bus Centre, Taff's Well, Mid Glamorgan, CF15 7QR 02922 362375

British Cheesemakers

INDEX OF CHEESEMAKERS

Dairy / Retailer	Cheesemaker/monger	County	Milk				Page

A

Dairy / Retailer	Cheesemaker/monger	County	C	G	S	O/B	Page
Abbey Farm Cottage	Suzanne & Jonty Birrell-Gray	North Yorkshire		G			24
Abbey Home Farm	Sarah Dibben	Gloucestershire	C			O	24
Aberdyfi Cheese Company	Roman Hackelsberger	Gwynedd			S		25
Abergavenny Fine Food Co	Commercial Cheesemaker	Monmouthshire		G			25
Alex James's Cheeses	Various Collaborations	Oxfordshire	C	G	S		25
Alsop & Walker	Arthur Alsop	East Sussex	C		S		26
Appleby Creamery	Maurice Walton	Cumbria	C	G	S		27
Appleby's	Paul Appleby	Shropshire	C				29
Argyll & Bute Cheeses	Ian Rutledge	Argyll & Bute	C				30
Artisan Farm	Commercial Cheesemaker	Lancashire	C				30

B

Dairy / Retailer	Cheesemaker/monger	County	C	G	S	O/B	Page
Balcombe Dairy	Chris Heyes	West Sussex	C				31
Ballochmyle Fine Cheese	Robert Shaw	Ayrshire	C				31
Ballylisk of Armagh	Dean Wright	Armagh	C				31
Barber's Farmhouse Cheese	Commercial Cheesemaker	Somerset	C				32
Batch Farm Cheesemakers	Jean Turner, M & S Dyer	Somerset	C	G			32
Bath Soft Cheese Co	Graham & Hugh Padfield	Somerset	C			O	33
Beenleigh Blue	Ben Harris	Devon			S		182
Bellevue Creamery	Calum Chaplin	Ayrshire	C				34
Belton Farm	Commercial Cheesemaker	Shropshire	C				35
Berkswell Cheese	Stephen Fletcher & Julie Hay	West Midlands			S		36
Bevistan Dairy	Beverley Beales	Bedfordshire			S		36
Black Cow	Jason Barber	Dorset	C				37
Blackwoods Cheese Company	David Holton	Kent	C			O	37
Blaenafon Cheddar Company	Woodhouse Family	Monmouthshire	C				38
Blue Sky Cheese	Jeremy & Becky Cooper	Lincolnshire			S		39
Book & Bucket Cheese Co	Peter & Mandy Morgan	Dorset	C		S		39
Bookham Harrison Farms	Rob Booker	West Sussex	C				41
Botton Creamery	Ruth Wells	North Yorkshire	C			O	41
Bradbury's Cheese	Commercial Cheesemaker	Derbyshire	C				42
Bradfields Farm Dairy	Clare Lambert	Essex	C				42
Briddlesford Farm Dairy	Griffin Family	Isle of Wight	C				43
Bridge Farm	Helen Archer	Borsetshire	C			O	44
Brinkworth Dairy	Ceri Collingborn	Wiltshire	C				44
Brooke's Wye Valley Dairy	Robert & Irene Brooke	Monmouthshire	C				45
Brue Valley	Simon Clapp	Somerset	C				46
Brunswick Blue	Ben Harris	Devon			S		182
Buckshaw Milk Sheep	Rachel Dustan	Dorset			S		46
The Buffalo Dairy	Duncan & Julie Aitkenhead	Cornwall	C			B	47
The Buffalo Farm	Steve Mitchell, Jim Ritchie	Fife				B	47

Burnside Cheese	Barry Graham	Orkney	C				47
Burt's Cheese	Claire Burt, Tom Partridge	Cheshire	C				48
Butlers Farmhouse Cheeses	Matthew & Daniel Hall	Lancashire	C	G	S		48

C

Caerfai Farm	Wyn & Christine Evans	Pembrokeshire	C			O	51
Caerphilly Cheese Company	Huw Rowlands, Deian Thomas	Caerphilly	C				51
Caledonian Creamery (Lactalis)	Commercial Cheesemaker	Dumfries & Galloway	C				51
Calon Wen	Commercial Cheesemaker	Carmarthenshire	C			O	52
Cambridge Cheese Company	Jacky & Paul Sutton-Adam	Cambridgeshire	C	G			52
Cambus O'May Cheese Co	Alex Reid	Aberdeenshire	C				53
Carron Lodge	Adrian Rhodes	Lancashire	C	G		B	53
Caws Cenarth	Carwyn Adams	Carmarthenshire	C		S	O	55
Caws Penhelyg	Roger Yorke	Ceredigion	C			O	57
Caws Rhyd Y Delyn	Menai & Malden Jones	Anglesey	C				57
Caws Teifi	John Savage-Onstwedder	Ceredigion	C			O	58
Cerney Cheese	Avril Pratt	Gloucestershire		G			59
Chapel Cross Tea Room	Rosie Adams	Somerset		G			59
Charles Martell & Son	Charles Martell	Gloucestershire	C				60
Cheddar Gorge Cheese Co.	Cheddar Gorge Cheese Team	Somerset	C				61
Cheese Cellar Dairy (H&B)	George Bramham	Worcestershire	C	G			61
Cheese Geek	Edward Hancock	London	C				62
Cheese on The Wey	John Brown	Surrey	C				63
Cheesemakers of Canterbury	Jane Bowyer	Kent	C	G	S		64
Cheshire Cheese Company	Commercial Cheesemaker	Cheshire	C				66
The Chuckling Cheese Company	Stuart & Emma Colclough	Lincolnshire	C				66
Coachyard Creamery	Mark Samuelson	Durham	C				67
Colston Bassett Dairy	Billy Kevan	Nottinghamshire	C				67
Connage Highland Dairy	Jill & Callum Clark	Highland	C			O	67
Cornish Cheese Company	Phil Stansfield	Cornwall	C	G			69
Cornish Gouda Company	Giel Sprierings	Cornwall	C				69
Cosyn Cymru	Carrie Rimes	Gwynedd			S		69
Cote Hill Farm	Mary, Michael, Joe Davenport	Lincolnshire	C				70
Cotherstone Dairy	Joan & Alwin Cross	Durham	C				71
The Cotswold Cheese Company	Jon & Lisa Goodchild	Gloucestershire	C				71
Country Cheeses	Jungheim Family, Rebecca Cleave	Devon	C	G			71
Cow Close Farm	Sophie & James Summerlin	Derbyshire	C				73
Croome Cheese	Nick Hodgetts	Worcestershire	C				73
Cropwell Bishop Creamery	Robin Skailes	Nottinghamshire	C				74
Cryer & Stott	Richard & Clare Holmes	West Yorkshire	C	G	S		75
Curds & Croust	Martin Gaylard	Cornwall	C	G			77
Curlew Dairy	Ben & Sam Spence	North Yorkshire	C				78
Curworthy Cheese	Rachel Stephens, Richard Drake	Devon	C				78

D

The Dairy Door	Millie Preece	Shropshire	C			79
Dairy Produce Packers	Commercial Cheesemaker	Armagh	C			80
Daltons Dairy	Dalton Family	Staffordshire	C			80
The Damn Fine Cheese Co.	Tracey Smedley	Highland	C			80
Dart Mountain Cheese	Julie & Kevin Hickey	Derry	C	G		81
David Williams Cheese	David Williams	Cheshire	C			82
Davidstow Creamery (Saputo)	Commercial Cheesemaker	Cornwall	C			82
Daylesford Organics	Peter Kindel, Sasha Serebrinsky	Gloucestershire	C		O	82
Defaid Dolwerdd	Nick & Wendy Holthan	Pembrokeshire		S		84
Delamere Dairy	Commercial Cheesemaker	Cheshire		G		84
Devon Blue	Ben Harris	Devon	C			182
Dewlay Cheesemakers	Nick & Richard Kenyon	Lancashire	C			85
Doddington Cheese	Maggie Maxwell	Northumberland	C			86
Draycott Blue	Webber Family	Somerset	C			182
Dromona	Commercial Cheesemaker	Tyrone	C			87
Drumturk Cheeses	Denise Ferguson	Perthshire		G		88
Dunlop Dairy	Ann Dorward	Ayrshire	C	G		89

E

Eldwick Creamery	Laura Greenwood	West Yorkshire	C			90
Errington Cheese	Selina Cairns	Lanarkshire		G	S	90
The Ethical Dairy	David & Wilma Finlay	Dumfries & Galloway	C		O	92
Ewenique Dairy	Bryn Perry, Rebecca Morris	Pembrokeshire		S		93

F

Farmview Dairies	Davide Tani	Antrim	C			93
Fayrefield Foods	Commercial Cheesemaker	Denbighshire	C			93
Feltham's Farm Cheeses	Marcus Fergusson, Penny Nagle	Somerset	C		O	94
Fen Farm Dairy	Jonny Crickmore	Suffolk	C			94
Ferndale Norfolk Farm Cheeses	Arthur Betts	Norfolk	C			95
Ffynnon Wen Farm	Harriet Cooke	Carmarthenshire		S		98
Fielding Cottage	Sam Steggles	Norfolk	C	G		95
Ford Farm Cheesemakers	Commercial Cheesemaker	Dorset	C	G	S	96
Fowler's of Earlswood	Adrian Fowler	Warwickshire	C		S	97

G

Galloway Farmhouse Cheese	Alan & Helen Brown	Dumfries & Galloway	C	G	S	O	99
Godminster	Commercial Cheesemaker	Somerset	C		O	99
Godsells Cheese	Liz Godsell	Gloucestershire	C			100
Golden Cross Cheese Company	Kevin & Alison Blunt	East Sussex		G	S	101
Goodwood Home Farm	Bruce Rowan	West Sussex	C		O	102

			C	G	S	B/O	
The Great British Cheese Co	Commercial Cheesemaker	Cheshire	C				102
Greenfields Dairy Products	Steven Proctor	Lancashire	C	G	S		104
Greens of Glastonbury	Lloyd Green	Somerset	C	G	S		103
Grimbister Farm Cheese	Anne Seator	Orkney	C				105
Guernsleigh Cheese	Ernie Durose	Staffordshire	C	G		B	106

H

Hamm Tun Fine Foods	Gary Bradshaw	Northamptonshire	C				107
Hampshire Cheeses	Stacey Hedges, Charlotte Spruce	Hampshire	C				107
Hancocks Meadow Farm	Pauline Healey	Herefordshire			S		108
Hand Stretched Cheese	Holly Bull	Carmarthenshire	C			O	108
Harbourne Blue	Ben Harris	Devon		G			182
Hartington Creamery	Diana Alcock	Derbyshire	C				108
Hayfields Dairy	Rob Huntbach	Cheshire	C				109
High Weald Dairy	Mark & Sarah Hardy	West Sussex	C	G	S	O	110
Highland Fine Cheeses	Rory Stone	Ross-shire	C				113
Hill Farm Real Food	Elaine Aidley	Cheshire	C				114
Hinxden Farm Dairy	Richard & Dee Manford	Kent	C				115
Holden Farm Dairy	Sam & Rachel Holden	Ceredigion	C			O	115
Hollis Mead Organic Dairy	Oliver Hemsley	Dorset	C			O	115
Homewood Cheeses	Tim Homewood, Angela Morris	Somerset			S		116
Honour Natural Foods	Hannah Loades	Kent	C			O	117

I

Inverloch Cheese Co	David & Grace Eaton	Argyll & Bute	C				118
The Island Smokery	Callum & Fiona MacInnes	Orkney	C				119
Isle of Mull Cheese	Brendan Reade	Argyll & Bute	C				119
Isle of Wight Cheese Company	Richard Hodgson	Isle of Wight	C				120

J

James's Cheese	James McCall	Dorset	C				121
J J Sandham	Commercial Cheesemaker	Lancashire	C	G			120
Jonathan Crump's Glouc Cheeses	Jonathan Crump	Gloucestershire	C				122
Jones' Cheese Company	Mark Jones	Ceredigion	C				123
Joseph Heler Cheese	Commercial Cheesemaker	Cheshire	C				123

K

Kappacasein	Bill Oglethorpe	London	C			O	124
The Kedar Cheese Co	Gavin & Jane Lochhead	Dumfries & Galloway	C				124
Keen's Cheddar	George & James Keen	Somerset	C				125
King Stone Dairy	David Jowett	Gloucestershire	C			O	125
Kingcott Dairy	Karen, Steve, Frank Reynolds	Kent	C				126

L

La Latteria	Simona di Vietri	London	C				127
Lacey's Cheese	Simon Lacey	North Yorkshire	C		S		127
Larkton Hall Cheese	Anne Clayton	Cheshire	C	G			128
Laverstoke Park Farm	Martin McCallum	Hampshire				B O	128
Leicestershire Handmade Cheese	Jo, David, Will Clarke	Leicestershire	C				129
Lightwood Cheese	Haydn Roberts	Worcestershire	C	G	S		129
Lincolnshire Poacher Cheese	Simon & Tim Jones, Richard Tagg	Lincolnshire	C				130
Llaeth Y Bont	Llewelyn Williams	Powys	C				131
Trefaldwyn Cheese	Clare Jones	Powys	C				185
Loch Arthur Creamery	Barry Graham	Dumfries & Galloway	C			O	131
Lockerbie Creamery (Arla)	Commercial Cheesemaker	Dumfries & Galloway	C				132
Long Clawson Dairy	Commercial Cheesemaker	Leicestershire	C				132
Long Lane Dairy	Katie Cordle	Herefordshire			S		134
Longman's	Cheesemonger	Somerset	C				134
Lubborn Creamery (Lactalis)	Commercial Cheesemaker	Somerset	C	G			135
Ludlow Farm Shop	Paul Bedford	Shropshire	C				136
Lyburn Farmhouse Cheese	Mike Smales	Wiltshire	C				136
Lye Cross Farm	Alvis Family	Somerset	C				137
Lymn Bank Cheese Company	Commercial Cheesemaker	Lincolnshire	C				138
Lynher Dairies Cheese Company	Catherine Mead	Cornwall	C				138

M

Marlow Cheese Company	James Hill	Buckinghamshire	C		S		139
Mike's Fancy Cheese	Michael Thomson	Down	C				140
Millbrook Dairy	David Evans, Kevin Beer	Devon	C				140
Monkey Chop Cheese	Jason Barber	Dorset	C				140
Monkland Cheese Dairy	Dean Storey	Herefordshire	C				141
Monkton Wyld Court	Simon Fairlie	Dorset	C				141
Monmouth Shepherd	Isabel Coates	Monmouthshire			S		142
Montgomery's Cheeses	Jamie Montgomery	Somerset	C				142
Moyden's Handmade Cheese	Martin & Beth Moyden	Shropshire	C				143
Mrs Bourne's Cheshire Cheese	Hugo Bourne	Cheshire	C				144
Mrs Kirkham's Lancashire	Graham Kirkham	Lancashire	C				144
Mrs Temple's Cheese	Catherine Temple	Norfolk	C				145

N

Naked White Cheese (Bradbury)	Commercial Cheesemaker	Nottinghamshire	C				146
Neal's Yard Creamery	Charlie Westhead	Herefordshire	C	G			146
Nettlebed Creamery	Rose Grimond	Oxfordshire	C			O	147
Norbury Park Farm Cheese Co.	Michaela & Neil Allam	Surrey	C				147
Norseland	Commercial Cheesemaker	Somerset	C				148
Norsworthy Dairy Goats	Dave & Marilyn Johnson	Devon		G			148

Name	People	County	C	G	S	B	O	Page
Northampton Cheese Company	Steve Reid, Mark Rogers	Northamptonshire	C					149
Northumberland Cheese Co	Martin Atkinson	Northumberland	C	G	S			150
Norton and Yarrow Cheese	Fraser Norton, Rachel Yarrow	Oxfordshire		G				151
Nortons Dairy	Ruth Norton	Norfolk	C					151
Nut Knowle Farm	Lyn & Jenny Jenner	East Sussex		G				152
Nutfield Dairy	Bessie Edge & Matthew Elphick	Surrey	C					154

O

Name	People	County	C	G	S	B	O	Page
The Old Cheese Room	Julianna Sedli	Wiltshire	C				O	154
The Open Air Dairy	Tom Foot, Neil Grigg	Dorset	C					155
Orkney Cheese Company	John Bruce	Orkney	C					155
Ottinge Court Dairy	Judy Wilson	Kent	C					155
Oxford Cheese Company	Baron Robert Pouget	Oxfordshire	C					156

P

Name	People	County	C	G	S	B	O	Page
Padstow Cheese Company	Lawrence & Rosea Reynolds	Cornwall	C					157
Pant Mawr Farmhouse Cheeses	David, Cynthia, Jason Jennings	Pembrokeshire	C					157
Paxton & Whitfield	Cheesemonger	London	C	G	S			158
Pevensey Cheese Company	Martin & Hazel Tkalez	East Sussex	C					159
Pextenement Cheese Company	Sandra Evans, Carl Warburton	West Yorkshire	C				O	159
Plaw Hatch Farm	Dom Lawrance	West Sussex	C				O	160
Polmarkyn Dairy	Katie Wood	Cornwall		G				161

Q

Name	People	County	C	G	S	B	O	Page
Quicke's Traditional	Mary Quicke, Malcolm Mitchell	Devon	C	G	S			161

R

Name	People	County	C	G	S	B	O	Page
Rennet and Rind	Perry Wakeman, Mark Hulme	Cambridgeshire	C					162
Ribblesdale Cheese Company	Commercial Cheesemaker	North Yorkshire		G	S			163
Rosary Goat's Cheese	Chris & Claire Moody	Wiltshire		G				164
Rowcliffe	Cheesemonger	Kent	C					165

S

Name	People	County	C	G	S	B	O	Page
Sharpham Dairy	Greg Parsons, Peter Howarth	Devon	C	G	S			165
Shepherds Purse Cheeses	Katie Madden	North Yorkshire	C		S	B		166
Shorrocks Cheese	Andrew Shorrock	Lancashire	C					167
Simon Weaver Organic	Simon Weaver	Gloucestershire	C				O	168
Slack House Farm	Eric & Dianne Horn	Cumbria	C				O	168
Smart's Traditional	Rod Smart	Gloucestershire	C					169
Snowdonia Cheese Company	Commercial Cheesemaker	Denbighshire	C					169

			C	G	S	B	O	
Somerset Cheese Company	Philip Rainbow, Anita Robinson	Somerset	C	G	S	B		170
South Caernarfon Creameries	Mark Edwards	Gwynedd	C					171
St Andrews Cheese Company	Jane Stewart	Fife	C					173
St Ives Cheese	John Sugden	Cambridgeshire			S			173
St James Cheese	Martin Gott, Nicola Robinson	Cumbria	C	G	S			173
St Jude Cheese	Julie Cheyney, Blake Bowden	Suffolk	C					174
Staffordshire Cheese Co.	Mary Button, Vitali Bespalovs	Staffordshire	C					175
Stamford Artisan Cheese	Alison Williamson	Cambridgeshire	C					176
Stichelton Dairy	Joe Schneider	Nottinghamshire	C					176
Stonebeck Cheese	Andrew & Sally Hattan	North Yorkshire	C					176
Strathearn Cheese Co.	Drew Watson, Pierre Leger	Perthshire	C					176
Suffolk Farmhouse Cheeses	James Salisbury	Suffolk	C					177
Swaledale Cheese Company	Richard Darbishire	North Yorkshire	C					178

T

			C	G	S	B	O	
Taw Valley Creamery (Arla)	Commercial Cheesemaker	Devon	C					178
Teesdale Cheesemakers	Allison & Jonathan Raper	Durham	C	G				179
Tenacres Cheese	Gillian Clough	West Yorkshire		G				180
Thornby Moor Dairy	Carolyn & Leonie Fairbairn	Cumbria	C	G				181
Ticklemore Cheese Dairy	Ben Harris	Devon	C	G	S			182
Times Past Cheese Dairy	Webber Family	Somerset	C					182
Torpenhow Farmhouse Dairy	Jenny & Mark Lee	Cumbria	C				O	183
The Traditional Cheese Dairy	Ben Cottingham, Andy Delves	East Sussex	C		S			184
Trefaldwyn Cheese	Clare Jones	Powys	C					184
Trethowan Brothers	Todd, Maugan & Kim Trethowan	Somerset	C				O	185
Treveador Farm Dairy	Alastair & Bernadette Rogers	Cornwall	C					185
Tuxford & Tebbutt (Arla)	Commercial Cheesemaker	Leicestershire	C					186
Two Hoots Cheese	Sandy & Andy Rose	Berkshire	C					186
Tŷ Caws	Owen Davies	Cardiff	C		S			186

V

			C	G	S	B	O	
Velocheese	Davide Tani	Antrim	C				O	187
Village Maid Cheese	Anne, Andy & Jake Wigmore	Berkshire	C		S			187

W

			C	G	S	B	O	
Wacky Wedge Cheese Company	Brad & Beth Cunningham	Gwynedd		G				188
Wandering Ewe Dairy	Hugh & Pippa Stables	Somerset			S			189
Weardale Cheese	Simon Raine	Durham	C					189
Wensleydale Creamery (Saputo)	Commercial Cheesemaker	North Yorkshire	C					190
West Country Water Buffalo	Jonathan Corpe	Somerset				B		191
Westcombe Dairy	Tom Calver, R Howard, J Coles	Somerset	C					191
Whalesborough Cheese	James Smith & Lucy Jones	Cornwall	C	G				192
Whin Yeats Dairy	Tom & Clare Noblett	Cumbria	C					194

White Lake Cheese	Roger Longman	Somerset	C	G	S		194
Wildcroft Dairy	Tracey & Graham Longhurst	Surrey		G			198
Wilton Farm	Becky Enefer	Norfolk			S		198
Windrush Valley Goat Dairy	Renee & Richard Loveridge	Gloucestershire		G			199
Winterdale Cheesemakers	Robin Betts	Kent	C				199
Woodbridge Farm	Mike & Emily Davies	Dorset	C				199
Woodlands Dairy	Shane Herbert	Dorset			S	O	200
Wookey Farm	Sarah Davies	Somerset		G			200
Wyke Farms	Clothier Family	Somerset	C				201

Y

Y Cwt Caws	Nigel, Rhian & Ffion Jefferies	Anglesey		G			201
Yellison Farm	Sharron & Edward Parker	North Yorkshire		G			202
Yester Farm Dairies	Simon & Jacky McCreery	East Lothian	C				203
Yorkshire Dama Cheese	Razan Alsous	West Yorkshire	C	G	S		203
Yorkshire Fine Cheese	Ruth Baker	West Yorkshire	C				204
Yorkshire Organic Cheesemakers	Andrew Foley	North Yorkshire	C			O	204
Yorkshire Pecorino	Mario Olianas	West Yorkshire			S		204

British Cheeses

INDEX OF CHEESES

MILK :

C = Cow   G = Goat   S = Sheep   B = Buffalo

TREATMENT :

U = Unpasteurised   P = Pasteurised   T = Thermised   U/P = Unpasteurised or Pasteurised

RENNET :

A = Animal (Traditional)   V = Vegetarian   L = Lactic   A/V = Both Animal and Vegetarian versions

ORGANIC

O = Organic

Name of Cheese	Dairy	County		Milk			Page

#

| 1057 Extra Mature Scottish Cheddar | Millbrook Dairy | Devon | C | P | V | | 140 |
| 1780 Aged Reserve Stilton PDO | Tuxford & Tebbutt (Arla) | Leicestershire | C | P | V | | 186 |

A

Abbey Home Farm Halloumi Style	Abbey Home Farm	Gloucestershire	C	P	V	O	24
Abbey Home Farm Soft Cheese	Abbey Home Farm	Gloucestershire	C	P	V	O	24
Abaty	Caws Pen Helyg	Ceredigion	C	U	V	O	57
Abaty Glas	Caws Pen Helyg	Ceredigion	C	U	V	O	57
Abbot's Gold	Wensleydale Creamery (Saputo)	North Yorkshire	C	P	V		190
Adlestrop	Daylesford Organics	Gloucestershire	C	P	V	O	82
Admiral Collingwood	Doddington Cheese	Northumberland	C	U	A		86
Aiket	Dunlop Dairy	Ayrshire	C	P	V		89
Ailsa Craig	Dunlop Dairy	Ayrshire	G	P	V		89
Airedale	Eldwick Creamery	West Yorkshire	C	P	V		90
Alex James No. 1 Cheddar	Ford Farm Cheesemakers	Dorset	C	P	V		25
Alex James No. 2 Blue Monday	Shepherds Purse Cheeses	North Yorkshire	C	P	V		25
Alex James No. 3 Valley Brie	Caws Cenarth	Carmarthenshire	C	P	V		26
Alex James No. 4 Goat's	Rosary Goats Cheese	Wiltshire	G	P	V		26
Alex James No. 5 Grunge	Nettlebed Creamery	Oxfordshire	C	P	A	O	26
Alex James No. 6 Sheep	High Weald Dairy	West Sussex	S	P	V	O	26
Alfred's Yellow Jersey	Cheese on The Wey	Surrey	C	T	V		63
Allerdale	Thornby Moor Dairy	Cumbria	G	U	A		181
Allison's Garlic Special	Teesdale Cheesemakers	Durham	C	P	V		179
Alpine Goat's Salad Cheese	Polmarkyn Dairy	Cornwall	G	U	V		161
Amalthea	Lightwood Cheese	Worcestershire	G	U	A		129
Ancient Ashmore	Cheesemakers of Canterbury	Kent	C	U	V		64
Angiddy	Brooke's Wye Valley Dairy	Monmouthshire	C	P	V		45
Anster	St Andrews Cheese Company	Fife	C	U	A		173
Apatha	St James Cheese	Cumbria	G	U	A		173

Appleby's Cheshire	Appleby's	Shropshire	C	U	A		29
Appleby's Double Gloucester	Appleby's	Shropshire	C	U	A		29
Applewood	Norseland	Somerset	C	P	V		148
Ardmore	Cambus O'May Cheese Co.	Aberdeenshire	C	U	A		53
Arran Blue	Bellevue Creamery	Ayrshire	C	P	V		34
Arran Camembert	Bellevue Creamery	Ayrshire	C	P	V		34
Arran Mist	Bellevue Creamery	Ayrshire	C	P	V		34
Ashcombe	King Stone Dairy	Gloucestershire	C	P	A	O	125
Ashdown Foresters	High Weald Dairy	West Sussex	C	P	V	O	110
Ashlynn	Cheese Cellar Dairy	Worcestershire	G	P	V		61
Ashmore Farmhouse	Cheesemakers of Canterbury	Kent	C	U	V		64
Aspire	Nut Knowle Farm	East Sussex	G	P	V		152
Auld Reekie	Cambus O'May Cheese Co.	Aberdeenshire	C	U	A		53
Aur Preseli	Defaid Dolwerdd	Pembrokeshire	S	P	V		84
Austen	Book & Bucket Cheese Co.	Dorset	S	P	V		39
Avebury	Brinkworth Dairy	Wiltshire	C	P	V		44
Aveline	Homewood Cheeses	Somerset	S	T	V		116
Ayrshire Dunlop PGI	Dunlop Dairy	Ayrshire	C	P	V		89
Ayrshire Farmhouse Brie	Ballochmyle Fine Cheese	Ayrshire	C	P	V		31

B

Bagborough Brie	White Lake Cheese	Somerset	C	P	V	O	194
Balcombe Breeze	Balcombe Dairy	West Sussex	C	P	V		31
Bakesy Meadow	Country Cheeses	Devon	G	P	V		71
Banagher Bold	Dart Mountain Cheese	Derry	C	P	V		81
Bara Brith	Blaenafon Cheddar Company	Monmouthshire	C	P	V		38
Barber's 1833 Vintage Reserve	Barber's Farmhouse Cheese	Somerset	C	P	V		32
Barber's Farmhouse Cheddar	Barber's Farmhouse Cheese	Somerset	C	P	V		32
Barber's Haystack Tasty	Barber's Farmhouse Cheese	Somerset	C	P	V		32
Barber's Mature Cheddar Truckle	Barber's Farmhouse Cheese	Somerset	C	P	V		32
Barber's Red Leicester	Barber's Farmhouse Cheese	Somerset	C	P	V		32
Barkham Blue	Two Hoots Cheese	Berkshire	C	P	V		186
Barlocco Blue	The Ethical Dairy	Dumfries & Galloway	C	P	V	O	92
Barncliffe Blue	Yorkshire Fine Cheese	West Yorkshire	C	P	V		204
Barncliffe Brie	Yorkshire Fine Cheese	West Yorkshire	C	P	V		204
Barncliffe Truffled	Yorkshire Fine Cheese	West Yorkshire	C	P	V		204
Barney Brie	Teesdale Cheesemakers	Durham	C	P	V		179
Baron Bigod	Fen Farm Dairy	Suffolk	C	P	A		94
Baronet	The Old Cheese Room	Wiltshire	C	P	V	O	154
Barrel Aged	Paxton & Whitfield	London	S	P	V		158
Batch Farm Cheese Curds	Batch Farm Cheesemakers	Somerset	C	U	V		32
Batch Farm Clothbound Cheddar	Batch Farm Cheesemakers	Somerset	C	U	V		33
Batch Farm Farmhouse Cheddar	Batch Farm Cheesemakers	Somerset	C	P	A		33
Batch Farm Goat's Cheese	Batch Farm Cheesemakers	Somerset	G	U	V		33

Cheese	Maker	County					Page
Batch Farm Mild Cheddar	Batch Farm Cheesemakers	Somerset	C	P	V		33
Batch Farm Somerset Red Cheddar	Batch Farm Cheesemakers	Somerset	C	P	V		33
Batch Farm Waxed Cheddar	Batch Farm Cheesemakers	Somerset	C	U	V		33
Bath Blue	Bath Soft Cheese Company	Somerset	C	P	A	O	33
Bath Soft	Bath Soft Cheese Company	Somerset	C	P	A	O	34
Baywell	Daylesford Organics	Gloucestershire	C	P	V	O	83
Beacon Blue	Butlers Farmhouse Cheeses	Lancashire	G	P	V		48
Beacon Fell PDO	Dewlay Cheesemakers	Lancashire	C	P	V		85
Beauvale	Cropwell Bishop Creamery	Nottinghamshire	C	P	A		74
Becca	Caws Cenarth	Carmarthenshire	S	P	V		55
Beckets Brie	Northampton Cheese Company	Northants	C	P	V	O	149
Beenleigh Blue	Ticklemore Cheese Dairy	Devon	S	P	V		182
Bell End Blue	Abbey Farm Cottage	North Yorkshire	G	U	V		24
Belstone	Curworthy Cheese	Devon	C	P	V		78
Belton Farm Caerphilly	Belton Farm	Shropshire	C	P	V		35
Belton Farm Cheddar	Belton Farm	Shropshire	C	P	V		35
Belton Farm Cheshire	Belton Farm	Shropshire	C	P	V		35
Belton Farm Double Gloucester	Belton Farm	Shropshire	C	P	V		35
Belton Farm Lancashire	Belton Farm	Shropshire	C	P	V		35
Belton Farm Port Wine Derby	Belton Farm	Shropshire	C	P	V		35
Belton Farm Red Leicester	Belton Farm	Shropshire	C	P	V		35
Belton Farm Sage Derby	Belton Farm	Shropshire	C	P	V		36
Belton Farm Wensleydale	Belton Farm	Shropshire	C	P	V		36
Benville	Hollis Mead Organic Dairy	Dorset	C	P	V	O	115
Berkswell	Berkswell Cheese	West Midlands	S	U	A		36
Bermondsey Frier	Kappacasein	London	C	U	A	O	124
Bermondsey Hard Pressed	Kappacasein	London	C	U	A	O	124
Bertha	Pextenement Cheese Company	West Yorkshire	C	P	V	O	159
Berwick Edge	Doddington Cheese	Northumberland	C	U	A		86
Bevistan Blue	Bevistan Dairy	Bedfordshire	S	U	V		36
Bevistan Smoked	Bevistan Dairy	Bedfordshire	S	P	V		37
Bevistan Tomme	Bevistan Dairy	Bedfordshire	S	P	V		37
Big Nick	Chapel Cross Tea Room	Somerset	G	U	V		59
Biggar Blue	Errington Cheese	Lanarkshire	G	U	V		90
Billie's Goat Cheese	Ford Farm Cheesemakers	Dorset	G	P	V		96
Binham Blue	Mrs Temple's Cheese	Norfolk	C	P	V		145
Binsey Red	Torpenhow Farmhouse Dairy	Cumbria	C	P	V	O	183
Birdoswald	Slack House Farm	Cumbria	C	P	V	O	168
Bisham	Marlow Cheese Company	Buckinghamshire	C	P	V		139
Bix	Nettlebed Creamery	Oxfordshire	C	P	A	O	147
Black and Blue	Staffordshire Cheese Company	Staffordshire	C	P	V		175
Black Bomber Extra Mature	Snowdonia Cheese Company	Denbighshire	C	P	V		169
Black Cow Cheddar	Black Cow	Dorset	C	P	V		37
Black Crowdie (Gruth Dhu)	Highland Fine Cheeses	Ross-shire	C	P	V		113

Black Dub Blue	Appleby Creamery	Cumbria	C	P	V		27
Black Jack	Nut Knowle Farm	East Sussex	G	P	V		152
Black Sheep	Caws Cenarth	Carmarthenshire	S	P	V		55
Blackfriar	Cheese on The Wey	Surrey	C	T	V		63
Blackjack Vintage Charcoal	Greenfields Dairy Products	Lancashire	C	P	V		104
Blackmount	Errington Cheese	Lanarkshire	G	U	A		90
Blacksticks Blue	Butlers Farmhouse Cheeses	Lancashire	C	P	V		48
Blackstone	Joseph Heler Cheese	Cheshire	C	P	V		123
Blackthorn Crumble	Drumturk Cheeses	Perthshire	G	P	V		88
Blackwater	Bradfields Farm Dairy	Essex	C	P	V		42
Blaenafon	Blaenafon Cheddar Company	Monmouthshire	C	P	V		38
Blaenafon Caerphilly	Blaenafon Cheddar Company	Monmouthshire	C	P	V		38
Blaenafon Oak Smoked Mature	Blaenafon Cheddar Company	Monmouthshire	C	P	V		38
Blanche	Cheese Cellar Dairy	Worcestershire	G	P	V		61
Bledington Blue	Daylesford Organics	Gloucestershire	C	P	V	O	83
Blencathra	Appleby Creamery	Cumbria	C	P	V		28
Bliss	Country Cheeses	Devon	C	P	V		71
Blue Bay	Country Cheeses	Devon	C	P	V		72
Blue Clouds	Balcombe Dairy	West Sussex	C	P	V		31
Blue Goat	Ribblesdale Cheese Company	North Yorkshire	G	P	V		163
Blue Knowle	Nut Knowle Farm	East Sussex	G	P	V		152
Blue Millie	Cheese on The Wey	Surrey	C	T	V		63
Blue Monk	Monkland Cheese Dairy	Herefordshire	C	U	V		141
Blue Murder	Highland Fine Cheeses	Ross-shire	C	P	V		113
Blue Wenalt	Brooke's Wye Valley Dairy	Monmouthshire	C	P	V		46
Blue Whinnow	Thornby Moor Dairy	Cumbria	C	U	A		181
Bluebell	The Ethical Dairy	Dumfries & Galloway	C	P	V	O	92
Blueberry Fayre	Long Clawson Dairy	Leicestershire	C	P	V		132
Bluemin White	Shepherds Purse Cheeses	North Yorkshire	C	P	V		166
Blyton	Book & Bucket Cheese Co.	Dorset	C	P	V		39
Bonnet	Dunlop Dairy	Ayrshire	G	P	V		89
Bonnington Linn	Errington Cheese	Lanarkshire	G	U	A		91
Border Riever	Appleby Creamery	Cumbria	C	P	V		28
Boresisle	Honour Natural Foods	Kent	C	P	V	O	117
Borsetshire Blue	Bridge Farm	Borsetshire	C	U	V	O	44
Bosworth Field	Leicestershire Handmade	Leicestershire	C	U	A		129
Botton Gouda	Botton Creamery	North Yorkshire	C	U	V	O	41
Bowland	David Williams Cheese	Cheshire	C	P	V		82
Bowyer's	Cheesemakers of Canterbury	Kent	C	P	V		64
Boy Laity	Curds and Croust	Cornwall	C	P	A		77
Bradbury's Waxed Truckles	Bradbury's Cheese	Derbyshire	C	P	V		42
Brefu Bach	Cosyn Cymru	Gwynedd	S	U	V		69
Briddlesford Cheddar	Briddlesford Farm Dairy	Isle of Wight	C	P	V		43
Briddlesford Fetter	Briddlesford Farm Dairy	Isle of Wight	C	P	V		43

Briddlesford Gouda	Briddlesford Farm Dairy	Isle of Wight	C	P	V		43
Briddlesford Halloumi	Briddlesford Farm Dairy	Isle of Wight	C	P	V		44
Briddlesford Red	Briddlesford Farm Dairy	Isle of Wight	C	P	V		44
Brie a Dale	Weardale Cheese	Durham	C	P	V		189
Brie by Gum	Eldwick Creamery	West Yorkshire	C	P	V		90
Brighton Blue	High Weald Dairy	West Sussex	C	P	V	(O)	110
Brighton Ewe	High Weald Dairy	West Sussex	S	P	V		111
Brightwell Ash	Norton and Yarrow Cheese	Oxfordshire	G	U	A		151
Bringewood	Ludlow Farm Shop	Shropshire	C	P	V		136
Brinkworth Blue	Brinkworth Dairy	Wiltshire	C	P	V		44
Bristol Button	Homewood Cheeses	Somerset	S	T	V		116
Britannia	Cryer & Stott	West Yorkshire	C	P	V		75
Brother Michael	High Weald Dairy	West Sussex	C	P	V	O	111
Brunswick Blue	Ticklemore Cheese Dairy	Devon	S	P	V		182
Bruton Beauty	Godminster Cheese	Somerset	C	P	V	O	99
Bruton Brie	Longman's Cheese	Somerset	C	P	V	O	134
Bucks Blue	Marlow Cheese Company	Buckinghamshire	C	P	V		139
Buckshaw Blewe	Buckshaw Milk Sheep	Dorset	S	U	V		46
Buckshaw Crumbly	Buckshaw Milk Sheep	Dorset	S	U	V		46
Buckshaw Fela	Buckshaw Milk Sheep	Dorset	S	U	V		46
Buckshaw Hallewemi	Buckshaw Milk Sheep	Dorset	S	U	V		47
Buckshaw White	Buckshaw Milk Sheep	Dorset	S	U	V		47
Buffalicious Mozzarella	West Country Water Buffalo	Somerset	B	U	V		191
Buffalo Blue	Shepherds Purse Cheeses	North Yorkshire	B	P	V		166
Buffaloumi	Laverstoke Park Farm	Hampshire	B	P	V	O	128
Burcott	Wookey Farm	Somerset	G	U	V		200
Bure's Essex	Bradfields Farm Dairy	Essex	C	P	V		42
Burland Bloom	Butlers Farmhouse Cheeses	Lancashire	C	P	V		49
Burns	Book & Bucket Cheese Co.	Dorset	S	P	V		40
Burnside	Burnside Cheese	Orkney	C	P	V		47
Burrow Mump	White Lake Cheese	Somerset	S	T	V		195
Burt's Blue	Burt's Cheese	Cheshire	C	P	V		48
Burwash Rose	The Traditional Cheese Dairy	East Sussex	C	P	V		184
Button Mill	Butlers Farmhouse Cheeses	Lancashire	C	P	V		49
Buxton Blue PDO	Staffordshire Cheese Company	Staffordshire	C	P	V		175
Bybrook	The Old Cheese Room	Wiltshire	C	P	V	O	154

C

Caboc	Highland Fine Cheeses	Ross-shire	C	P	V		113
Caer Caradoc	Moyden's Handmade Cheese	Shropshire	C	U	V		143
Caerfai Caerffili	Caerfai Farm	Pembrokeshire	C	U	V	O	51
Caerfai Cheddar	Caerfai Farm	Pembrokeshire	C	U	V	O	51
Caerphilly Caerphilly	Caerphilly Cheese Company	Glamorganshire	C				51
Cairnsmore Cow	Galloway Farmhouse Cheese	Dumfries & Galloway	C	U	V	O	99

Cairnsmore Ewe	Galloway Farmhouse Cheese	Dumfries & Galloway	S	U	V	99
Cairnsmore Goat	Galloway Farmhouse Cheese	Dumfries & Galloway	G	U	V	99
Calon Wen Cheddar	Calon Wen	Carmarthenshire	C	P	V	O	52
Cam	Bradfields Farm Dairy	Essex	C	P	V	43
Cambridge Bleat	Cambridge Cheese Company	Cambridgeshire	G	P	A	52
Cambridge Blue	Cambridge Cheese Company	Cambridgeshire	C	U	A	52
Cambus O'May	Cambus O'May Cheese Co.	Aberdeenshire	C	U	A	53
Campbelltown Loch	Inverloch Cheese Company	Argyll & Bute	C	P	V	118
Canterbury Cobble	Cheesemakers of Canterbury	Kent	C	U	V	64
Capability Brown	Doddington Cheese	Northumberland	C	U	A	87
Capel Newydd	Blaenafon Cheddar Company	Monmouthshire	C	P	V	38
Capercaillie	Drumturk Cheeses	Perthshire	G	P	V	88
Capricorn Goat	Lubborn Creamery (Lactalis)	Somerset	G	P	V	135
Caprini	Nut Knowle Farm	East Sussex	G	P	V	152
Carlton	Bevistan Dairy	Bedfordshire	S	P	V	37
Carlton Crowdie	Yellison Farm	North Yorkshire	G	P	L	202
Carnival	Long Clawson Dairy	Leicestershire	C	P	V	132
Carraig Bán	Dart Mountain Cheese	Derry	G	P	V	81
Carrick	The Ethical Dairy	Dumfries & Galloway	C	U	V	O	92
Carron Lodge Double Gloucester	Carron Lodge	Lancashire	C	P	V	53
Carron Lodge Goat Cheddar	Carron Lodge	Lancashire	G	P	V	54
Carron Lodge Lancashire	Carron Lodge	Lancashire	C	P	V	54
Carron Lodge Red Leicester	Carron Lodge	Lancashire	C	P	V	54
Castello Tickler	Taw Valley (Arla)	Devon	C	P	V	178
Castlerigg	St James Cheese	Cumbria	S	U	A	173
Cathedral City Cheddar	Davidstow Creamery (Saputo)	Cornwall	C	P	V	82
Caws Calan	Cosyn Cymru	Gwynedd	S	U	A	69
Caws Cenarth Cheddar	Caws Cenarth	Carmarthenshire	C	P	V	O	55
Caws Cerwyn	Pant Mawr Farmhouse Cheeses	Pembrokeshire	C	P	V	157
Caws Chwaral	Cosyn Cymru	Gwynedd	S	U	A	70
Caws Dyfi	Aberdyfi Cheese Company	Gwynedd	S	P	A	25
Caws Preseli	Pant Mawr Farmhouse Cheeses	Pembrokeshire	C	P	V	157
Caws y Bugail	Aberdyfi Cheese Company	Gwynedd	S	P	A	25
Celeste	Country Cheeses	Devon	C	U	V	72
Celtic Promise	Caws Teifi	Ceredigion	C	U	A	O	58
Cenarth Brie	Caws Cenarth	Carmarthenshire	C	P	V	O	55
Cerne Abbas Cheddar	Oxford Cheese Company	Oxfordshire	C	P	V	156
Cerney Mini Ash	Cerney Cheese	Gloucestershire	G	U	V	59
Cerney Pyramid	Cerney Cheese	Gloucestershire	G	U	V	59
Chabis	Golden Cross Cheese Company	East Sussex	G	U	V	101
Chalvedon	Bradfields Farm Dairy	Essex	C	P	V	43
Chapelhouse	Pextenement Cheese Company	West Yorkshire	C	P	V	O	159
Charcoal Briquette	Carron Lodge	Lancashire	C	P	V	54
Chardown Hill	James's Cheese	Dorset	C	P	V	121

Charlton	Goodwood Home Farm	West Sussex	C	P	V	O	102
Charnwood	Long Clawson Dairy	Leicestershire	C	P	V		132
Chattox	Homewood Cheeses	Somerset	S	T	V		116
Chaucers	Cheesemakers of Canterbury	Kent	C	P	V		64
Cheddar Gorge Flavoured Cheddar	Cheddar Gorge Cheese Co.	Somerset	C	U	V		61
Cheddar Gorge Traditional Cheddar	Cheddar Gorge Cheese Co.	Somerset	C	U	V		61
Cheddar Gorge Waxed Cheddar	Cheddar Gorge Cheese Co.	Somerset	C	U	V		61
Cheddleton	Staffordshire Cheese Company	Staffordshire	C	P	V		175
Chelwood	Norsworthy Dairy Goats	Devon	G	U	V		148
Chemmy	Country Cheeses	Devon	G	P	V		72
Cheney's Fortune	Godminster Cheese	Somerset	C	P	V	O	99
Cheshire Cheese Cheddar	Cheshire Cheese Company	Cheshire	C	P	V		66
Cheshire Cheese Cheshire	Cheshire Cheese Company	Cheshire	C	P	V		66
Cheshire Cheese Royal Blue	Cheshire Cheese Company	Cheshire	C	P	V		66
Cheshire Cheese Smokewood	Cheshire Cheese Company	Cheshire	C	P	V		66
Chesterwood	Northumberland Cheese Co	Northumberland	G	P	V		150
Chilli con Cheddar	Greenfields Dairy Products	Lancashire	C	P	V		104
Chilli Marble	High Weald Dairy	West Sussex	C	P	V		111
Chiltern Cloud	Marlow Cheese Company	Buckinghamshire	S	P	V	O	139
Chipple	Curworthy Cheese	Devon	C	P	V		78
Christmas Pudding	Inverloch Cheese Company	Argyll & Bute	C	P	V		118
Chuckling Cheese Cheddar Truckles	The Chuckling Cheese Company	Lincolnshire	C	P	V		66
Chuckling Cheese Large Truckles	The Chuckling Cheese Company	Lincolnshire	C	P	V		66
Clara	Cheese Cellar Dairy	Worcestershire	G	P	V		61
Clarabel	Fowler's of Earlswood	Warwickshire	C	P	V		97
Clawson Reserve Blue Stilton PDO	Long Clawson Dairy	Leicestershire	C	P	V		132
Clawson Reserve Rutland Red	Long Clawson Dairy	Leicestershire	C	P	V		133
Clawson Reserve Shropshire Blue	Long Clawson Dairy	Leicestershire	C	P	V		132
Clawson Reserve White Stilton PDO	Long Clawson Dairy	Leicestershire	C	P	V		133
Clerkland Crowdie	Dunlop Dairy	Ayrshire	C	P	V		89
Clickers	Northampton Cheese Company	Northants	C	P	V	O	149
Clothbound Cheshire	Mrs Bourne's Cheshire Cheese	Cheshire	C	U/P	V		144
Coastal Cheddar	Ford Farm Cheesemakers	Dorset	C	P	V		96
Cobbett	Monkton Wyld Court	Dorset	C	U	A		141
Cobblers Nibble	Hamm Tun Fine Foods	Northants	C	U	V		107
Cockadilly Chilli	Godsells Cheese	Gloucestershire	C	P	V		100
College White	Oxford Cheese Company	Oxfordshire	C	P	V		156
Coleraine Cheddar	Dairy Produce Packers	Armagh	C	P	V		80
Colliers Mature Celtic Cheddar	Fayrefield Foods	Denbighshire	C	P	V		93
Colliers Powerful Cheddar	Fayrefield Foods	Denbighshire	C	P	V		93
Colston Bassett Shropshire Blue	Colston Bassett Dairy	Nottinghamshire	C	P	VA		67
Colston Bassett Stilton PDO	Colston Bassett Dairy	Nottinghamshire	C	P	VA		67
Colwey	Cheese on The Wey	Surrey	C	T	V		63
Connage Cheddar	Connage Highland Dairy	Highland	C	P	V	O	67

Connage Clava Brie	Connage Highland Dairy	Highland	C	P	V	O	68
Connage Cromal	Connage Highland Dairy	Highland	C	P	V	O	68
Connage Crowdie	Connage Highland Dairy	Highland	C	P	V	O	68
Connage Dunlop	Connage Highland Dairy	Highland	C	P	V	O	68
Connage Gouda	Connage Highland Dairy	Highland	C	P	V	O	68
Copys Cloud	Mrs Temple's Cheese	Norfolk	C	P	V		145
Corinium	Paxton & Whitfield	London	C	P	A	O	158
Cornish Blue	Cornish Cheese Company	Cornwall	C	P	V		68
Cornish Blue Goat's Cheese	Polmarkyn Dairy	Cornwall	G	U	V		161
Cornish Brie	Cornish Cheese Company	Cornwall	C	P	V		68
Cornish Camembert	Cornish Cheese Company	Cornwall	C	P	V		69
Cornish Cheddar	Cornish Cheese Company	Cornwall	C	P	V		69
Cornish Crumbly	Whalesborough Cheese	Cornwall	C	P	V		192
Cornish Gouda	Cornish Gouda Company	Cornwall	C	P	A		69
Cornish Grey Goat's Cheese	Polmarkyn Dairy	Cornwall	G	U	V		161
Cornish Herbert	Whalesborough Cheese	Cornwall	C	P	V		192
Cornish Jack	Padstow Cheese Company	Cornwall	C	P	A		157
Cornish Kern	Lynher Dairies Cheese Company	Cornwall	C	P	A		138
Cornish Nanny	Cornish Cheese Company	Cornwall	G	P	V		69
Cornish Smuggler	Whalesborough Cheese	Cornwall	C	P	V		193
Cornish White Goat's Cheese	Polmarkyn Dairy	Cornwall	G	U	V		161
Cornish Yarg	Lynher Dairies Cheese Company	Cornwall	C	P	V		139
Coronation Gold	Whalesborough Cheese	Cornwall	C	P	V		193
Corra Linn	Errington Cheese	Lanarkshire	S	U	A		91
Corscombe	Hollis Mead Organic Dairy	Dorset	C	P	V	O	115
Cote Hill Blue	Cote Hill Farm	Lincolnshire	C	U	V		70
Cote Hill Lindum	Cote Hill Farm	Lincolnshire	C	U	V		70
Cote Hill Red	Cote Hill Farm	Lincolnshire	C	U	V		70
Cote Hill White	Cote Hill Farm	Lincolnshire	C	U	V		70
Cote Hill Yellow	Cote Hill Farm	Lincolnshire	C	U	V		70
Cotherstone	Cotherstone Dairy	Durham	C	P	V		71
Cotswold	Long Clawson Dairy	Leicestershire	C	P	V		133
Cotswold Blue Veined Brie	Simon Weaver Organic	Gloucestershire	C	P	V	O	168
Cotswold Brie	Simon Weaver Organic	Gloucestershire	C	P	V	O	168
Crabtree	Larkton Hall Cheese	Cheshire	C	U	A		128
Cranborne Blue	Book & Bucket Cheese Co.	Dorset	C	P	V		40
Cremet	Sharpham Dairy	Devon	GC	P	V		165
Cricket St Thomas Brie	Lubborn Creamery (Lactalis)	Somerset	C	P	V		135
Cricket St Thomas Camembert	Lubborn Creamery (Lactalis)	Somerset	C	P	V		135
Crimson	Long Clawson Dairy	Leicestershire	C	P	V		133
Crofter	Ford Farm Cheesemakers	Dorset	S	P	V		96
Crofton	Thornby Moor Dairy	Cumbria	CG	U	A		181
Crookwheeel	St James Cheese	Cumbria	S	U	A		174
Croome Flavoured Cheddar	Croome Cheese	Worcestershire	C	P	V		73

Croome Waxed Truckles	Croome Cheese	Worcestershire	C	P	V		73
Cropwell Bishop Blue Shropshire	Cropwell Bishop	Nottinghamshire	C	P	V		74
Cropwell Bishop Stilton PDO	Cropwell Bishop Creamery	Nottinghamshire	C	P	A/V		74
Cropwell Bishop White Stilton PDO	Cropwell Bishop Creamery	Nottinghamshire	C	P	V		74
Crump's Double Gloucester	Jonathan Crump's	Gloucestershire	C	U	V		122
Crump's Single Gloucester PDO	Jonathan Crump's	Gloucestershire	C	U	V		122
Crwys	Tŷ Caws	Glamorgan	CS	P	V		186
Cryer & Stott Coverdale	Cryer & Stott	West Yorkshire	C	P	V		75
Cryf	Caws Cenarth	Carmarthenshire	C	P	V		55
Cuddy's Cave	Doddington Cheese	Northumberland	C	U	A		87
Cullum	Paxton & Whitfield	London	S	P	V		158
Cumberland Farmhouse	Thornby Moor Dairy	Cumbria	C	U	A		181
Curthwaite	Thornby Moor Dairy	Cumbria	G	U	V		181
Curworthy	Curworthy Cheese	Devon	C	P	A		78
Cybi Melyn	Y Cwt Caws	Anglesey	G	P	V		201
Cygnet	Marlow Cheese Company	Buckinghamshire	C	P	V		139
Cymru Crunch	Blaenafon Cheddar Company	Monmouthshire	C	P	V		38

D

Dale End Cheddar	Botton Creamery	North Yorkshire	C	U	V	O	41
Daltons Dovedale Blue PDO	Daltons Dairy	Staffordshire	C	P	V		80
Daltons Staffordshire PDO	Daltons Dairy	Staffordshire	C	P	V		80
Dambuster	Carron Lodge	Lancashire	C	P	V		54
Damn Fine Waxed Cheddar	The Damn Fine Cheese Co.	Highland	C	P	V		80
Dargate Dumpy	Cheesemakers of Canterbury	Kent	S	P	V		65
Darling Blue	Doddington Cheese	Northumberland	C	P	A		87
Darling Howe	Torpenhow Farmhouse Dairy	Cumbria	C	P	V	O	183
Dart Mountain Dusk	Dart Mountain Cheese	Derry	C	P	V		81
Dartmoor Chilli	Curworthy Cheese	Devon	C	P	A		78
Davidstow Cheddar	Davidstow Creamery (Saputo)	Cornwall	C	P	V		82
Daylesford Blue	Daylesford Organics	Gloucestershire	C	P	A	O	83
Daylesford Cheddar	Daylesford Organics	Gloucestershire	C	P	A	O	83
Daylesford Double Gloucester	Daylesford Organics	Gloucestershire	C	P	A	O	83
Daylesford Single Gloucester PDO	Daylesford Organics	Gloucestershire	C	P	A	O	83
Dazel Ash	Rosary Goat's Cheese	Wiltshire	G	P	V		164
Delamere Farmhouse Mild Goat	Delamere Dairy	Cheshire	G	P	V		84
Delamere Medium Goat's Cheese	Delamere Dairy	Cheshire	G	P	V		85
Delilah	Cheese Cellar Dairy	Worcestershire	C	P	V		62
Demeter	Wildcroft Dairy	Surrey	G	U	A		198
Devil's Dance	Godminster Cheese	Somerset	C	P	V	O	99
Devil's Rock Blue	Pextenement Cheese Company	West Yorkshire	C	P	V	O	159
Devon Blue	Ticklemore Cheese Dairy	Devon	C	P	V		183
Devon Maid	Curworthy Cheese	Devon	C	P	V		78
Devon Oke	Curworthy Cheese	Devon	C	P	A		79

Devon Sage	Country Cheeses	Devon	C	P	V		72
Devonshire Gold	Hartington Creamery	Derbyshire	C	P	V		108
Devonshire Red	Quicke's Traditional	Devon	C	P	V		161
Dewlay Cheddar	Dewlay Cheesemakers	Lancashire	C	P	V		85
Dewlay Cheshire	Dewlay Cheesemakers	Lancashire	C	P	V		85
Dewlay Double Gloucester	Dewlay Cheesemakers	Lancashire	C	P	V		85
Dewlay Lancashire Creamy	Dewlay Cheesemakers	Lancashire	C	P	V		85
Dewlay Lancashire Crumbly	Dewlay Cheesemakers	Lancashire	C	P	V		85
Dewlay Red Leicester	Dewlay Cheesemakers	Lancashire	C	P	V		86
Dewlay Wensleydale	Dewlay Cheesemakers	Lancashire	C	P	V		86
Dirty Vicar	Norbury Park Farm Cheese Co.	Surrey	C	U	V		147
DiVine	Burt's Cheese	Cheshire	C	P	V		48
Doddington	Doddington Cheese	Northumberland	C	U	A		87
Dol Las	Caws Cenarth	Carmarthenshire	S	P	V		56
Dol Wen	Caws Cenarth	Carmarthenshire	S	P	V		56
Doris	Teesdale Cheesemakers	Durham	C	P	V		179
Dorking Cock	Norbury Park Farm Cheese Co.	Surrey	C	U	V		147
Dorset Blue Vinny	Woodbridge Farm	Dorset	C	P	V		199
Dorset Goat	Paxton & Whitfield	London	G	P	V		158
Dorset Red	Ford Farm Cheesemakers	Dorset	C	P	V		96
Dorstone	Neal's Yard Creamery	Herefordshire	G	P	A		146
Double Barrel	Lincolnshire Poacher Cheese	Lincolnshire	C	U	A		130
Double Berkeley	Charles Martell and Son	Gloucestershire	C	P	A		60
Double Devonshire	Quicke's Traditional	Devon	C	P	V		162
Double Yorkshire	Wensleydale Creamery (Saputo)	North Yorkshire	C	P	V		190
Dovedale Blue PDO	Staffordshire Cheese Company	Staffordshire	C	P	V		175
Dragon Welsh Caerphilly	South Caernarfon Creameries	Gwynedd	C	P	V		171
Dragon Welsh Cheddar	South Caernarfon Creameries	Gwynedd	C	P	V		171
Dragon's Breath	Blaenafon Cheddar Company	Monmouthshire	C	P	V		38
Draycott Blue	Times Past Cheese Dairy	Somerset	C	P	V		183
Drewi Sant	Pant Mawr Farmhouse Cheeses	Pembrokeshire	C	P	V		158
Driftwood	White Lake Cheese	Somerset	G	T	V		195
Dromona Cheddar	Dromona	Tyrone	C	P	V		87
Drumturk Goat's Curd	Drumturk Cheeses	Perthshire	G	P	V		88
Drunken Burt	Burt's Cheese	Cheshire	C	P	V		48
Duckett's Caerphilly	Westcombe Dairy	Somerset	C	U	A		191
Duddleswell	High Weald Dairy	West Sussex	S	P	V		111
Duke of Wellington	Cryer & Stott	West Yorkshire	C	P	V		75
Durham Blue	Teesdale Cheesemakers	Durham	C	P	V		179
Dutchman	Plaw Hatch Farm	West Sussex	C	U	V	O	160

E

Earl of Arden	Fowler's of Earlswood	Warwickshire	S	P	V		97
East Lee	Pextenement Cheese Company	West Yorkshire	C	P	V	O	159

Eastwood	Cheese Geek	London	C	P	V		62
Ebbor Gorge	Wookey Farm	Somerset	G	P	V		200
Eden Chieftain	Appleby Creamery	Cumbria	C	P	V		28
Eden Ivory	Appleby Creamery	Cumbria	S	P	V		28
Eden Pearl	Appleby Creamery	Cumbria	S	P	V		28
Eden Smokie	Appleby Creamery	Cumbria	C	P	V		28
Eden Sunset	Appleby Creamery	Cumbria	C	P	V		28
Eden Valley Brie	Appleby Creamery	Cumbria	C	P	V		28
Edgedale	Coachyard Creamery	Durham	S	U	V		67
Edmund Tew	Blackwoods Cheese Company	Kent	C	U	A	O	37
Effin Hot	Hayfields Dairy	Cheshire	C	P	V		109
Ele, The Original	Padstow Cheese Co	Cornwall	C	P	V		157
Elgar Mature	Lightwood Cheese	Worcestershire	C	U	V		130
Ellie's Goat	Cheesemakers of Canterbury	Kent	G	P	V		65
Elmhirst	Sharpham Dairy	Devon	C	T	V		164
Elrick Log	Errington Cheese	Lanarkshire	G	U	V		91
Elsdon	Northumberland Cheese Co.	Northumberland	G	P	V		150
Endeavour	Cryer & Stott	West Yorkshire	C	P	V		75
Equinox	White Lake Cheese	Somerset	G	T	V		195
Essex Soft	Bradfields Farm Dairy	Essex	C	P	V		43
Ethical Dairy Cheddar	The Ethical Dairy	Dumfries & Galloway	C	U	V	O	92
Eve	White Lake Cheese	Somerset	G	T	V		195
Evenlode	King Stone Dairy	Gloucestershire	C	P	A	O	126
Ewe Beauty	Cryer & Stott	West Yorkshire	C	P	V		75
Ewe Blue	Ewenique Dairy	Pembrokeshire	S	P	V		93
Ewe Eat Me	Alsop & Walker	East Sussex	S	P	V		26
Ewe-mi	Yorkshire Pecorino	West Yorkshire	S	P	V		204

F

Fallen Monk	Lacey's Cheese	North Yorkshire	S	U	V		127
Farley	The Dairy Door	Shropshire	C	P	V		79
Farley	Village Maid Cheese	Berkshire	G	T	V		187
Farmhouse Caerphilly	Carron Lodge	Lancashire	C	P	V		54
Fat Cow	Highland Fine Cheeses	Ross-shire	C	P	V		113
Father Thames	Marlow Cheese Company	Buckinghamshire	C	P	V		140
Federia	Larkton Hall Cheese	Cheshire	C	U	A		128
Fedw	Brooke's Wye Valley Dairy Co.	Monmouthshire	C	P	V		46
Fellstone	Whin Yeats Dairy	Cumbria	C	U	A		194
Fetish	White Lake Cheese	Somerset	S	T	V		195
Ffetys	Y Cwt Caws	Anglesey	G	P	V		201
Ffili	Caws Cenarth	Carmarthenshire	C	P	V	O	56
Finn	Neal's Yard Creamery	Herefordshire	C	P	V	O	146
Fior di Latte Mozzarella	Brue Valley	Somerset	C	P	V		46
Flakebridge	Appleby Creamery	Cumbria	C	P	V		29

Flaming Pepper	Long Clawson Dairy	Leicestershire	C	P	V		133
Flatcapper Brie	Cryer & Stott	West Yorkshire	C	P	V		75
Fleet Valley Blue	The Ethical Dairy	Dumfries & Galloway	C	U	V	O	92
Flower Marie	Golden Cross Cheese Company	East Sussex	S	U	V		101
Forest Blue	Fowler's of Earlswood	Warwickshire	C	P	V		97
Fosse Way Fleece	Somerset Cheese Company	Somerset	S	P	V		170
Fountains Gold	Wensleydale Creamery (Saputo)	North Yorkshire	C	P	V		190
Fowler's	Fowler's of Earlswood	Warwickshire	C	P	V		97
Fowler's Flavour Added	Fowler's of Earlswood	Warwickshire	C	P	V		97
Fowler's Sage Derby	Fowler's of Earlswood	Warwickshire	C	P	V		97
Francis	James's Cheese	Dorset	C	P	V		121
Fremlin's Kentish Log	Cheesemakers of Canterbury	Kent	G	P	V		65
Frenni	Defaid Dolwerdd	Pembrokeshire	S	P	V		84
Fresh Ewe's Cheese	Homewood Cheeses	Somerset	S	T	V		116
Frowsbury Hill	Wildcroft Dairy	Surrey	G	U	A		198

G

Gafr Goch (Red Goat)	Wacky Wedge Cheese Company	Gwynedd	G	U	A		188
Gafr Wen (White Goat)	Wacky Wedge Cheese Company	Gwynedd	G	U	A		189
Gallipot Eyes	Brinkworth Dairy	Wiltshire	C	P	V		45
Galloway Cheddar	Caledonian Creamery (Lactalis)	Dumfries & Galloway	C	P	V		51
Gallybagger	Isle of Wight Cheese Company	Isle of Wight	C	U	V		120
Garstang Blue	Dewlay Cheesemakers	Lancashire	C	P	V		86
Gert Lush	Feltham's Farm Cheeses	Somerset	C	P	V	O	94
Glas	Defaid Dolwerdd	Pembrokeshire	S	P	V		84
Glaston Tile	White Lake Cheese	Somerset	G	T	V		195
Glazert	Dunlop Dairy	Ayrshire	G	P	V		89
Go T' Foot of T' Stairs	Eldwick Creamery	West Yorkshire	G	P	V		90
Goatisan	Ribblesdale Cheese Company	North Yorkshire	G	P	V		163
Goatlloumi	Polmarkyn Dairy	Cornwall	G	U	V		161
Godsells Double Gloucester	Godsell's Cheese	Gloucestershire	C	P	V		100
Godsells Single Gloucester PDO	Godsell's Cheese	Gloucestershire	C	P	V		100
Golden Brie	Guernsleigh Cheese	Staffordshire	C	P	V		106
Golden Cenarth	Caws Cenarth	Carmarthenshire	C	P	V	O	56
Golden Cross	Golden Cross Cheese Company	East Sussex	G	U	V		101
Golding	Book & Bucket Cheese Co.	Dorset	S	P	V		40
Goodweald Smoked	The Traditional Cheese Dairy	East Sussex	C	U	V		184
Goosnargh Gold	Butlers Farmhouse Cheeses	Lancashire	C	P	V		49
Gorwydd Caerphilly	Trethowan Brothers	Somerset	C	U	A	O	185
Gouda Gold	Ribblesdale Cheese Company	North Yorkshire	G	P	V		163
Gouda Mon	Caws Rhyd Y Delyn	Anglesey	C	P	V		57
Grace's Goats Cheese	Greenfields Dairy Products	Lancashire	G	P	V		104
Graceburn	Blackwoods Cheese Company	Kent	C	U	A	O	37
Granite	Drumturk Cheeses	Perthshire	G	P	V		88

Great British Flavoured Cheddar	The Great British Cheese Co.	Cheshire	C	P	V			102
Great British Flavoured Cheshire	The Great British Cheese Co.	Cheshire	C	P	V			102
Great British Flavoured Red Leicester	The Great British Cheese Co.	Cheshire	C	P	V			102
Great British Flavoured Wensleydale	The Great British Cheese Co.	Cheshire	C	P	V			103
Great British Lancaster Bomber	The Great British Cheese Co.	Cheshire	C	P	V			103
Great White	Ffynnon Went Farm	Carmarthenshire	S	P	V			98
Green's Cheddar	Greens of Glastonbury	Somerset	C	U/P	V	(O)		103
Green's Double Gloucester	Greens of Glastonbury	Somerset	C	P	V	(O)		103
Green's Sheep	Greens of Glastonbury	Somerset	S	P	V	(O)		103
Green's Traditional Cheddar	Greens of Glastonbury	Somerset	C	U/P	A	(O)		103
Green's Traditional Goat	Greens of Glastonbury	Somerset	G	P	A	(O)		103
Green's Twanger	Greens of Glastonbury	Somerset	C	P	V			104
Greenfields Cheddar	Greenfields Dairy Products	Lancashire	C	P	V			104
Greenfields Cheshire	Greenfields Dairy Products	Lancashire	C	P	V			104
Greenfields Crumbly Lancashire	Greenfields Dairy Products	Lancashire	C	P	V			105
Greenfields Double Gloucester	Greenfields Dairy Products	Lancashire	C	P	V			104
Greenfields Lancashire	Greenfields Dairy Products	Lancashire	C	P	V			105
Greenfields Red Leicester	Greenfields Dairy Products	Lancashire	C	P	V			105
Greenfields Wensleydale	Greenfields Dairy Products	Lancashire	C	P	V			105
Greta	Cheese Cellar Dairy	Worcestershire	C	P	V			62
Greystones Single Gloucester PDO	Simon Weaver Organic	Gloucestershire	C	P	V	O		168
Grimbister	Grimbister Farm Cheese	Orkney	C	U	V			105
Groovy Goat	Ribblesdale Cheese Company	North Yorkshire	G	P	V			163
Gruff	Cheesemakers of Canterbury	Kent	G	U	V			65
Guernsleigh Blue	Guernsleigh Cheese	Staffordshire	C	P	V			106
Guernsleigh Buffalo Cheddar	Guernsleigh Cheese	Staffordshire	B	P	V			106
Guernsleigh Goat Cheddar	Guernsleigh Cheese	Staffordshire	G	P	V			106
Guernsleigh Original	Guernsleigh Cheese	Staffordshire	C	P	V			106
Guernsleigh Soft	Guernsleigh Cheese	Staffordshire	C	P	V			106
Guinevere	Somerset Cheese Company	Somerset	B	P	V			170
Gun Hill	Nut Knowle Farm	East Sussex	G	P	V			152
Gunstone	Norsworthy Dairy Goats	Devon	G	U	V			149
Gurney's Gold	Mrs Temple's Cheese	Norfolk	C	P	V			145
Gwyn Bach	Caws Teifi	Ceredigion	C	U	A	O		58

H

Hadston	Northumberland Cheese Co.	Northumberland	C	P	V			150
Hafod	Holden Farm Dairy	Ceredigion	C	U/P	A	O		115
Hal-Ewe-Mee	Blue Sky Cheese	Lincolnshire	S	U	V			39
Hallernie	Guernsleigh Cheese	Staffordshire	C	P	V			106
Halwmi	Defaid Dolwerdd	Pembrokeshire	S	P	V			84
Hambledon Hill	James's Cheese	Dorset	C	P	V			122
Hamstone	White Lake Cheese	Somerset	C	P	V	O		195
Harbourne Blue	Ticklemore Cheese Dairy	Devon	G	P	V			183

Hardy's	Book & Bucket Cheese Co.	Dorset	S	P	V		40
Harefield	Smart's Traditional	Gloucestershire	C	U	V		169
Harlech	Croome Cheese	Worcestershire	C	P	V		73
Harley	The Dairy Door	Shropshire	C	P	V		79
Harrogate Blue	Shepherds Purse Cheeses	North Yorkshire	C	P	V		166
Hartington Dovedale Blue PDO	Hartington Creamery	Derbyshire	C	P	V		108
Hartington Shropshire Blue	Hartington Creamery	Derbyshire	C	P	V		109
Hartington Stilton PDO	Hartington Creamery	Derbyshire	C	P	V		109
Hatherton Smoked	Joseph Heler Cheese	Cheshire	C	P	V		123
Hay-on-Wye	Neal's Yard Creamery	Herefordshire	G	P	A		146
Hayfields Cheddar	Hayfields Dairy	Cheshire	C	P	V		109
Hayfields Cheshire	Hayfields Dairy	Cheshire	C	P	V		110
Hayfields Crunch	Hayfields Dairy	Cheshire	C	P	V		110
Hayfields Dbl Glouc Chive & Onion	Hayfields Dairy	Cheshire	C	P	V		110
Hayfields Red Leicester	Hayfields Dairy	Cheshire	C	P	V		110
Haytor	Curworthy Cheese	Devon	C	P	V		79
Hebden Goat	Tenacres Cheese	West Yorkshire	G	U	A		180
Hebridean Blue	Isle of Mull Cheese	Argyll & Bute	C	U	A		119
Heckfield	Village Maid Cheese	Berkshire	C	T	V		188
Helford Blue	Treveador Farm Dairy	Cornwall	C	P	V		185
Helford Camembert	Treveador Farm Dairy	Cornwall	C	P	V		185
Helford Sunrise	Treveador Farm Dairy	Cornwall	C	P	V		185
Helford White	Treveador Farm Dairy	Cornwall	C	P	V		185
Heligan Gold	Whalesborough Cheese	Cornwall	C	P	V		193
Hello Ewe	Homewood Cheeses	Somerset	S	T	V		116
Hendrix	Cheese Geek	London	C	P	V		62
Hereford Hop	Charles Martell and Son	Gloucestershire	C	P	A		60
Hereford Sage	Monkland Cheese Dairy	Herefordshire	C	U	V		141
Herefordshire Frier	Long Lane Dairy	Herefordshire	S	P	V		134
High Weald Halloumi	High Weald Dairy	West Sussex	SC	P	V	O	111
High Weald Ricotta	High Weald Dairy	West Sussex	S	P	V	O	111
Highland Brie	Highland Fine Cheeses	Ross-shire	C	P	V		113
Highland Camembert	Highland Fine Cheeses	Ross-shire	C	P	V		113
Highmoor	Nettlebed Creamery	Oxfordshire	C	P	A	O	147
Hiraeth	Tŷ Caws	Glamorgan	S	P	V		187
Hobnail	Northampton Cheese Company	Northamptonshire	C	P	V	O	149
Hod Hill	James's Cheese	Dorset	C	P	V		122
Holbrook	St James Cheese	Cumbria	G	U	A		174
Hollywell	Monmouth Shepherd	Monmouthshire	S	P	V		142
Holmbury Vintage Cheddar	Rowcliffe	Kent	C	P	V		165
Holy Smoked	Godsells Cheese	Gloucestershire	C	P	V		100
Homewood Ricotta	Homewood Cheeses	Somerset	S	T	V		116
Hooded Monk	Godsells Cheese	Gloucestershire	C	P	V		100
Hootenanny	Appleby Creamery	Cumbria	G	P	V		29

Hotspur	Doddington Cheese	Northumberland	C	U	A		87
How's Yer Father	Artisan Farm	Lancashire	C	P	V		30
Howgate Kintyre Blue	Inverloch Cheese Company	Argyll & Bute	C	P	A		118
Howgate Kintyre Brie	Inverloch Cheese Company	Argyll & Bute	C	P	V		118
Howling Hound	Godminster Cheese	Somerset	C	P	V	O	100
Huntsman	Long Clawson Dairy	Leicestershire	C	P	V		133
Huxley	Book & Bucket Cheese Co.	Dorset	C	P	V		40

I

Idle Hour	Alsop & Walker	East Sussex	C	P	V		26
Ilchester Cheddar	Norseland	Somerset	C	P	V		148
Inglewhite Buffalo	Carron Lodge	Lancashire	B	P	V		54
Ingot	St James Cheese	Cumbria	G	U	A		174
Innkeepers Choice	Long Clawson Dairy	Leicestershire	C	P	V		133
Inverloch Goat	Inverloch Cheese Company	Argyll & Bute	G	P	V		118
Ironbridge	Moyden's Handmade Cheese	Shropshire	C	U	V		143
Isle of Kintyre Gigha Fruit Cheese	Inverloch Cheese Company	Argyll & Bute	C	P	V		118
Isle of Kintyre Magnus' Hammer	Inverloch Cheese Company	Argyll & Bute	C	P	V		118
Isle of Kintyre Wax Cheddar	Inverloch Cheese Company	Argyll & Bute	C	P	V		119
Isle of Mull Cheddar	Isle of Mull Cheese	Argyll & Bute	C	U	A		119
Isle of Wight Blue	Isle of Wight Cheese Company	Isle of Wight	C	P	V		120
Isle of Wight Soft	Isle of Wight Cheese Company	Isle of Wight	C	P	V		120
Ivy's Reserve Vintage Cheddar	Wyke Farms	Somerset	C	P	V		201

J

John Bourne's Blue Cheshire	Mrs Bourne's Cheshire Cheese	Cheshire	C	P	V		144
Joseph Heler Cheddar	Joseph Heler	Cheshire	C	P	V		123
Joseph Heler Cheshire	Joseph Heler	Cheshire	C	P	V		123
Joseph Heler Gloucester	Joseph Heler	Cheshire	C	P	V		123
Joseph Heler Leicester	Joseph Heler	Cheshire	C	P	V		124
Jubilee Blue	Mrs Bourne's Cheshire Cheese	Cheshire	C	P	V		144
Just Jane to Fly Again	Lymn Bank Farm Cheese Co.	Lincolnshire	C	P	V		138

K

Kappacasein Ricotta	Kappacasein	London	C	U	A	O	124
Katherine	White Lake Cheese	Somerset	G	U	A		195
Katy's White Lavender	Shepherds Purse Cheeses	North Yorkshire	S	P	V		167
Kearney Blue	Farmview Dairies	Antrim	C	P	A		93
Kedar Halloumi Style Cheese	The Kedar Cheese Company	Dumfries & Galloway	C	P	V		124
Kedar Mozzarella	The Kedar Cheese Company	Dumfries & Galloway	C	P	V		125
Kedar Ricotta	The Kedar Cheese Company	Dumfries & Galloway	C	P	V		125
Kedar Tomme	The Kedar Cheese Company	Dumfries & Galloway	C	P	V		125
Keen's Cheddar	Keen's Cheddar	Somerset	C	U	A		125

Kelly's Canterbury Goat	Cheesemakers of Canterbury	Kent	G	U	V		65
Kelston Park	Bath Soft Cheese Company	Somerset	C	P	V	O	34
Keltic Gold	Whalesborough Cheese	Cornwall	C	P	V		193
Kentish Blue	Kingcott Dairy	Kent	C	U	V		126
Kidderton Ash	Butlers Farmhouse Cheeses	Lancashire	G	P	V		49
Kilcreen	Dart Mountain Cheese	Derry	C	P	V		81
King Charles III Truffle Cheddar	Cryer & Stott	West Yorkshire	C	P	V		75
King of the Castle	White Lake Cheese	Somerset	G	T	V		196
King's Blue	Hartington Creamery	Derbyshire	C	P	V		109
Kingcott Blue	Kingcott Dairy	Kent	C	U	V		126
Kisdon Ewe	Lacey's Cheese	North Yorkshire	S	U	V		127
Kit Calvert Wensleydale PGI	Wensleydale Creamery (Saputo)	North Yorkshire	C	P	V		190
Knuckleduster	Lincolnshire Poacher Cheese	Lincolnshire	C	U	A		130

L

La Fresca Margarita	Feltham's Farm Cheeses	Somerset	C	P	V	O	94
La Latteria Fior di Latte	La Latteria	London	C	P	A		127
Lacey's Brie	Lacey's Cheese	North Yorkshire	C	P	V		127
Lacey's Mature Cheddar	Lacey's Cheese	North Yorkshire	C	P	V		127
Lacey's Wensleydale	Lacey's Cheese	North Yorkshire	C	P	V		127
Lady Grey	St James Cheese	Cumbria	G	U	A		174
Lady Halton Smoked	Ludlow Farm Shop	Shropshire	C	P	V		136
Lady Mary's Bairn	Strathearn Cheese Company	Perthshire	C	P	V		176
Lady Prue	Quicke's Traditional	Devon	CG	P	V		162
Laganory	The Ethical Dairy	Dumfries & Galloway	C	U	V	O	92
Lairig Ghru	Cambus O'May Cheese Co.	Aberdeenshire	C	U	A		53
Lamb Leer	Homewood Cheeses	Somerset	S	T	V		117
Lamyatt	Westcombe Dairy	Somerset	C	U/P	A		191
Lanark Blue	Errington Cheese	Lanarkshire	S	U	V		91
Lanark White	Errington Cheese	Lanarkshire	S	U	V		91
Lancashire Bomb	Shorrocks Cheese	Lancashire	C	P	V		167
Largie	Argyll and Bute Cheeses	Argyll & Bute	C	P	V		30
Laughton Log	Golden Cross Cheese Company	East Sussex	G	U	V		101
Laverstoke Park Mozzarella	Laverstoke Park Farm	Hampshire	B	P	V	O	129
Leckford	Nettlebed Creamery	Oxfordshire	C	P	A	O	147
Leeds Blue	Yorkshire Pecorino	West Yorkshire	S	P	A		205
Lemon Zest	Long Clawson Dairy	Leicestershire	C	P	V		133
Leno	Hand Stretched Cheese	Carmarthenshire	C	P	V	O	108
Leonard Stanley	Godsells Cheese	Gloucestershire	C	P	V		100
Levin Down	Goodwood Home Farm	West Sussex	C	P	V	O	102
Lightwood Chaser	Lightwood Cheese	Worcestershire	C	P	V		130
Lillibet Blue	Cryer & Stott	West Yorkshire	C	P	V		76
Limestone	White Lake Cheese	Somerset	G	T	V		196
Lincoln Blue	Carron Lodge	Lancashire	C	P	V		54

Lincoln Imp	Carron Lodge	Lancashire	C	P	V		55
Lincolnshire Poacher	Lincolnshire Poacher Cheese	Lincolnshire	C	U	A		130
Lincolnshire Red	Lincolnshire Poacher Cheese	Lincolnshire	C	U	V		131
Lion Hotel 1868 Cheddar	Blaenafon Cheddar Company	Monmouthshire	C	P	V		39
Little Benet	Chapel Cross Tea Room	Somerset	G	U	V		59
Little Bertie	Hamm Tun Fine Foods	Northamptonshire	C	U	V		107
Little Burtles	Burt's Cheese	Cheshire	C	P	V		48
Little Colonel	James's Cheese	Dorset	C	P	V		122
Little Derby	Fowler's of Earlswood	Warwickshire	C	P	V		98
Little Herbert	Padstow Cheese Company	Cornwall	C	P	V		157
Little Hereford	Monkland Cheese Dairy	Herefordshire	C	U	V		141
Little Lepe	Rosary Goat's Cheese	Wiltshire	G	P	V		164
Little Lilly	White Lake Cheese	Somerset	G	T	V		196
Little She	White Lake Cheese	Somerset	S	T	V		196
Little Stinky	Country Cheeses	Devon	C	P	V		72
Little Sussex	High Weald Dairy	West Sussex	S	P	V	O	111
Little Truffle	Nut Knowle Farm	East Sussex	G	P	V		152
Little Wheal	Whalesborough Cheese	Cornwall	C	P	V		193
LLaeth y Bont Blue Cheese	Llaeth Y Bont	Powys	C	P	V		131
LLaeth y Bont Brie Type Cheese	Llaeth Y Bont	Powys	C	P	V		131
LLaeth y Bont Caerphilly Style Cheese	Llaeth Y Bont	Powys	C	P	V		131
Llain	Caws Cenarth	Carmarthenshire	C	P	V	O	56
Loch Arthur Farmhouse	Loch Arthur Creamery	Dumfries & Galloway	C	U	V	O	131
Lochnagar	Cambus O'May Cheese Co.	Aberdeenshire	C	U	A		54
Lockerbie Cheddar	Lockerbie Creamery (Arla)	Dumfries & Galloways	C	P	V		132
London Raclette	Kappacasein	London	C	U	A	O	124
Long Lane Ricotta	Long Lane Dairy	Herefordshire	S	P	V		134
Longbow	White Lake Cheese	Somerset	G	T	V		196
Longman's Cheddar	Longman's Cheese	Devon	C	P	V		135
Lord London	Alsop & Walker	East Sussex	C	P	V		26
Lord Nelson	Cambridge Cheese Company	Cambridgeshire	G	U	A		52
Lord of The Hundreds	The Traditional Cheese Dairy	East Sussex	S	U	V		184
Lovable Rogue	Monkey Chop Cheese	Dorset	C	P	V		140
Ludlow Red	Ludlow Farm Shop	Shropshire	C	U	A		136
Luna	Cheese Cellar Dairy	Worcestershire	G	P	V		62
Lyburn Gold	Lyburn Farmhouse Cheese	Wiltshire	C	P	V		136
Lye Cross Cheddar	Lye Cross Farm (Alvis Bros)	Somerset	C	P	V		137
Lye Cross Double Gloucester	Lye Cross Farm (Alvis Bros)	Somerset	C	P	V	(O)	137
Lye Cross Grass-Fed Organic Cheddar	Lye Cross Farm (Alvis Bros)	Somerset	C	P	V		137
Lye Cross Organic Cheddar	Lye Cross Farm (Alvis Bros)	Somerset	C	P	V		137
Lye Cross Red Leicester	Lye Cross Farm (Alvis Bros)	Somerset	C	P	V	(O)	138
Lymn Bank Flavoured Cheddar	Lymn Bank Farm Cheese Co.	Lincolnshire	C	P	V		138
Lymn Bank Signature Barrels	Lymn Bank Farm Cheese Co.	Lincolnshire	C	P	V		138
Lypiatt	The Old Cheese Room	Wiltshire	C	P	V	O	154

M

Maida Vale	Village Maid Cheese	Berkshire	C	T	V		188
Marmite Cheddar	Norseland	Somerset	C	P	V		148
Martell Double Gloucester	Charles Martell and Son	Gloucestershire	C	U/P	V		60
Martell Single Gloucester PDO	Charles Martell and Son	Gloucestershire	C	U/P	V		60
Martlet Gold	Nut Knowle Farm	East Sussex	G	P	V		152
Marvel	Hollis Mead Organic Dairy	Dorset	C	P	V	O	116
Mature Goat	Ribblesdale Cheese Company	North Yorkshire	G	P	V		163
May Hill Green	Charles Martell and Son	Gloucestershire	C	P	V		60
Mayfield	Alsop & Walker	East Sussex	C	P	V		27
Medita	High Weald Dairy	West Sussex	S	P	V	O	111
Medleys	The Old Cheese Room	Wiltshire	C	P	V	O	154
Meeny Hill	Dart Mountain Cheese	Derry	G	P	V		81
Meeny Hill Blue	Dart Mountain Cheese	Derry	G	P	V		81
Megique	Drumturk Cheeses	Perthshire	G	P	V		88
Melbury	Woodlands Dairy	Dorset	S	P	V	O	200
Meldon	Curworthy Cheese	Devon	C	P	V		79
Merry Wife	Bath Soft Cheese Company	Somerset	C	P	V	O	34
Mexicana	Norseland	Somerset	C	P	V		148
Michael's Mount	White Lake Cheese	Somerset	G	T	V		196
Millie	Cheese on The Wey	Surrey	C	T	V		63
Minger	Highland Fine Cheese	Ross-shire	C	P	V		114
Mini Mogul	Chapel Cross Tea Room	Somerset	G	U	V		59
Miss Muffet	Whalesborough Cheese	Cornwall	C	P	V		193
Miss Thymed	Whalesborough Cheese	Cornwall	C	P	V		193
Miss Wenna	Curds and Croust	Cornwall	C	P	V		77
Molecomb Blue	Goodwood Home Farm	West Sussex	C	P	V	O	102
Mon Las	Caws Rhyd Y Delyn	Anglesey	C	P	V		57
Mon Wen	Y Cwt Caws	Anglesey	G	P	V		201
Monkland	Monkland Cheese Dairy	Herefordshire	C	U	V		141
Montgomery's Cheddar	Montgomery's Cheeses	Somerset	C	U	A		142
Moorland Tomme	Botton Creamery	North Yorkshire	C	U	V	O	41
Morangie Brie	Highland Fine Cheeses	Ross-shire	C	P	V		114
Moreton	King Stone Dairy	Gloucestershire	C	P	A	O	126
Morn Dew	White Lake Cheese	Somerset	C	P	V		196
Mount's Bay Mozzarella	The Buffalo Dairy	Cornwall	B	P	V		47
Mouse House Flavoured Cheddar	Lymn Bank Farm Cheese Co.	Lincolnshire	C	P	V		138
Mouth Almighty	Artisan Farm	Lancashire	C	P	V		30
Mrs Bell's Blue	Shepherds Purse Cheeses	North Yorkshire	S	P	V		167
Mrs Bell's Salad Cheese	Shepherds Purse Cheeses	North Yorkshire	S	P	V		167
Mrs Bournes Mature Cheshire	Mrs Bourne's Cheshire Cheese	Cheshire	C	P	V		144
Mrs Butlers	Butlers Farmhouse Cheeses	Lancashire	C	P	V		49
Mrs Kirkham's Lancashire	Mrs Kirkham's Lancashire	Lancashire	C	U	A		144
Muldoon's Picnic	Artisan Farm	Lancashire	C	P	V		30

N

Naked White Stilton	Naked White Cheese Company	Nottinghamshire	C	P	V		146
Nanny Blue	Teesdale Cheesemakers	Durham	G	P	V		180
Nanny Florrie	Curds and Croust	Cornwall	G	P	V		77
Nanny McBrie	Appleby Creamery	Cumbria	G	P	V		29
Nanny Muffet	Whalesborough Cheese	Cornwall	G	P	V		193
Nattercrop	Pextenement Cheese Company	West Yorkshire	C	P	V	O	159
Newport	Moyden's Handmade Cheese	Shropshire	C	U	V		143
Nicky Nook	Dewlay Cheesemakers	Lancashire	C	P	V		86
Norbury Blue	Norbury Park Farm Cheese Co.	Surrey	C	U	V		148
Norfolk Dapple	Ferndale Norfolk Cheeses	Norfolk	C	U	V		95
Norfolk Mardler	Fielding Cottage	Norfolk	G	P	V		95
Norfolk Pinkfoot	Ferndale Norfolk Cheeses	Norfolk	C	U	V		95
Norfolk Tawny	Ferndale Norfolk Cheeses	Norfolk	C	U	A		95
Norfolk White Lady	Wilton Farm	Norfolk	S	P	V		198
Norsworthy	Norsworthy Dairy Goats	Devon	G	U	V		149
Northamptonshire Blue	Hamm Tun Fine Foods	Northants	C	U	V		107
Northern Balls	Cryer & Stott	West Yorkshire	C	P	V		76
Northern Blue	Shepherds Purse Cheeses	North Yorkshire	C	P	V		167
Northern Goat's	Cryer & Stott	West Yorkshire	G	P	V		76
Nortons Soft Cheese	Nortons Dairy	Norfolk	C	P	V		151
Northumberland	Northumberland Cheese Co.	Northumberland	C	P	V		151
Nutfield Cheddar	Nutfield Dairy	Surrey	C	P	V		154

O

Oakly Park	Ludlow Farm Shop	Shropshire	C	P	A/V		136
Oakwood	Ford Farm Cheesemakers	Dorset	C	P	V		96
Ogleshield	Montgomery's Cheeses	Somerset	C	U	A		142
Okeford Beacon	James's Cheese	Dorset	C	P	V		122
Old Applebian	Appleby Creamery	Cumbria	C	P	V		29
Old Demdike	Homewood Cheeses	Somerset	S	T	V		117
Old Winchester	Lyburn Farmhouse Cheese	Wiltshire	C	P	V		137
Olde Sussex	The Traditional Cheese Dairy	East Sussex	C	U	V		184
Olde York	Shepherds Purse Cheeses	North Yorkshire	S	P	V		167
Olwyn Fawr	Cosyn Cymru	Gwynedd	S	U	A		70
Organic Monterey Jack	Pextenement Cheese Company	West Yorkshire	C	P	V	O	160
Original Goat	Ribblesdale Cheese Company	North Yorkshire	G	P	V		163
Original Sheep	Ribblesdale Cheese Company	North Yorkshire	S	P	V		164
Orkney Cheddar PGI	Orkney Cheese Company	Orkney	C	P	V		155
Orkney Flavoured Mature Cheddar	The Island Smokery	Orkney	C	P	V		119
Orwell	Book & Bucket Cheese Co.	Dorset	S	P	V		40
Ottinge Bramshill	Ottinge Court Dairy	Kent	C	U	A		155
Ottinge Mutschli	Ottinge Court Dairy	Kent	C	U	A		155
Ottinge Oaxaca	Ottinge Court Dairy	Kent	C	U	A		155

Owd Ewe	Ribblesdale Cheese Company	North Yorkshire	S	P	V		164
Oxford Blue	Oxford Cheese Company	Buckinghamshire	C	P	V		156
Oxford Dolce	Oxford Cheese Company	Buckinghamshire	C	P	V		156
Oxford Isis	Oxford Cheese Company	Buckinghamshire	C	P	V		156
Oxonlees	Westcombe Dairy	Somerset	C	U/P	A		192

P

Paddy's Milestone	Dunlop Dairy	Ayrshire	C	P	V		89
Pagewood	Hill Farm Real Food	Cheshire	C	U	A		114
Pant ys Gawn	Abergavenny Fine Food Co.	Monmouthshire	G	P	V		25
Park House Cheddar	Torpenhow Farmhouse Dairy	Cumbria	C	P	V	O	183
Parkapella	Monmouth Shepherd	Monmouthshire	S	P	V		142
Parlick Brie	Butlers Farmhouse Cheeses	Lancashire	S	P	V		49
Parlick Original	Butlers Farmhouse Cheeses	Lancashire	S	P	V		49
Parys	Y Cwt Caws	Anglesey	G	P	V		202
Patience	Abbey Home Farm	Gloucestershire	C	P	V	O	24
Pavé Cobble	White Lake Cheese	Somerset	S	T	V		196
Paxton & Whitfield Cave Aged	Paxton & Whitfield	London	C	P	V		158
Paxton & Whitfield Smoked Ceodre	Paxton & Whitfield	London	C	P	V		158
Peakland Blue	Hartington Creamery	Derbyshire	C	P	V		109
Peakland White	Hartington Creamery	Derbyshire	C	P	V		109
Pendragon	Somerset Cheese Company	Somerset	B	P	V		170
Pennard Red	Somerset Cheese Company	Somerset	G	P	V		170
Pennard Ridge	Somerset Cheese Company	Somerset	G	P	V		170
Pennard Vale	Somerset Cheese Company	Somerset	G	P	V		170
Penyston Brie	Daylesford Organics	Gloucestershire	C	U	V	O	83
Perl Las	Caws Cenarth	Carmarthenshire	C	P	V	O	56
Perl Wen	Caws Cenarth	Carmarthenshire	C	P	V	O	56
Perroche	Neal's Yard Creamery	Herefordshire	G	P	V		146
Pevensey Blue	Pevensey Cheese Company	East Sussex	C	P	A		159
Pexo Blanco	Pextenement Cheese Company	West Yorkshire	C	P		O	160
Pexommier	Pextenement Cheese Company	West Yorkshire	C	P	V	O	160
Phipps Firkin	The Northampton Cheese Co.	Northants	C	P	V	O	150
Pickled Ewe's Cheese	Homewood Cheeses	Somerset	S	T	V		117
Pike's Delight	Pextenement Cheese Company	West Yorkshire	C	P	V	O	160
Pitchfork Cheddar	Trethowan Brothers	Somerset	C	U	A	O	185
Plaw Hatch Cheddar	Plaw Hatch Farm	West Sussex	C	U	V	O	160
Pomfret Monk	Cryer & Stott	West Yorkshire	C	P	V		76
Posbury	Norsworthy Dairy Goats	Devon	G	U	V		149
Potter	Book & Bucket Cheese Co.	Dorset	C	P	V		40
Ptarmigan	Drumturk Cheeses	Perthshire	G	P	V		88
Preseli	Defaid Dolwerdd	Pembrokeshire	S	P	V		84
Prince Bishop	Weardale Cheese	Durham	C	P	V		189
Pwll Ddu	Blaenafon Cheddar Company	Monmouthshire	C	P	V		39

Pyramid	Nut Knowle Farm	East Sussex	G	P	V	153

Q

Queso Fresco	Yorkshire Dama Cheese	West Yorkshire	C	P	V	203
Quicke's Cheddar	Quicke's Traditional	Devon	C	P	A/V	162
Quicke's Elderflower	Quicke's Traditional	Devon	C	P	V	162
Quicke's Ewe Cheddar	Quicke's Traditional	Devon	S	P	A	162
Quicke's Goat Cheddar	Quicke's Traditional	Devon	G	P	V	162

R

Rachael Reserva	White Lake Cheese	Somerset	G	T	V		197
Rachel	White Lake Cheese	Somerset	G	T	V		197
Ragstone	Neal's Yard Creamery	Herefordshire	G	P	A		146
Rainbows Gold	Somerset Cheese Company	Somerset	C	P	V		171
Rainton Tomme	The Ethical Dairy	Dumfries & Galloway	C	U	V	O	92
Ramps Hill	Brinkworth Dairy	Wiltshire	C	P	V		45
Ramsey	Cheesemakers of Canterbury	Kent	S	U	V		66
Ravens Oak	Butlers Farmhouse Cheeses	Lancashire	G	P	V		49
Rebel Nun	Feltham's Farm Cheeses	Somerset	C	P	V	O	94
Red Fox	Belton Farm	Shropshire	C	P	V		36
Red Lakes	Fowler's of Earlswood	Warwickshire	C	P	V		98
Red Storm	Snowdonia Cheese Company	Denbighshire	C	P	V		169
Redesdale	Northumberland Cheese Co.	Northumberland	S	P	V		151
Regatta	Marlow Cheese Company	Buckinghamshire	C	P	V		140
Reggie Red Crunch	Hayfields Dairy	Cheshire	C	P	V		110
Remembered Hills	Ludlow Farm Shop	Shropshire	C	P	V		136
Renegade Monk	Feltham's Farm Cheeses	Somerset	C	P	V	O	94
Rhuby Crumble	Cryer & Stott	West Yorkshire	C	P	V		76
Richmond Blue	Lacey's Cheese	North Yorkshire	C	P	V		128
Riseley	Village Maid Cheese	Berkshire	S	T	V		188
Rock Star Cave Aged Cheddar	Snowdonia Cheese Company	Denbighshire	C	P	V		169
Roding Red	Bradfields Farm Dairy	Essex	C	P	V		43
Rokke	Padstow Cheese Company	Cornwall	C	P	V		157
Rollright	King Stone Dairy	Gloucestershire	C	P	A	O	126
Ronnie	Teesdale Cheesemakers	Durham	C	P	V		180
Rosary	Rosary Goat's Cheese	Wiltshire	G	P	V		164
Rosedale	Abbey Farm Cottage	North Yorkshire	G	U	V		24
Rossett Red	Calon Wen	Carmarthenshire	C	P	V	O	52
Rothbury Red	Butlers Farmhouse Cheeses	Lancashire	C	P	V		50
Royal Bassett Blue	Brinkworth Dairy	Wiltshire	C	P	V		45
Rushmore	Sharpham Dairy	Devon	CG	T	V		165

S

Saint George	Nut Knowle Farm	East Sussex	G	P	V		153
Saint Giles	High Weald Dairy	West Sussex	C	P	V	(O)	112
Sandham Cheddar	J J Sandham	Lancashire	C	P	V		120
Sandham Coverdale	J J Sandham	Lancashire	C	P	V		120
Sandham Lancashire	J J Sandham	Lancashire	C	P	V		120
Sandham Lancashire Bomb	J J Sandham	Lancashire	C	P	V		121
Sandham Ogden Original	J J Sandham	Lancashire	C	P	V		121
Sandham Old King Coal	J J Sandham	Lancashire	C	P	V		121
Sandham Red Crunch	J J Sandham	Lancashire	C	P	V		121
Sandham Wensleydale	J J Sandham	Lancashire	C	P	V		121
Saval	Caws Teifi	Ceredigion	C	U	A	O	58
Savour	Sharpham Dairy	Devon	CG	T	V		165
Saxon Cross	Bradbury's Cheese	Derbyshire	C	P	V		42
Scarlet	Long Clawson Dairy	Leicestershire	C	P	V		134
Scottish Buffalo Mozzarella	The Buffalo Farm	Fife	B	P	V		47
Scrumpy Sussex	The Traditional Cheese Dairy	East Sussex	C	U	V		184
Sergeant Pepper	Whalesborough Cheese	Cornwall	C	P	V		194
Seriol Wyn	Y Cwt Caws	Anglesey	G	P	V		202
Seriously Cheddar	Caledonian Creamery (Lactalis)	Dumfries & Galloway	C	P	V		52
Seven Sisters	High Weald Dairy	West Sussex	S	P	V	(O)	112
Shaggy's Beard	Ellie's Dairy	Kent	G	P	V		65
Shakespeare	Book & Bucket Cheese Co.	Dorset	S	P	V		40
Sharpham Brie	Sharpham Dairy	Devon	C	T	V		165
Sharpham Camembert	Sharpham Dairy	Devon	C	T	V		166
Sharpham Rustic	Sharpham Dairy	Devon	C	T	V		166
Shawn	Ellie's Dairy	Kent	S	U	V		65
Sheep Rustler	White Lake Cheese	Somerset	S	T	V		197
Sheffield Forge	Cryer & Stott	West Yorkshire	C	P	V		76
Shipston Blue	Carron Lodge	Lancashire	B	P	V		55
Shoalgate	Country Cheeses	Devon	C	U	V		72
Shoetown Blue	Hamm Tun Fine Foods	Northants	C	U	V		107
Shorthorn Blue	Yorkshire Organic Cheese	North Yorkshire	C	P	V	O	204
Shrewsbury Fretta	Moyden's Handmade Cheeses	Shropshire	C	U	V		143
Singing Granny	Godsells Cheese	Gloucestershire	C	P	V		101
Sinodun Hill	Norton and Yarrow Cheese	Oxfordshire	G	U	A		151
Sir Lancelot	Errington Cheese	Lanarkshire	S	U	A		91
Sister Sarah	High Weald Dairy	West Sussex	G	P	V		112
Six Spires	Somerset Cheese Company	Somerset	C	U	V		171
Sizzler	Plaw Hatch Farm	West Sussex	C	U	V	O	160
Skinny Cheese	The Ethical Dairy	Dumfries & Galloway	C	U	V	O	93
Skinny Crowdie	Highland Fine Cheeses	Ross-shire	C	P	V		114
Skyver	The Northampton Cheese Co.	Northants	C	P	V	O	150
Slack-ma-Girdle	Charles Martell and Son	Gloucestershire	C	P	V		60

Slate Cavern Aged Cheddar	South Caernarfon Creameries	Gwynedd	C	P	V		172
Slate Cavern Aged Red Leicester	South Caernarfon Creameries	Gwynedd	C	P	V		172
Smart's Double Gloucester	Smart's Traditional	Gloucestershire	C	U	V		169
Smart's Single Gloucester PDO	Smart's Traditional	Gloucestershire	C	U	V		169
Smelly Ha'peth	Artisan Farm	Lancashire	C	P	V		30
Smokey Duke	Curds and Croust	Cornwall	C	P	V		77
Smouldering Ember	Butlers Farmhouse Cheeses	Lancashire	C	P	V		50
Snowdonia Flavoured Cheddar	Snowdonia Cheese Company	Denbighshire	C	P	V		170
Snowdrop	Cote Hill Farm	Lincolnshire	C	U	V		70
Soft Bard	Fowler's of Earlswood	Warwickshire	C	P	V		98
Soft Joyce	Ffynnon Went Farm	Carmarthenshire	S	P	V		98
Solstice	White Lake Cheese	Somerset	C	P	V		197
Solway Mountain	The Kedar Cheese Company	Dumfries & Galloway	C	P	V		125
Somerset Chilli	Somerset Cheese Company	Somerset	C	P	V		171
Somerset Goat Halloumi	White Lake Cheese	Somerset	G	T	V		197
Somerset Herb & Cider	Somerset Cheese Company	Somerset	C	P	V		171
South Caernarfon Caerphilly	South Caernarfon Creameries	Gwynedd	C	P	V		172
South Caernarfon Cheddar	South Caernarfon Creameries	Gwynedd	C	P	V		172
South Caernarfon Double Gloucester	South Caernarfon Creameries	Gwynedd	C	P	V		172
South Caernarfon Monterey Jack	South Caernarfon Creameries	Gwynedd	C	P	V		172
South Caernarfon Red Leicester	South Caernarfon Creameries	Gwynedd	C	P	V		172
South Caernarfon Wensleydale	South Caernarfon Creameries	Gwynedd	C	P	V		172
Sparkenhoe Blue	Leicestershire Handmade	Leicestershire	C	U	A		129
Sparkenhoe Red Leicester	Leicestershire Handmade	Leicestershire	C	U	A		129
Sparkenhoe Shropshire Blue	Leicestershire Handmade	Leicestershire	C	U	A		129
Special Reserve Tasty Lancashire	Dewlay Cheesemakers	Lancashire	C	P	V		86
Spenwood	Village Maid Cheese	Berkshire	S	T	V		188
Sperrin Blue	Dart Mountain Cheese	Derry	C	P	V		81
Spitfire	Oxford Cheese Co mpany	Buckinghamshire	C	P	A		156
Squeaky Goat's Cheese	Yorkshire Dama Cheese	West Yorkshire	G	P	V		203
Squeaky Sheep's Cheese	Yorkshire Dama Cheese	West Yorkshire	G	P	V		203
St Andrews Cheddar	St Andrews Cheese Company	Fife	C	U	A		173
St Barties	The Dairy Door	Shropshire	C	P	V		79
St Bees	Thornby Moor Dairy	Cumbria	G	U	V		181
St Benedict	Lacey's Cheese	North Yorkshire	S	U	V		128
St Cera	St Jude Cheese	Suffolk	C	U	A		174
St Crispin	Hamm Tun Fine Foods	Northants	C	U	V		107
St Cuthbert	Weardale Cheese	Durham	C	P	V		189
St Ella	Rosary Goat's Cheese	Wiltshire	G	P	V		164
St Helena	St Jude Cheese	Suffolk	C	U	A		175
St Ivo	St Ives Cheese	Cambridgeshire	S	P	V		173
St James	St James Cheese	Cumbria	S	U	A		174
St Jude	St Jude Cheese	Suffolk	C	U	A		175
St Ludoc	Caws Cenarth	Carmarthenshire	C	P	V	O	56

St Michael's	Honour Natural Foods	Kent	C	P	V	O	117
St Michael's Blue	Honour Natural Foods	Kent	C	P	V	O	117
St Sunday	St James Cheese	Cumbria	C	P	V		174
St Thom	Lightwood Cheese	Worcestershire	G	U	A		130
Staffordshire PDO	Staffordshire Cheese Company	Staffordshire	C	P	V		175
Stanage Millstone	Cow Close Farm	Derbyshire	C	P	V		73
Sterling Gold	Bridge Farm	Borsetshire	C	U	V		44
Stichelton	Stichelton Dairy	Nottinghamshire	C	U	A		176
Stinking Bishop	Charles Martell and Son	Gloucestershire	C	P	V		60
Stithians	Lynher Dairies Cheese Company	Cornwall	C	P	A		139
Stonebeck	Stonebeck Cheese	North Yorkshire	C	U	A		176
Stoney Cross	Lyburn Farmhouse Cheese	Wiltshire	C	P	V		137
Stottie	Cryer & Stott	West Yorkshire	G	P	V		76
Stow Blue	The Cotswold Cheese Company	Gloucestershire	C	P	V		71
Stratford Blue	Butlers Farmhouse Cheeses	Lancashire	C	P	V		50
Strathdon Blue	Highland Fine Cheeses	Ross-shire	C	P	V		114
Stripey	Greenfields Dairy Products	Lancashire	C	P	V		105
Suffolk Blue	Suffolk Farmhouse Cheeses	Suffolk	C	P	V		177
Suffolk Blue Brie	Suffolk Farmhouse Cheeses	Suffolk	C	P	V		177
Suffolk Brie	Suffolk Farmhouse Cheeses	Suffolk	C	P	V		177
Suffolk Gold	Suffolk Farmhouse Cheeses	Suffolk	C	P	V		177
Summerfield Alpine	Botton Creamery	North Yorkshire	C	U	V	O	42
Sunburst	Long Clawson Dairy	Leicestershire	C	P	V		134
Sunday Best	Butlers Farmhouse Cheeses	Lancashire	C	P	V		50
Superior Goat	Ribblesdale Cheese Company	North Yorkshire	G	P	V		164
Surrey Red	Nutfield Dairy	Surrey	C	P	V		154
Sussex Blossom	High Weald Dairy	West Sussex	S	P	V	O	112
Sussex Blue	Alsop & Walker	East Sussex	C	P	V		27
Sussex Brie	Alsop & Walker	East Sussex	C	P	V		27
Sussex Camembert	Alsop & Walker	East Sussex	C	P	V		27
Sussex Charmer	Bookham Harrison	West Sussex	C	P	V		41
Sussex Farmhouse	Alsop & Walker	East Sussex	C	P	V		27
Sussex Marble	High Weald Dairy	West Sussex	C	P	V	(O)	112
Sussex Slipcote	High Weald Dairy	West Sussex	S	P	V	O	112
Sussex Squire	Nut Knowle Farm	East Sussex	G	P	V		153
Sussex Velvet	High Weald Dairy	West Sussex	C	P	V	O	112
Sussex Yeoman	Nut Knowle Farm	East Sussex	G	P	V		153
Swaledale	Swaledale Cheese Company	North Yorkshire	C	P	V		178
Swaledale Blue	Swaledale Cheese Company	North Yorkshire	C	P	V		178
Sweet Charlotte	Country Cheeses	Devon	C	P	V		72
Swift	Cheese Geek	London	C	P	V		62
Sykes Fell	Greenfields Dairy Products	Lancashire	S	P	V		105

T

Taffy Apple	Blaenafon Cheddar Company	Monmouthshire	C	P	V			39
Taid	Y Cwt Caws	Anglesey	G	P	V			202
Tain Cheddar	Highland Fine Cheeses	Ross-shire	C	P	V			114
Tam's Tipple	Cheesemakers of Canterbury	Kent	C	U	V			115
Taw Valley Cheddar	Taw Valley Creamery (Arla)	Devon	C	P	V			178
Taw Valley Churnton	Taw Valley Creamery (Arla)	Devon	C	P	V			178
Taw Valley Double Gloucester	Taw Valley Creamery (Arla)	Devon	C	P	V			179
Taw Valley Red Leicester	Taw Valley Creamery (Arla)	Devon	C	P	V			179
Taw Valley Tasty	Taw Valley Creamery (Arla)	Devon	C	P	V			179
Teesdale Blue	Teesdale Cheesemakers	Durham	C	P	V			180
Teesdale Goat	Teesdale Cheesemakers	Durham	G	P	V			180
Teifi	Caws Teifi	Ceredigion	C	U	A	O		58
Teifi Caerphilly PGI	Caws Teifi	Ceredigion	C	U	A	O		58
Teifi Halloumi	Caws Teifi	Ceredigion	C	U	V	O		58
The Cheese with no Name	Brinkworth Dairy	Wiltshire	C	P	V			45
The Cheese with no Name	Larkton Hall Cheese	Cheshire	CG	U	A			128
The Duchess	Rennet and Rind	Cambridgeshire	C	U	V			162
The Duke	Rennet and Rind	Cambridgeshire	C	U	V			163
The English Pecorino	White Lake Cheese	Somerset	S	T	V			197
The Lady Mary	Strathearn Cheese Company	Perthshire	C	P	V			177
The Other Monk	Monkland Cheese Dairy	Herefordshire	C	U	V			141
The Single Rose	Ballylisk of Armagh	Armagh	C	P	V			31
The Strathearn	Strathearn Cheese Company	Perthshire	C	P	V			177
The Truffler	Curds and Croust	Cornwall	C	P	V			77
The Wedge	The Dairy Door	Shropshire	C	P	V			79
Thelma's Traditional Caerffili	Caws Cenarth	Carmarthenshire	C	P	V	O		57
This Is Proper Double Gloucester	Butlers Farmhouse Cheeses	Lancashire	C	P	V			50
This Is Proper Goat's Cheese	Butlers Farmhouse Cheeses	Lancashire	C	P	V			50
This Is Proper Lancashire	Butlers Farmhouse Cheeses	Lancashire	C	P	V			50
This Is Proper Red Leicester	Butlers Farmhouse Cheeses	Lancashire	C	P	V			50
Thornby Moor	Thornby Moor Dairy	Cumbria	G	U	V			181
Three Virgins	Godsells Cheese	Gloucestershire	C	P	V			101
Tibb	Homewood Cheeses	Somerset	S	T	V			117
Ticklemore	Sharpham Dairy	Devon	G	P	V			166
Tillerton	Norsworthy Dairy Goats	Devon	G	U	V			149
Tilston Blue	Cheese on The Wey	Surrey	C	T	V			63
Times Past Farmhouse Cheddar	Times Past Cheese Dairy	Somerset	C	P	V			183
Times Past Mature Cheddar	Times Past Cheese Dairy	Somerset	C	P	V			183
Times Past Traditional Cheddar	Times Past Cheese Dairy	Somerset	C	P	V			183
Tintern	Croome Cheese	Worcestershire	C	P	V			74
Tinto	Errington Cheese	Lanarkshire	G	U	V			91
Tirkeeran	Dart Mountain Cheese	Derry	C	P	A			82
Togglers	The Northampton Cheese Co.	Northants	C	P	V	O		150

Tommie	Cheese on The Wey	Surrey	C	T	V		64
Tongue Taster	The Northampton Cheese Co.	Northants	C	P	V	O	150
Tor	White Lake Cheese	Somerset	G	T	V		197
Tovey	Thornby Moor Dairy	Cumbria	G	U	A		182
Trefaldwyn Blue	Trefaldwyn Cheese	Powys	C	P	V		184
Trehill	Country Cheeses	Devon	C	P	V		72
Tremains	High Weald Dairy	West Sussex	C	P	V	O	112
Triple Rose	Ballylisk of Armagh	Armagh	C	P	V		31
Trothy	Monmouth Shepherd	Monmouthshire	S	P	V		142
Trotter Hill	Butlers Farmhouse Cheeses	Lancashire	C	P	V		51
Truffle Ewe	High Weald Dairy	West Sussex	S	P	V		113
Truffle Gloucester	Simon Weaver Organic	Gloucestershire	C	P	V	O	168
Truffler	Ford Farm Cheesemakers	Dorset	C	P	V		96
Truffler	Somerset Cheese Company	Somerset	C	P	V		171
Trufflynn	Cheese Cellar Dairy	Worcestershire	G	P	V		62
Trusmadoor	Torpenhow Farmhouse Dairy	Cumbria	C	P	V	O	183
Tunworth	Hampshire Cheeses	Hampshire	C	P	A		107
Tuxford & Tebbutt Shropshire Blue	Tuxford & Tebbutt (Arla)	Leicestershire	C	P	V		186
Tuxford & Tebbutt Stilton PDO	Tuxford & Tebbutt (Arla)	Leicestershire	C	P	V		186
Tynedale	Northumberland Cheese Co.	Northumberland	C	P	V		151
Tysilio	Y Cwt Caws	Anglesey	G	P	V		202
Tysul Blue	Jones' Cheese Company	Ceredigion	C	P	V		123

V

Vale of Camelot Blue	Longman's Cheese	Devon	C	P	V		135
Valley Drover	Hancocks Meadow Farm	Herefordshire	S	U	A		108
Velocheese Burrata	Velocheese	Antrim	C	P	A	O	187
Velocheese Fior di Latte	Velocheese	Antrim	C	P	A	O	187
Velocheese Scamorza	Velocheese	Antrim	C	P	A	O	187
Velocheese Stracciatella	Velocheese	Antrim	C	P	A	O	187
Village Gossip	Godsells Cheese	Gloucestershire	C	P	V		101
Vintage Trelawny	Whalesborough Cheese	Cornwall	C	P	V		194
Volesdale	Coachyard Creamery	Durham	C	U	V		67

W

Walsingham	Mrs Temple's Cheese	Norfolk	C	P	V		145
Wandering Ewe	Wandering Ewe Dairy	Somerset	S	U	A		189
Warwickshire	Fowler's of Earlswood	Warwickshire	C	P	V		98
Wash Stone	Whin Yeats Dairy	Cumbria	C	U	A		194
Washbourne	Sharpham Dairy	Devon	S	P	V		166
Washington	Cheese Geek	London	C	P	V		63
Waterloo	Village Maid Cheese	Berkshire	C	T	V		188
Wave	Cryer & Stott	West Yorkshire	C	P	V		76
Wealden	Nut Knowle Farm	East Sussex	G	P	V		153

Wealden Hard	Nut Knowle Farm	East Sussex	G	P	V		153
Wealdway	Nut Knowle Farm	East Sussex	G	P	V		153
Wealdway Mature	Nut Knowle Farm	East Sussex	G	P	V		153
Weardale	Weardale Cheese	Durham	C	P	V		190
Wedmore	Westcombe Dairy	Somerset	C	U	A		192
Wee Comrie	Strathearn Cheese Company	Perthshire	C	P	V		177
Wells Alpine	Mrs Temple's Cheese	Norfolk	C	P	V		145
Wensleydale Double Gloucester	Wensleydale Creamery (Saputo)	North Yorkshire	C	P	V		190
Wensum White	Fielding Cottage	Norfolk	G	P	V		95
West Country Mature Cheddar	The Open Air Dairy	Dorset	C	P	V		155
Westcombe Cheddar	Westcombe Dairy	Somerset	C	U	A		192
Westcombe Red	Westcombe Dairy	Somerset	C	U	A		192
Westcombe Ricotta	Westcombe Dairy	Somerset	C	U	A		192
Weywood	Cheese on The Wey	Surrey	C	T	V		64
Whin Yeats Farmhouse	White Yeats Dairy	Cumbria	C	U	A		194
White Fox	Belton Farm	Shropshire	C	P	V		36
White Heart	White Lake Cheese	Somerset	G	T	V		197
White Hilton	Teesdale Cheesemakers	Durham	C	P	V		180
White Nancy	White Lake Cheese	Somerset	G	T	V		198
White Wood	White Lake Cheese	Somerset	G	T	V		198
Whitehill	Monmouth Shepherd	Monmouthshire	S	P	V		142
Whyte Witch	Stamford Artisan Cheese	Cambridgeshire	C	U	A		176
Wiggold Cheddar	Abbey Home Farm	Gloucestershire	C	P	V	O	24
Wighton	Mrs Temple's Cheese	Norfolk	C	P	V		145
Wigmore	Village Maid Cheese	Berkshire	S	T	V		188
Wild Garlic Yarg	Lynher Dairies Cheese Company	Cornwall	C	P	V		139
Wilde	Book & Bucket Cheese Co.	Dorset	C	P	V		41
Wiltshire Blue	Brinkworth Dairy	Wiltshire	C	P	V		45
Wiltshire Loaf	Brinkworth Dairy	Wiltshire	C	P	V		45
Winchester	Lyburn Farmhouse Cheese	Wiltshire	C	P	V		137
Windrush	Windrush Valley Goat Dairy	Gloucestershire	G	P	V		199
Windrush Greek Style	Windrush Valley Goat Dairy	Gloucestershire	G	P	V		199
Windsor Red	Long Clawson Dairy	Leicestershire	C	P	V		134
Winnie's Wheel	Cheesemakers of Canterbury	Kent	C	P	V		115
Winslade	Hampshire Cheeses	Hampshire	C	P	A		108
Winterdale Shaw	Winterdale Cheesemakers	Kent	C	U	A		199
Wissington	Wilton Farm	Norfolk	S	P	V		198
Witheridge	Nettlebed Creamery	Oxfordshire	C	P	A	O	147
Withybrook	Country Cheeses	Devon	G	P	V		73
Woodside Red	Alsop & Walker	East Sussex	C	P	V		27
Wookey Hole Cheddar	Ford Farm Cheesemakers	Dorset	C	P	V		96
Wookey Hole Goat Cheese	Ford Farm Cheesemakers	Dorset	G	P	V		97
Wookey Salad Cheese	Wookey Farm	Somerset	G	P	V		200
Wookey Soft Goats Cheese	Wookey Farm	Somerset	G	P	V		200

Worcester Blue	Lightwood Cheese	Worcestershire	C	P	A		130
Worcestershire Hop	Croome Cheese	Worcestershire	C	P	V		74
Wordsworth	Book & Bucket Cheese Co.	Dorset	C	P	V		41
Worthy Farm Reserve Cheddar	Wyke Farms	Somerset	C	P	V		201
Wrekin Blue	Moyden's Handmade Cheese	Shropshire	C	U	V		143
Wrekin White	Moyden's Handmade Cheese	Shropshire	C	U	V		143
Wyfe of Bath	Bath Soft Cheese Company	Somerset	C	P	V	O	34
Wyke Farms Cheddar	Wyke Farms	Somerset	C	P	V		201

Y

Y Cwt Caws Goat Curd	Y Cwt Caws	Anglesey	G	P	V		202
Y-Fenni	Croome Cheese	Worcestershire	C	P	V		74
Yarley	Wookey Farm	Somerset	G	P	V		200
Yarlington	King Stone Dairy	Gloucestershire	C	P	A	O	126
Yarlington Blue	Longman's Cheese	Devon	C	P	V		135
Yellison Soft Goat's Cheese	Yellison Farm	North Yorkshire	G	P	V		202
Yester Mozzarella Fior di Latte	Yester Farm Dairies	East Lothian	C	P	V		203
Yoredale	Curlew Dairy	North Yorkshire	C	U	A/V		78
Yorkshire	Swaledale Cheese Company	North Yorkshire	C	P	V		178
Yorkshire Blue	Shepherds Purse Cheese	North Yorkshire	C	P	V		167
Yorkshire Cask	Cryer & Stott	West Yorkshire	C	P	V		77
Yorkshire Extra Mature Cheddar	Wensleydale Creamery (Saputo)	North Yorkshire	C	P	V		190
Yorkshire Kay-Soa	Eldwick Creamery	West Yorkshire	C	P	V		90
Yorkshire Pecorino Fiore	Yorkshire Pecorino	West Yorkshire	S	P	A		205
Yorkshire Pecorino Fresco	Yorkshire Pecorino	West Yorkshire	S	P	A		205
Yorkshire Red	Wensleydale Creamery (Saputo)	North Yorkshire	C	P	V		191
Yorkshire Ricotta	Yorkshire Dama Cheese	West Yorkshire	C	P	V		203
Yorkshire Ricotta	Yorkshire Pecorino	West Yorkshire	S	P	A		205
Yorkshire Squeaky Cheese	Yorkshire Dama Cheese	West Yorkshire	C	P	V		203
Yorkshire Wensleydale PGI	Wensleydale Creamery (Saputo)	North Yorkshire	C	P	V		191
Yorkshire Wensleydale Blue	Wensleydale Creamery (Saputo)	North Yorkshire	C	P	V		191
Young Buck	Mike's Fancy Cheese Company	Down	C	U	A		140
Young Louis	Chapel Cross Tea Room	Somerset	G	U	V		59
Yr Afr (The Goat)	Wacky Wedge Cheese Company	Gwynedd	G	U	A		189

www.steveparkercheeseandwine.com

steve@steveparkercheeseandwine.com

Twitter : @stevecheesewine

Instagram : stevecheesewine

FUTURE BOOKS FROM STEVE PARKER

☐ COOKING WITH BRITISH CHEESE

☐ WINESPOTTING

☐ BRITISH CHEESE AND WINE PAIRING

☐ THE CHEESE AND WINE SHOP (A Novel)

Printed in Great Britain
by Amazon

28534883R00149